The Buddhist Vision
An Introduction to the Theory and Practice of Buddhism

Alex Kennedy
(Dharmachari Subhuti)

RIDER

London Melbourne Sydney Auckland Johannesburg

Rider and Company

An imprint of the Hutchinson Publishing Group

17–21 Conway Street, London W1P 6JD

Hutchinson Publishing Group (Australia) Pty Ltd
P O Box 496, Hawthorn, Melbourne, Victoria 3122

Hutchinson Group (N Z) Ltd
P O Box 40–086, Glenfield 10, Auckland

Hutchinson Group (S A) Pty Ltd
P O Box 337, Bergvlei, 2012 South Africa

First published 1985

© Alex Kennedy 1985

Set by Colset Private Limited, Singapore in 11/12 Compugraphic Bembo

Printed and bound in Great Britain by
Anchor Brendon Ltd,
Tiptree, Essex

British Library Cataloguing in Publication Data

Library of Congress Cataloging in Publication Data

ISBN 0 7126 1084 7

Contents

Acknowledgements

Chris Krupa, Kit Emmett, and Dharmachari Aloka prepared the diagrams in this book. Dharmachari Dharmapriya at short notice read through and corrected the manuscript. Dharmacharini Srimala, Su Lawson, and Vida Browning compiled the Index. I am very grateful to them and to those many others who have helped in various ways.

List of Illustrations

Preface

There are many, many books available on the subject of Buddhism and to write another requires some justification. For a number of years, I have been lecturing on Buddhism and teaching Buddhist meditation and during this time I found a lack of the kind of work that I can wholeheartedly recommend to people who have had little acquaintance with the Buddha's teachings. Such a book must combine a number of different qualities and it is these that I have set out to incorporate into this volume.

Firstly, it should be accessible to the complete newcomer to Buddhism, explaining its principal teachings from basics. I have therefore avoided complex technicalities and all but six or seven terms from the canonical languages of Buddhism. The foreign words, like 'Buddha' and 'Dharma', that I have retained are simply not translatable and will have to be accepted as a kind of Buddhist English. I might be accused of having oversimplified some complex teachings but my assumption is that those who want to know more will do some further reading (for which purpose I have provided a booklist).

Secondly, it seems that a complete overview of the Buddhist vision of existence is required, so that the reader can see what a Buddhist considers human life is, its relation to the universe as a whole and its ultimate significance. The Wheel of Life, the Spiral, and the Mandala of the Five Buddhas, which I have used as the framework of my exposition, explore and relate every facet of existence, and I have used the concept of evolution as an explanatory thread to tie them all together. Once these three groups of symbols are grasped, the reader should have a general picture of how a Buddhist sees life.

Man is made of many parts: he is heart as well as head. Buddhism speaks to the whole man and an account of Buddhism must present as many of its facets as possible. I have, therefore, chosen symbols to provide the structure of my book in the hope that they will yield solid psychological and philosophical information and, at the same time, some insights of a more imaginative and poetic kind. Too many works on Buddhism are dry and academic; it has been my wish to bring some feeling to what is, after all, the Buddhist *vision* of reality.

Lastly, and perhaps most importantly of all, what is needed is a book by a committed Buddhist, practising in the modern world. I have been a member of the Western Buddhist Order for more than ten years and I try to devote my whole life to following the Buddhist Path. Since I became a member of the Order I have been working with my teacher and fellow Order members to create a Buddhist movement that will help people to follow the Buddhist way of life, here and now. My account of Buddhism is, therefore, unashamedly convinced. I write as one who sincerely believes in, and tries to practise, the subject of his writing. I hope that this will show that Buddhism is a *practical* teaching of great significance to modern man – as it has been, and will be, to all men of any time.

At the same time, I am an Englishman, born and bred in the West, and I have never been further East than the other side of the beautiful Greek island where this book was written. My Western background will, I hope, mean that the work is accessible to other Westerners.

Since this book consists, for the most part, of my understanding of the Buddha's vision as expounded by my teacher, the Ven. Sangharakshita, I can truly say that I am only responsible for the faults and distortions. The creative vision has already been unfolded; I have simply tried to set it out as faithfully and clearly as I can. I hope that I have succeeded and that it will open many people's minds and hearts to the evolutionary potential which is theirs.

I am, in this as in most worthwhile things in my life, deeply grateful to the Ven. Sangharaskshita for providing the teachings on which this book is based, encouraging me to write it, and putting up with the inconvenience of a diminished secretariat while I have been away. So great is my debt to him that I think I have probably quoted him verbatim in my text on a number of occasions without noticing it. All the teachings contained herein come more or less directly from him.

I wish also to express my thanks to my friends and colleagues, Dharmacharis Vessantara, Bodhiraja, and Ratnaprabha, who have cheerfully shouldered the extra work which my absence has entailed. Robert Stainton has, once more, allowed me the use of his Greek villa which is truly a writer's haven; we have never met and I am therefore all the more appreciative of his disinterested generosity. Finally, Dharmachari Jayadeva has been my companion in my island retreat and has shopped and cooked for me, kept the house in order, put up with the times when my pen would not write and with my uncommunicative absorbtion when it would. Without the help of these friends I would never have been able to write this book.

Dharmachari Subhuti
Skopelos, Greece

7 April 1984
The sixteenth anniversary of the founding of the Western
Buddhist Order

1
Everyone Has a View

Everyone has a view, a perspective on existence. These views govern the direction of our lives; they are often almost entirely unconscious, forming a substructure to our minds, made up of unthinking assumptions about ourselves and our world. Though we may be unaware of our views and may never give them articulate expression, nevertheless, in everything we do and say, we betray our basic perspectives. Our views may be self-contradictory, unfounded, untrue but, because we are so closely identified with them, we never see them for what they are. It might even be said that we *are* our views.

Views range from the most casual opinions about everyday matters to theories about ultimate metaphysical issues. At bottom, everyone's system of values is founded upon some view about the purpose of life, however vague, inarticulate or inconsistent; for example, we consider life to be the survival of the fittest, or a test for a higher life to come, or simply without any point at all. Usually, our views remain a more or less loosely associated jumble of assumptions, prejudices, opinions and beliefs, yet they may be elaborated into complex and dazzling philosophies.

Even when built up in this way into finely spun structures of thought, the basis of our views is emotional. Our most fundamental views are not so much concepts, though they may find conceptual expression, as powerful myths which give form to our desires and passions, like, for instance, the myth of Aryan supremacy, or of the historical process inevitably leading to the perfect society, or of the redemption of man by a saviour god. 'Myth' here does not mean a mere legend or fiction but an archetypal patterning of the psyche which shapes reason and emotion into a whole, thrusting in a single direction. It is these myths, together with the whole mass of our views, which move us.

11

Broadly, views are acquired in two ways: either we generate them for ourselves or we inherit them from the culture which surrounds us. The acquisition is usually unconscious and we exercise little discrimination in what we allow to structure our minds and lives. The views which we develop for ourselves are often but rationalizations by which we provide ourselves with reasons for following our desires. Those we inherit from others are often picked up partly from a felt need to conform to the views of our families, friends and the social groups within which we live and partly because they suit our wants. We are being fed with views all the time: by our educational institutions, mass media and our everyday contacts. The very shapes of our houses and manner of our dress affects the way we see the world.

Once views are adopted, they may have a very strong influence upon the whole course of our lives. Having given shape to our emotions and thoughts, they mould our actions. We order the world in conformity with our longings and then we live in that world we have ourselves created. Clearly, the views we hold have consequences for us, either good or bad. They may lead us into ever-recurring cycles of confusion and pain or they may give rise to greater freedom and happiness. It is of the greatest importance that we clarify our minds and distinguish those views which are wholesome and helpful from those which are diseased and harmful since our very lives depend upon it.

Such a clarification of our mental contents requires intensive self-examination. We must learn to be aware of our thoughts and motives. We must see what it is that influences us and to what end. We must begin to take responsibility for our own views, to see what emotions underlie them and where they tend to lead us. Thus far, the work is negative and consists largely in clearing away confusion. But how *shall* we see the world? – that is the question which now confronts us. We can either try to develop for ourselves a more comprehensive and satisfying view of things or we can open ourselves to the influence of one which is already developed. Both options have their attendant dangers and difficulties. We may be deceived by ourselves in the first case and by others in the second. Both may have either a successful or a disastrous outcome. It is, however, to the guidance of others that we must, almost inevitably, turn. Unless we cut ourselves off from human society altogether (which is almost impossible to do today, even were it desirable) then we must always be under some cultural influence from which it will be hard for us to disentangle ourselves. Besides, if others have, with great effort perhaps, and even suffering, managed to achieve a breadth of view far greater than our own, we would be foolish not to allow ourselves to be taught by them. Our own efforts would be greatly accelerated if we, wisely and with circumspection, let ourselves be influenced by the most enriching views in our human culture.

Our own times are probably unprecedented in the diversity of views of life available to us. In the West, our traditional, Christian-based culture is still extant, though now much on the defensive, and there is the new 'consumer culture', with its instant material satisfactions, which finds more and more adherents the world over. Besides these, a vast range of 'alternative' views is developing, drawn from Eastern religion and Western science, psychology and philosophy, or various combinations of these. Among all these views we must choose what influences we want.

But how can we evaluate? Would not our evaluation itself be based upon a view? Are we not simply predisposed to select what most suits our own immediate desires, for better or worse? How can we evaluate values? We are thrown back on our own experience. But our own experience must be carefully and critically examined. To begin with, we must be sure that we have correctly understood the view we are investigating and that we are not prematurely judging it in the light of our preconceptions about it. That done, we can ask ourselves whether or not it makes reasoned sense, whether the view is self-consistent and conforms to experience. Then, we can try to see what the likely consequences might be of that view if put into practice. We can examine the lives of those of its adherents we might encounter. We can even experiment to see what its effects are within our own lives.

Not only can we make a very cool and reasoned examination but also we must take into account our own immediate responses to the view. Here we must, of course, be self-critical, distinguishing our own superficial partialities from a genuine intuition. If we are healthy and straightforward, we will find that some views seem to constrict and confine us, as if we cannot think and feel at our fullest within them. Such views are too narrow to do justice to our potential as human beings. Other views, we will find, seem dark and twisted, distorting our natures into bizarre and unnatural shapes. Others again seem to lighten our hearts, open up our minds, and give us room to expand and breathe new air. They reveal vistas of limitless horizons and undreamt-of possibilities towards which we feel irresistibly drawn.

13

The evaluative criterion is within our own experience. If we know ourselves well enough and are sincere in our enquiry then we will find that we recognize an increase in genuine happiness, friendliness and mental clarity on the one hand, and of suffering, alienation from others and confusion on the other. We can see what views tend to the former and what to the latter. Those that tend to produce more positive and wholesome states are, in Buddhist terms, 'right views' and those that engender negative states are 'wrong views'.

The view that is to be presented in this book is a Buddhist view of life and it is upon the above criterion that it asks to be evaluated. It offers itself as a way of viewing life which will help the individual to become happier, to experience greater harmony with others and to see things with a purer understanding. In essence, this is Buddhism: a view of the infinite possibilities of human development. No ceiling confines us; there is, for Buddhism, no God for ever above and beyond man's reach. We may, if we choose to make the effort, break through barrier after barrier in our lives in an unending spiral of intensifying happiness, wisdom and love.

The founder of the Buddhist tradition, known by the title 'The Buddha', meaning 'The Awakened One', required no blind belief from his disciples but expressly urged them to 'test my words as the goldsmith tests gold in the fire'. Again and again, in the Buddhist texts, we are called upon to weigh up what we hear before we place any reliance upon it. We should approach this Buddhist view wide-awake, responsibly, separating our own thoughts and feelings from the mass of our inherited assumptions. We should be careful neither to accept blindly and uncritically nor to reject through prejudice. We should listen to that view carefully and sympathetically, and evaluate it in the light of our own reason, intuition and experience.

Essential as this initial appraisal is, it is only the first step. Critical evaluation and intellectual assent are not enough, for Buddhism demands action of its followers. They must put it into practice, act upon it and make it their own. Yet even this is not enough. The Buddhist view may enable one to cultivate within oneself higher and nobler states of mind and to function more and more beneficially but still, at this stage, it is not something one sees directly for oneself. It is reasonable to one, intuitively one responds to it, and all one's experience bears it out but it is still, as it were, an influence upon one from outside. The ultimate aim of the Buddhist view is to produce in those

14

who respond to it a corresponding *vision* so that they see for themselves, by direct experience, the truth of that view. In a sense, then, one no longer has a view at all, for view has been replaced by direct vision.

For Buddhism, the final criterion for evaluating views is whether or not they lead to the transcendence of views, that is, to vision. Wrong views distort and stunt the lives of those who hold them, right views promote the cultivation of more and more positive mental states but, above all, followed to their conclusion they lead to that direct experience of the nature of things which is vision. Vision lies at the heart of Buddhism. For Buddhists, it was first seen by an historical individual, Siddhartha Gautama, some 2,500 years ago, in North India. In attaining that vision he became the Buddha. He saw that every human being has the potential to become a Buddha and he spent the remainder of his life trying to help others to realize his vision. The tradition we know of as Buddhism is the continuing attempt of the Buddha's successors to communicate that same vision of reality to others.

The Buddha's vision is beyond particular time and place. It is as relevant today as at any point in the long history of the tradition which he founded. In accordance with the changing cultures and ages within which it has been conveyed, it has been constantly renewed and re-expressed. The tradition is a rich treasury of the many forms which its communication has taken. Each of these forms has had its own power to move men to make profound changes in themselves and their world.

Our own times are characterized by a disintegration of common values. We are faced with a melting pot of views about which there is no general agreement. An increasingly prevalant view is the materialist one. The supernatural and the other-worldly, heaven and hell, or other possible dimensions of being play little part in the conscious attitude of most people today. No doubt, much superstition and unreason has been cleared away, but we are left with drastically limited horizons. It is a flat, one-dimensional world in which we live out our brief span between birth and death. Much of our time is taken up with elaborate housekeeping and the business of physical survival, albeit in ever-increasing comfort and convenience. Whatever time is left we devote to entertainment. To those who feel that such a view of life leaves something in them unanswered, this Buddhist vision is offered.

2
A Vision of Existence

The ascertainable historical facts of the Buddha's life provide but a bare outline. We know that he was born, Siddhartha Gautama, in the sixth century BC, at Lumbini on the modern Indo-Nepalese border. His father was a leading nobleman (sometimes, it is said, the head) of a prosperous warrior clan, the Shakyans. His mother died a few days after his birth and he was nurtured by his aunt. He was married to a cousin at an early age and had by her a son, Rahula. He underwent, in his early manhood, a deep spiritual crisis which he later spoke of in these terms:

And I too, before awakening, being liable to birth because of self, sought what was likewise liable to birth because of self; being liable to ageing, disease, dying, sorrow and impurity sought what was likewise liable to ageing, disease, dying, sorrow and impurity. Then it occurred to me, 'Why do I, being liable to all these things myself, seek after them? Why don't I, liable as I am to birth, ageing, decay, dying, sorrow and impurity, seek the unborn, the unageing, the undecaying, the undying, the sorrowless, the pure, the uttermost security from the bonds – Nirvana?'*

Siddhartha Gautama felt a deep revulsion for the emptiness of his life as a prosperous citizen and, leaving home in accordance with the practice of the times, took up the life of a wandering seeker after truth. After studying under various teachers from whom he failed to gain effective guidance and after practising austerities for a number of years, he decided to make his effort, on his own, by the path of meditation. Beneath a peepul tree at Bodhgaya, he gained Enlightenment and became a Buddha.

We are told that, after his Enlightenment, he could not see any way

Ariyapariyesanasutta, Majjhima-Nikaya, I. 163.

to communicate his experience, the gap between his own Enlightened mind and that of the rest of humanity being, in a sense, infinite. Yet the very essence of his experience was a deep feeling of compassion for every living creature. He knew that his vision would remove for ever all their sufferings if only they could perceive its full depth and splendour. He now saw, in imagination, the whole of humanity like lotus plants growing in a vast lake. Some were buried deep in the mud at the bottom of the lake; some pushed their buds up through the water; whilst others stood clear of the water, their petals beginning to open to the radiance of the sun. Beings were, he saw, in different stages of development. There were some whose hearts were already ripe for his teaching and others, again, whom he must encourage to mature until they could absorb the full experience of Enlightenment. For the remainder of his life he devoted himself solely to this task and with great skill and unfailing patience he developed a whole system of teaching to suit all temperaments and levels of development. According to tradition, many of his immediate disciples did gain Enlightenment and, throughout the ages, many more have done so under his inspiration. For 2,500 years, Buddhism has retained within itself, despite decay and atrophy in some of its institutional forms, a living tradition of direct spiritual experience stretching back to the Buddha himself.

What was the Buddha's vision of existence? Both the vision itself and the attempt to communicate it to others, by whatsoever means, are known to Buddhists as the Dharma. This is a Sanskrit word (in Pali, another important language of early Buddhism, it is *Dhamma*) with a number of complex meanings. For present purposes, Dharma means the Truth as experienced by the Buddha and as taught by him. This is a key word in Buddhism, best left untranslated. It is as the Dharma that Buddhists speak of Buddhism, referring to themselves as 'followers of the Dharma'. Our question, then, becomes, 'What is the Dharma?' In a sense, of course, it is not possible to say. The Dharma cannot be known by the intellect alone, it must be experienced, face to face. Yet expression of the experience in conceptual terms may help us to gain, at least, a rational understanding of its scope. Symbols and images have the further power to stir us in the deeper faculty of imagination so that we appreciate something of the beauty and range of the Buddha's insight. In this book we will be using a blend of both concepts and images to convey a general account of the Dharma. We will be examining, primarily, three great symbols, or rather groups of symbols: the

Wheel of Life, the Spiral Path and the Mandala of the Five Buddhas. These will form the framework of our exposition. First of all, however, it is necessary to explain some of the basic principles of the Dharma.

The main conceptual formula used by the Buddha to convey his vision is known as 'The Principle of Universal Conditionality' or, more strictly, though less intelligibly, 'The Law of Conditioned Co-production':

This being, that becomes; from the arising of this, that arises; this not becoming, that does not become; from the ceasing of this, that ceases.

These words are deceptively easy to comprehend with the intellect yet they contain a depth of meaning which few attain. They teach us that the entire universe is made up of processes, each of which arises in dependence on a network of conditions. When the conditions which have brought about any particular process are no longer present, it ceases. Each process, itself the product of conditions, in its turn conditions new processes. The Buddha saw everything, both in man and in the world, as a complex of these interrelated processes. Life is a ceaseless swirl of motion. Nothing remains still for a single instant: either it is forming or decaying. What we call 'things' are, in reality, processes. The world appears to us as if it consisted of solid, stable entities, virtually permanent and unchanging. This way of seeing things is necessary for everyday practical purposes but we proceed to turn practical convenience into rigid belief and behave in the world as if we, and it, were fixed everlasting entities. But everything, human beings included, is a process and, though there may be continuity within that ever-changing process, there is nothing that is eternally stable.

From one point of view the impermanent nature of conditioned things is horrifying. It means we can never wholly reply or depend on anything conditioned because whatever we depend on is liable to inevitable decay. Material objects can be lost, stolen or broken. People are subject to shifting moods and will themselves, at some point, die. Nothing in the phenomenal universe is ultimately substantial. There is nothing that can, as it were, take the full weight of our reliance. If we do build ourselves upon things which are conditioned then we are doomed, sooner or later, to experience frustration and pain.

The fact of impermanence has, however, another side to it. It means that everything must change and, if it must do so, it may change for the better. For the flow of conditioned processes may function in two different ways. It may, on the one hand, form a continuous oscillation, an ebb and flow of generation and decay or, on the other, it may move in a mounting curve of increasing development. It may function in cycles, going round and round like a wheel, or wind higher and higher in the manner of a spiral. Since we are ourselves conditioned processes then we, too, may function in the cyclic or the spiral fashion.

The cyclic kind of conditionality is purely quantitative. The play of conditions brings elements together for a while to form a stone, a tree or a horse. Sooner or later, conditions alter and the adhesion ceases. So, growth and decay follow each other inexorably. Though vast planets and organisms of astonishing complexity may be produced, sooner or later decay will set in and they will be scattered. This kind of conditionality is mechanical; once conditions are established, the consequence follows automatically just as does the turning of a clockwork motor from the winding of the spring. It is cyclic in that, though there be a rise, it is a rise only to fall again. Like a great wheel the chain of conditions rolls around, now up, now down. Fixed at the hub, it cannot move beyond its own circumference. Nothing new has come into being, only infinite rearrangements of the old.

Much of our own functioning is of this kind. Not only are our bodily processes governed by the cyclic type of conditionality but so is much of our mental activity. We think, speak and act as the product of a complex of conditions: physical, biological and social. We are largely what our environment has made us. In fact, much of our behaviour is explicable in terms of a stimulus-response model of Pavlovian simplicity: we simply react to things around us with little self-awareness. This type of mental functioning has been termed the 'reactive mind'.

The workings of the reactive mind do not account for all human behaviour. There is yet another way in which we can operate: by means of the 'creative mind'. This kind of mental functioning is characterized by ever-increasing *quality*, in accordance with the spiral type of conditionality. Rather than operating in cycles, the chain of conditions rises by successive augmentation, gaining in quality at each new level. Each factor surpasses the preceding one and is surpassed by the one that follows it. Each forms the basis for, but does not limit, the stage that grows out of it. When we function in this spiral-like way, we are creative. We take the conditions as presented to us – the world around us, our own feelings and emotions – and we invest them with some new value drawn from our own depths. A clear example of this spiral or creative mind is seen in the work of the artist. A sculptor, for instance, takes raw stone and the head of his subject as his conditions and produces a bust which is not merely a good likeness, displaying his technical skill, but also conveys a deeper insight into the nature of man. Not only has there been a quantitative change in the block of stone but also a qualitative one in the mind of the artist which he has managed to convey to his sculpture.

The creative mind is by no means the exclusive property of the artist. Whenever we transcend our conditioning to any extent, we act creatively. Whenever, for instance, we are activated by genuine altruism or generosity, whenever we bring new harmony and clarity into the situations we find ourselves in, then we act creatively. Creative behaviour is characterized by self-awareness, inspired spontaneity and positive emotions like friendliness, happiness and vigour. It is a continuous bursting of the boundaries of our conditioning at higher and higher levels.

The choice between reactive and creative behaviour faces us at every moment. We can either continue the cycle of our reactions or, by cultivating self-awareness, we can gradually establish a flow of creativity. The Dharma encourages us to make that transition from the reactive to the creative mind. It shows us that, to function reactively, is to experience continuous frustration and pain while the creative leads to ever-increasing happiness and fulfilment.

The reactive mind is represented by the symbol of the Wheel, the creative by the Spiral. The Wheel and the Spiral exist in different degrees in different people. Some make no effort to cultivate higher states within themselves. Their minds are dominated by the cyclic kind of conditionality, by the Wheel. Others do make some effort although they still function reactively to a greater or lesser extent. These belong partly to the Wheel and partly to the Spiral. Finally, there are beings whose lives are a continuous process of creative expansion. They are wholly of the Spiral. Buddhahood is the point at which the Spiral process separates itself completely from the cyclic and there is nothing but creativity.

From those who are making their first faltering steps on the Spiral to those who are on the threshold of Buddhahood stretches the Path of human development. Those treading that Path must be constantly watchful to allow the creative mind within them to unfold and to keep at bay the reactive mind. Time and again, they will falter and, over and over, they must renew their efforts. Midway on that Path there is, however, a vital point of transition. It is the point at which the Spiral within one just outweighs the Wheel. It is called the point of 'Stream Entry' because one has there entered the stream which inevitably leads now beyond the Wheel towards Buddhahood. It is a point of no-return because, although the reactive still functions within one, it can never possess one wholly again and one cannot but go forward on the Path. Up to that point, one can slip back, even give up the attempt altogether. The point of Stream Entry is an important intermediate goal for Buddhists because it is only from that point onwards that one's progress is assured.

Buddhism, then, holds up this vision of the universe as a process with two tendencies: the reactive and the creative. It shows us that human beings may ascend a Path of development which stretches from the Wheel to the point of Bhuddhahood, at which the Spiral unfolds free from all cyclic tendencies whatsoever. Buddhism not only has a vision of human potential, it offers guidance as one treads the Path: it describes the stages along the way and it has a vast treasury of methods which help one to tread it.

One of the most basic teachings of early Buddhism divides the Path into three successive stages and shows the work to be done at each. The 'Threefold Path' consists of the stages of morality, meditation and wisdom. We will be exploring each of these in later chapters of this book so only a preliminary account is necessary at this point.

When we first set our feet upon the Path, there is a vast gulf between our higher aspiration and our everyday behaviour. However sincerely we want to cultivate creative states of mind, our actions and our way of life are little different from those of anyone else. Sometimes, our work and the people we are closest to do not assist our efforts. It may even be that our friends and relations actively deride our interest in developing ourselves. We must, therefore, examine our lives to see what does and what does not contribute to our development. Not only may our way of life be hindering us to an extent, but our own behaviour may be working against our desire to grow. We may be acting so as to harm others, whether in great or small ways. In acting thus, we confirm the negative tendencies in our mind which keep the Wheel spinning. Such behaviour is defined as *unethical* in Buddhism because it binds us more and more tightly to the reactive mode of conditionality. So we begin our higher development by bringing our way of life into harmony with our pursuit of the Path, that is, by examining and improving our morality.

As aids to the cultivation of morality, Buddhist tradition gives various lists of precepts. Precepts are not commandments imposed upon us by an external authority. They are a description of the behaviour of one who is completely creative and they act as guidelines by which we may test and work upon our own actions. The commonest set of precepts is five-fold and describes what one who is perfectly creative does *not* do. Each one is taken as a principle to underlie our actions as we tread the Path:

I undertake the training principle of abstaining from harming living beings.
I undertake the training principle of abstaining from taking the not-given.
I undertake the training principle of abstaining from sexual misconduct.
I undertake the training principle of abstaining from false speech.
I undertake the training principle of abstaining from drink and drugs which cloud the mind.

Once one has freed oneself of the grosser unethical acts and one's way of living has begun to enhance one's development instead of detracting from it, then one's mind will begin to settle and clear, for the consequence of a truly ethical life is mental lightness and ease. One can now begin to work more directly upon the mind through meditation. In Buddhist terms, meditation is a way of raising the level of one's consciousness so that one experiences an unceasing progression of positive states. Through meditation, one purifies the mind of all distraction, superficiality and all negative tendencies. It is usually practised systematically by sitting in a secluded place and carrying out a simple exercise. Two basic practices of this kind are common to many of the different schools of Buddhism. The first is known as the 'Mindfulness of Breathing' in which, in a number of stages, one concentrates attention more and more upon the breath as it passes in and out of the body. Gradually the ceaseless chatter which usually dominates our minds calms down, leaving a feeling of deep stillness and harmony which is intensely pleasurable. The mind is poised and clear, vividly aware without any object to be aware of.

The second, complementary, practice is called the 'Development of

Loving Kindness'. One develops feelings of love and well-wishing towards oneself, first of all: then, stage by stage, towards a friend, a neutral person, an enemy and, finally, one expands one's love out gradually to embrace all creatures in all the directions of space. As one persists regularly with the practice of meditation, one becomes more and more accomplished so that one can quite quickly absorb oneself in these lofty and joyous states. Not only will one be enjoying them at the time of meditation but all the time, whatever one is doing.

Once this degree of skill in meditation has been reached, the mind will be in a very elevated state. All sub-conscious energies will be resolved into consciousness, all rigidity and prejudice will be overcome, and fear, hatred and craving will be suspended. All inner conflict will be ended and one will be free enough and concentrated enough to bring the full weight of one's being to bear on comprehending the very nature of existence. So the stage of meditation provides the basis for the stage of wisdom.

This stage is characterized either by reflecting upon some saying of the Buddha's which sums up his insight, by contemplating some symbolic expression of his vision, or by any of a number of other methods. Eventually, one breaks through from view to vision, one sees things as they really are. The attainment of wisdom is not merely a process of understanding. Integral to the experience is a dissolving of the barriers between oneself and other beings. No longer is one exclusively bound up with oneself, for one experiences no essential difference between oneself and others. One feels unbounded love and compassion equally strongly for all beings. The understanding of wisdom and the fellow-feeling of compassion are but two aspects of the one experience of vision.

The arising of vision marks the point of Stream Entry, the point at which the spiral tendencies outweigh the cyclic. From here until the final extinction of all reactive, wheel-like currents within one, at Buddhahood, one must permeate with vision every part of one's life. Gradually, vision transforms and reorders every level of one's being.

Buddhahood itself is not truly the end of the Path. In a sense, it is only the beginning for it is at Buddhahood that one is completely free of all fetters, even the subtlest, tying one to the Wheel. Buddhahood is the point at which the Path passes completely beyond our comprehension. Our own most exalted moments provide but the palest analogies for the triumphal progression which now ensues.

The picture we have given of the Threefold Path offers a glimpse of the stages through which we must ascend and the means by which we must travel. It is obviously a rather simplified picture. Few people's lives unfold in quite such an orderly manner; many people nowadays start their efforts on the Path with the practice of meditation before they have properly undertaken the stage of morality. It is also a picture from one particular viewpoint which stresses the individual's work to change *himself*. Taken by itself, it can make following of the Spiral Path seem a rather isolated and self-concerned life. Far from this being the case, our interaction with other people and the deepening of our relationships with them is crucial to our development. Through our contact with those more advanced than ourselves we gain the inspiration and the understanding to progress. Through contact with our peers we gain stimulation and challenge, encouragement and criticism and, above all, that indispensable feeling of brotherhood without which life is not truly human. In our contact with those less developed than we are, we learn to nurture and care for others. Other people prevent us from becoming lost in the fog of subjectivity where we see nothing but ourselves and our own needs. The Spiral Path could be seen as, essentially, consisting in the deepening of our friendship and love for others. The higher we climb on the Path, the more we will be able to enter into fellowship with others.

The ideal of friendship is of such centrality to Buddhists that, in its highest form, it becomes one of the three chief objects of veneration. These three, the 'Three Jewels', are the Buddha, Dharma and Sangha. The Buddha is reverenced as the goal towards which all beings are moving and also as the historical individual, Siddhartha Gautama, the founder of the whole Buddhist tradition. The Dharma is both the Truth which the Buddha perceived and the Path which he set forth in his teachings. The Sangha is the spiritual community. These Three Jewels, or 'Three Most Precious Things', are the basis of Buddhism. What renders one a Buddhist is 'Going for Refuge to the Three Jewels', the act of personal commitment to realizing in one's own life the ideals which the Three Jewels represent.

The Spiritual Community or Sangha, then, is one of the foundations of Buddhism. At its highest level it is the indescribable accord that exists between the spiritually attained – those who have reached or surpassed Stream Entry. Sharing the same creative vision and yet each a unique expression of it, they are the sublime example of harmony. Complete trust and perfect understanding mark their relations with one another. In Buddhist scriptures there are many, very moving examples of the love and sympathy which existed between the various members of the Buddha's company.

On a lower level, the Sangha refers to the community of all those who have Gone for Refuge to the Three Jewels. They all experience the Buddha's vision as the ultimate meaning of their lives and they are all committed to its realization. Since the Sangha at this level includes both those who have, and those who have not, passed the point of no return, many of its members are subject to the buffetings of the still-unquieted reactive mind. The bond between them may therefore be of a more fragile kind, but it is nonetheless deep and heartfelt. Going for Refuge to the Three Jewels usually finds expression in a simple ceremony. One is then a member of a Sangha in the sense of a fellowship, a brotherhood, an Order – a body of men and women, devoted to the Three Jewels, who form a spiritual community (although not necessarily living together under one roof). The word Sangha is sometimes used in a more restricted sense to refer to the monks and nuns alone, but more properly membership of the Sangha does not enjoin the following of any particular way of life – except that it be one that genuinely helps the individual to grow. Many members of the Sangha may live in residential communities either for men or for women, others will be married and have families, and others may live on their own. What they have in common is not their lifestyle but their common commitment to the Buddha's vision. That common vision makes the Sangha potentially a very powerful force for the transformation of the world.

The Sangha, on all its levels, makes up the Buddhist community and, whenever time and circumstances will permit, it manifests a whole culture which has the treading of the Path as its basis. Institutions and practices, customs and ceremonies, arts and crafts: a whole way of life for men and women at all stages on the Path and of all temperaments and talents will gradually evolve to help them in their development. Such Buddhist cultures have flourished many times and in many different forms in the East with great beauty and richness. A Buddhist way of life is beginning to emerge here in the West, unique in its manifestations yet based upon the same principles as those of the past.

So far we have presented the Buddhist vision of existence in terms derived from traditional expositions. But there are currents in Western thought which suggest close analogies to the Dharma and which can certainly be extended to convey its message. For instance, a number of modern thinkers have begun to suggest that the concept of evolution explains more than just the origins of species. There are still some people who contend that the world was created by God with all the species now on earth in the form we find them. These 'creationists' are few, however, and it is now widely accepted that all existing life-forms on the planet evolved over very long periods of time from simple organisms originating in the sea. That much seems to be more or less beyond controversy. The manner by which that evolution took place is still an open debate. Whether the mechanism of evolution can be explained in terms of the chance adaptations of natural selection or by some higher order of meaning working itself out through the evolutionary process is, of course, of the greatest significance. For present purposes, however, we may confidently assert the generally accepted thesis that man has evolved from life-forms which are lower, in the sense that they are of far simpler biological structure, without entering the lists of the debate about how it happened.

It has often been pointed out that the concept of evolution can be used to describe many of the phenomena in our universe. Galaxies and stars evolve no less than does the individual human being from conception to adulthood. That whole evolutionary trend running through the universe seems to culminate in man, the most complex and adaptable form of which we have empirical evidence. But is the mature human being the final product of evolution? Are we the goal towards which life has been moving?

Here, we must broaden the terms of our enquiry for, so far, we have seen evolution as an increasing complexity of physical and biological organization. But when we look at mankind we see that human cultures may be in a process of evolution (they can, of course, also be seen to decay). Furthermore, when we look at individual men and women, we find that, though they may share within broad limits a common physical form, they have very different psychological characteristics and are of varying aptitudes and abilities. We find, particularly, that there are some who, for their intellectual penetration, creative genius or nobility of heart, tower above their fellows. A rough hierarchy can be discerned of qualities and virtues – although it is not always easy, or even fruitful, to place anyone in their particular degree. Many of the great figures of human history, though they may have been born with uncommon gifts, have gone to considerable lengths to cultivate their talents and to improve themselves. They have, in Goethe's words, made something of themselves. Whatever excellence they have had beyond the rest of men they owe to their own efforts over and above the advantages conferred on them by nature or society. They could be said to have undertaken their own evolution beyond the stage of ordinary man. They seem therefore to point the way to the next phase of evolution.

Man, then, appears as a kind of watershed in the evolutionary process. He is the product of biological evolution both in the sense that his body has evolved from lower life-forms over billions of years and that it has, in its growth from zygote to mature adult, mirrored that evoluton. Biological evolution, by whatever mechanism, has brought him thus far without any conscious intervention on his part. But, from this point, he must make himself. This lower, 'quantitative' evolution prepares the basis for a Higher Evolution of quality. Looked at in this way, evolution is not primarily the development of more complex biological forms, but the development of higher and higher levels of consciousness.

The lower evolution consists in the elaboration of sense consciousness. From the rudimentary sentience of the most primitive, single-celled organism up to the sophisticated sensory awareness of the higher animals, there is a change of degree only, not of kind. The world is perceived in greater depth and detail the higher up the evolutionary ladder we climb. But there are no persons or individuals to whom the perceptions belong or to whom they are attached. The individual organism in whom such perceptions occur has not identified himself, does not know himself. Particular perceptions are, as it were, part of the undifferentiated mass of nature's consciousness.

But, probably from the higher animals upwards, a new kind of consciousness gradually emerges: reflexive or self-consciousness, which has the possibility of completion in man. The undifferentiated, primitive harmony of sense consciousness, in which all life is yet merged in one continuous sleep, has been broken. Consciousness has become its own object and the possessor of consciousness has identified himself; he is aware of his own awareness. As self-awareness matures, the individual – for such there now is – makes a fundamental split in his experience, between what is himself and what is other. From now on, the basic structure of his perception is the differentiation of those elements of experience which belong to himself and those that do not. He polarizes his consciousness into self and other.

With this split, a whole new range of possibilities opens up. Self-consciousness makes possible the infinite ascent of the higher evolution and is also the progenitor of cruelty and greed unknown in nature. With it, we are barred from the perfect, although entirely without reflexive awareness, balance of nature, yet we are given the possibility of a new and far higher harmony in the full flowering of consciousness. It is, perhaps, the fruit of the Tree of the Knowledge of Good and Evil which Adam and Eve were forbidden to eat. It was their disobedience and the ending of their primal innocence for which they were banished from Eden. The Buddhist is, however, strongly encouraged to eat of the fruit of the Tree and to go forth from Eden of his own agency without the need of angels with flaming swords. He is urged to take upon himself his human destiny by following through to the full the implications of self-consciousness.

Self-consciousness has a number of different aspects. Memory is perhaps the most important, for to be self-conscious is to have a sense of an identity continuing from the past. From this awareness of oneself as having an history is derived an awareness of the relationship between actions and effects, of oneself as author of one's actions, and thus of one's responsibility for their consequences. Out of self-consciousness, there emerges our moral sense.

Imagination, too, is a part of self-consciousness. In a sense, self-consciousness is itself an act of imagination because self-consciousness consists in one being oneself an object of one's own awareness and we cannot literally perceive ourselves as an object. Imagination frees us from our immediate situation and allows us to rove unfettered through the many possibilities of existence. As memory gives us a past so imagination gives us a future. Not only do we remember but we can anticipate. We can set ourselves goals and aims, we can see ourselves other than we now are.

Imagination is double-edged. As we will see in the following chapters, it gives rise to the distortions and perversions of self-consciousness which lead up grotesque and terrifying evolutionary cul-de-sacs. Yet it is through imagination that we can soar to new heights of being and can envision high ideals. Imagination is the source of creativity and reveals to us the Spiral of the Higher Evolution. When functioning in its purest form, imagination is the faculty whereby we apprehend spiritual truth.

Imagination allows us to enter into sympathetic communication with others. We have identified ourselves as centres of action and experience but now we are able to see that others also have selves. We are able to enter imaginatively into their lives and thus to understand and talk with them. This capacity for mutual understanding means that self-conscious beings may cooperate together both in the business of physical survival but, more especially, in the Higher Evolution itself. Mutual cooperation and communication are, indeed, among the hallmarks of a mature individuality.

With self-consciousness, then, comes individuality, self as distinct from other, subject from object. Up until that point, evolution has been a blind, unconscious process. It is whole groups and classes of living beings which evolve together, not particular individuals. With the dawning of individuality, evolution must be consciously undertaken. The individual becomes responsible for his own future growth and, without his own consistent effort, no natural forces will sweep him forward. No one can force us to evolve or do our growing for us, though others may be crucial guides and companions on the Path; as the Buddhist texts say, 'The Buddhas, too, but show the way.' No saviour can do one's growing for one. No guru, incarnation of God though he claims to be, can give one knowledge. It must be won by our own efforts with the inspiration and advice of those who have trodden the Path before us.

The full emergence and acceptance of our individuality is the first step in the Higher Evolution. To begin with, our sense of ourselves is often sketchy and incomplete. We are, as it were, amphibious, spending much of our time in the vast oceans of the lower evolution and making a few, usually intellectual, forays on to the dry land of the Higher Evolution. It is this transition that we must complete by drawing ourselves fully up on to the solid ground of self-awareness. What is involved is the fulfilling of our self-consciousness, bringing all aspects of being into awareness: physical, emotional and intellectual.

The distinction between self and other, subject and object, has first to be firmly established. Then it must be transcended. The ascent of the Spiral Path, the continuance of the Higher Evolution, draws the two poles of experience closer and closer together. For instance, our awareness of the beauty of an object draws us beyond the tight limits of our own self-hood in a kind of communion with the beautiful object. In profound thought – not compulsive intellection but 'the whole man wholly attending' – we penetrate to a level of understanding deeper

The Buddhist Vision

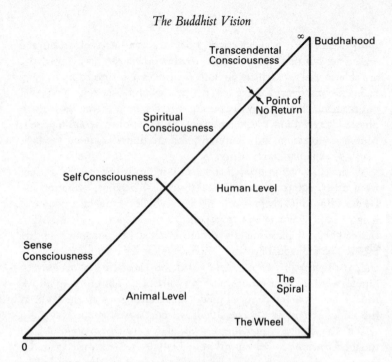

Fig. 1 The Triangle of the Evolution of Consciousness

than our normal perception of the duality of subject and object. In meditation, our purified and sharpened concentration give us access to dimensions in which consciousness is increasingly unified. In friendship, when cooperating with others, working for them, communicating intensely with them, we forget ourselves in our concern for them and gain access to a wider awareness.

The drawing together in our experience of subject and object and the relaxing of the tension between them belongs to a new kind of awareness: Spiritual Consciousness. Level upon level of ever more beautiful, joyous, and satisfying states of mind rise up one above the other. But, though the tension between self and other is being eased as they are drawn into greater harmony, there is still that same fundamental split in the structure of our perception. Spiritual Consciousness must give way to Transcendental Consciousness, in which the distinction between subject and object is finally dissolved. At this level,

30

consciousness is experienced in its wholeness as a total, absolute awareness, completely free and unobstructed, luminous and all-pervading.

It is hard for us to gain any understanding of what this state must be
like. It is to be without a self as we ordinarily understand it but not to
be immersed in the unconscious pre-selfhood of nature. Many inter-
preters of Buddhism have fallen into the trap of considering this Transcendental Consciousness to be a kind of ultimate blank – hardly a
desirable goal for the whole of evolution. It is perhaps best – although,
in a way, false or rather inadequate – to consider that, with Transcendental Consciousness, there is still, in some sense, a continuation of
the Spiral Path but functioning in a way that for the present we cannot
comprehend. All things are seen, as they are, in all their unique detail
and all are pervaded by an overwhelming Love and Compassion. This
Buddha-Consciousness is freed from all suffering and knows only the
'Great Bliss' which, needless to say, in comparison makes our everyday
happiness look like misery.

The process of evolution begins in the unconscious wholeness of
nature which is broken by the dawning of self-awareness. The split is
finally healed in the Transcendental Awareness of Buddhahood. As
men we stand at the mid-point of the great evolutionary drama that
begins with the single-celled organism and ends with the Buddha. We
cannot go back into the innocent darkness of natural ignorance and to
remain suspended where we are is to experience alienation and frustration. We must push on, by our own individual efforts, with the help
and guidance of friends and teachers, towards that goal of Buddhahood.

3

The Wheel and the Way

The origins of the Wheel of Life as a symbol of the Buddhist vision of mundane existence are to be found in the earliest phase of Indian Buddhism. One text*, belonging to the important Sarvastivada School, gives an account of the Buddha himself instructing that the Wheel be painted at the gateway of every monastery, and detailing how it should be done.

According to this text, Maudgalyayana, one of the Buddha's two foremost disciples, occasionally visited the beings in all the different realms of existence. All the Buddhist traditions attest to his mastery of psychic powers and this was but one of his abilities. He could see the beings in hell-like states or in heavenly worlds and in all other possible phases of being. He could see what had brought them to that condition, what the imperfections and sufferings of each state might be, and where they lead. He had, it seems, an extraordinary capacity to empathize with others, to see into their minds and their hearts, to feel their sufferings or joys, and to understand how they had come to be as they were.

With this ability to enter deeply into the lives of others, it is perhaps not surprising that he was also able to communicate very effectively. The text tells us that if any senior monk was having trouble with a disciple who was losing his inspiration he would send him to Maudgal-yayana who would 'exhort and teach him well' to such good effect that 'such dissatisfied monks would again lead the spiritual life with keen ardour, even distinguishing themselves with the higher attainments'. It seems that he had the power to reinvigorate flagging zeal by sharing his own deep insight into all the various conditions of existence.

So much in demand was he that he seemed to live surrounded by

* Sahasodgata Avadana, Divyavadana 21.

monks and nuns, laymen and women. The Buddha, noticing this, commented that there were not enough people like Maudgalyayana to teach all those who needed him. He, therefore, proposed that a picture should be made, representing Maudgalyayana's teaching and he instructed his followers to paint the Wheel of Life depicting the different realms of existence and the processes which underlie them, at the entrance to every monastery. At each, one monk was to be deputed to explain the imagery to visitors and novices.

This story is interesting from a number of points of view, not least because it shows the use of visual arts as a medium for the Dharma in the very early years of Buddhism. (The source is a text thought to have been compiled some time in the first century BC and almost certainly enshrining much earlier traditions.) Its chief interest lies in its spiritual message, however. Some may not find it easy to take literally the 'miraculous' element in the story. (Buddhism has always maintained that there is nothing miraculous about such matters, in the sense of a disruption of the laws of nature by an higher power. It considers, rather, that our own faculties and powers are limited by our own limited point of view and that, if we expand our minds, we may be able to do things that now seem impossible.) Even if one cannot accept that Maudgalyayana literally visited those other dimensions of being by the exercise of his psychic powers, it is possible to see that he had some sort of visionary insight into other people's states of mind and the way they experience things. His vision was no mere theory. He knew them for what they were, by his own immediate perception. Thus the basis of this symbolic representation, the Wheel of Life, is direct experience. The image attempts to convey that insight in visual terms. We should always bear this in mind and try to stretch beyond the confines of the symbol's structure to the Transcendental Vision which underlies it.

The other point of immediate interest in the story is the effect Maudgalyayana had on the dissatisfied disciples. Few who make some effort to tread the Path do not know moments when they feel no inspiration for any of the practices which will help them to grow. In those moments, in fact, they will probably feel little interest in the very idea of growth. It can all seem too much effort and struggle for little tangible result. At such moments, although we may be able to give a perfect account of Buddhist teaching and may be in full intellectual agreement with its conclusions, yet we have no zest for it. Emotional engagement is lacking and we feel little or no enthusiasm for the spiritual

Path. The world has become flat and two-dimensional and it is only in the little gratifications of everyday life that we can see any hope of happiness. Somehow, Maudgalyayana was able to rekindle the fires of inspiration in such cold ashes as these. Even from the scanty information in the story it is clear that he did not do so by giving a lucid, rational description of reality. Such a description might have roused the intellectual curiosity of some but it would hardly cause them to 'lead again the spiritual life with keen ardour' and even to distinguish themselves by the excellence of their attainments. He touched them in such a way that, not only were their understandings deepened, but their hearts were moved. He appealed, in other words, to their imaginations.

As we have seen, the faculty of imagination accompanies the emergence of self-consciousness. At its most general, it is simply the capacity to bring to mind images of what is not actually present to the senses. This general definition covers anything from fantasies about food or sex through dreams of world domination to the sublime vision of the artist or mystic. Clearly, this imaginative capacity can be used mechanically to produce images which are the picturing to ourselves of our egoistical desires in fantasy or what Freud termed 'hallucinatory wish-fulfilment'. Anyone who has tried to meditate will know how much of our mental activity is taken up with this kind of imagination, for one often experiences in learning to meditate a constant stream of fantasies before one is able to settle the mind to concentration. This kind of imaginative activity belongs to the reactive mind, to the Wheel.

Imagination also has a creative function through which we unfold higher potentialities from within ourselves. Its images are, in this case, the projection from our own depths of new levels of consciousness beyond those we ordinarily experience. From another point of view, the creative imagination is the faculty with which we respond to a higher level of reality. True works of art have the effect of stirring our imaginations, and it is with the faculty of creative imagination that we respond to spiritual vision and truth. In this sense, the creative imagination is not dissimilar from the faculty of 'Imagination' referred to in the literary criticism of the English Romantics, especially Coleridge. The Imagination or the 'Imaginal faculty' as a creative power of the human mind must be clearly distinguished from imagination as reactive fantasy.

The Imaginal faculty unites and transcends both thinking and feeling. In contrast, the psyche of many, if not most, people in modern, industrialized societies are deeply divided. Our intellectual faculties are to some extent differentiated and developed – although I do not wish to imply that they are usually developed to a high degree. Our emotions are, however, woefully immature. It is as if modern man has two personalities: one on the surface which is capable of reason and fairly sophisticated intellectual comprehension and a semi- or sub-conscious personality, consisting of retarded or even infantile emotions. A degree of alienation has developed between the two which leaves them usually at war with one another. Because of this split we have little conception of intellection which is, at the same time, full of feeling or of emotion which is suffused with intelligence. But the Imaginal faculty is of this kind. It is a function of the whole personality, integrated in feelingful understanding. When the Imagination is alive in us, we are whole individuals, reaching beyond ourselves to fresh heights of consciousness. It is a sad reflection on our times that we have no commonly accepted word for such a capacity. It is as if, having no name for it, we cannot experience it. But the Imaginal faculty is latent within us, as an ability to apprehend and appreciate higher dimensions of reality. Without such a faculty there could be no art and certainly no Spiral Path. It is to this faculty that Maudgalyayana appealed and it is because he did so that he had such success with those weary disciples.

The Imaginal faculty unites and transcends both emotion and thought. It unites them in so far as they no longer operate as autonomous sub-personalities within the overall person. They are but two aspects of one whole. They are transcended in that they are no longer 'thought' and 'emotion' as we normally know them. No longer does emotion consist of those crude and coarse outbursts and longings, often blind and impulsive, which characterize much of our emotional life. It is not negative and self-centred but positive and expansive, opening out beyond the tight confines of self-interest. It is the kind of inspired, uplifted, exalted emotion which is part of aesthetic experience, as when we are deeply absorbed in music or wonder at the flaming tints of the setting sun. And, since it is united with understanding, it is suffused with sensitivity, awareness and clarity.

Thought as a component of the Imaginal faculty is not merely the capacity to infer valid conclusions from given premises. It is the penetration and cognition of truth at higher levels. Poetry offers a clear example of this kind of intellection. School children are often asked to give a gloss on the meaning of a poem but the best poems will never entirely reduce to conceptual analysis of this kind. There are levels and shades of meaning which are lost in translation to such reasoned prose. Yet something in one understands what the poet says even if one cannot ever adequately expound or explain it. He has managed to distil into his lines his own perception of an higher level of truth which ordinary language cannot convey. One's apprehension of his meaning is not onesidedly cognitive, for it is to the Imaginal faculty that he speaks. He carries his meaning to us through our response both to Beauty and to Truth. The sensuous qualities of the poem, the power of the images, flow of words, rhythm and rhyme, speak to our emotions. The meaning of the words and the symbolism of the images they conjure up appeal to our intellect. But here, in the Imaginal faculty, thought and emotion are united and transcended. Beauty is Truth and Truth, Beauty.

At this point, it should be stressed that Buddhism does not under-value reason. It is an essential attribute of human life and an indispensable tool of human growth. We must be able to think clearly in ordering our worldly affairs, otherwise our decisions and predictions can only be based on guesswork and so-called intuition – often a very doubtful process amounting to little more than subjective prejudice. We must be able to gather and examine evidence to draw reasonable conclusions from what we know. But reason is not only essential for everyday functioning. We must use it to clarify the tangle of confused ideas that so often chokes our minds; those false views and wrong opinions which can have such a disastrous effect upon our lives. Much of this confusion arises because we have never examined our own assumptions in the light of reason. Through reason, also, we can get a preliminary grasp of the Buddhist vision as conceptually formulated and we can investigate it to see whether it makes sense. Again, until we can establish a deeper contact with other people, reason is the common ground on the basis of which we can relate to one another. The man who is incapable of reason is still immersed in the half-light of instinctual feeling and can only make magical, dreamlike connections among things. Reason, as has been said, distinguishes man from the animals. Yet the sphere of reason is strictly limited.

Reason, as I am using the term here, is the faculty by which we order concepts so that we can arrive at correct conclusions about our world. It is a function of our self-consciousness. Having split the world into what is self and what is other, we then divide what we regard as other into smaller and ever smaller units to which we attach word-labels.

Words allow us to hold in our minds, and to consider, the various objects to which they refer. Thus we are able to think about the constituents of our world and their interrelationships. In thus breaking up what is outside us into objects, we unconsciously follow a set of rules which determine *how* we break it up. For instance, if a portion of what we perceive consistently exhibits the same characteristics over a period of time we will interpret it to be one object which is different from all others.

These rules are basic assumptions which we are not usually conscious of applying. They are buried in our language and culture and in the very structure of our own minds. Reason, then, is part of the way in which we choose to see the world; it is a function of a subject/object dominated perception, oriented to the material world. Needless to say, we do not each of us determine for ourselves how we are going to see the world. We drink it in with our mother's milk.

The fact that reason rests upon assumptions which are part of the way in which we structure our experience does not mean that it is an illusion. Within their own sphere these assumptions will yield valid conclusions which will enable us to function effectively in the world. Most of us need to *develop* the rational faculty further and to apply it more consistently and thoroughly. Problems only arise when we try to apply reason outside its own limits. Reason cannot comprehend the fundamental nature of things because reality lies beyond the framework of subject and object which we impose upon it and which is the basis from which reason operates. To be able to reason about our world we must reduce it to manageable order, but in reducing and simplifying we lose the indescribable complexity of things, their full richness and wonder. The ultimate nature of things is beyond the reach of reason.

We have already seen that ordinary reason cannot provide us with an understanding of an inspired poem, although it may give us a basis of understanding from which our Imagination can take flight. A symbol or myth cannot be understood in its fullness by the use of the rational faculty, for a symbol may be at the same time one thing and its opposite – defying the Law of Non-contradiction! Reason can do no more than give us a working model of the world, effective for most practical purposes as long as it is not taken too literally. But a model is not the reality, and to get closer to reality we need to use another mode of cognition – found in the Imaginal faculty.

The Imagination can express itself through, and respond to, concepts when these are inspired or illumined. Some Buddhist philosophy is of this kind. The system itself may be rationally articulated yet it is not a speculative construct, erected purely on the basis of reason. It is the attempt to convey, in rational-conceptual form, the insights perceived by the Imagination using concepts as metaphors for a truth that lies beyond reason. On encountering a philosophy of this kind, one's own Imaginal faculty may be stirred to life. There are dangers, though, that this sort of philosophical expression degenerates, all to rapidly, into a rationalistic dogma as successive generations read it more and more literalistically and fail to raise themselves beyond the level of words to the vision which the words are meant to convey. This process of decay is certainly evident in some Buddhist schools. For this reason other schools have preferred to baffle the intellect with paradoxes and negations so that the rational mind is unable to fasten on to any concepts and solidify them into a fixed model. *Perhaps the main point is that the student of the Dharma should never mistake an understanding of the words used for an insight into truth.* He should always be striving for his own direct experience of the meaning behind the words.

It is in the arts that we are most accustomed to witness the functioning of the Imaginal faculty. Art which is anything more than decorative, merely interesting, or clumsily didactic draws us up to a new level of awareness which we share for a while with the artist. If we are moved in this manner, the way in which we perceive the world is affected and we may feel a new sense of wholeness and purpose. Images, symbols, myths, whether in art or our own dreams and visions, are the common language of the Imagination, able as they are to communicate many levels of meaning and, at the same time, call up a powerful emotional response.

The Imaginal faculty, finally, may go beyond images, however refined and subtle. Images, too, are a refraction of reality, not reality itself. The Imagination can rise to burst through all that veils us from the Truth. When it does so it is Insight, the direct perception of the nature of things in perfect, non-dual awareness. It is the dawning of this Insight which makes one a Stream Entrant and it is its full flowering which is Enlightenment.

Images are the common language of the faculty of Imagination and that faculty, as we have seen, has the power to move the heart as well as to illumine the mind. It is for these reasons that the Buddha caused Maudgalyayana's vision to be translated into the visual image of the Wheel of Life. For these same reasons the Wheel of Life and other symbols have been chosen as the framework for this exposition of the Dharma. To some extent, the images speak for themselves to that faculty of Imagination within every one of us. Perhaps all analysis should be abandoned and the different elements of the symbolism described and left to convey their own message. But that task requires a Buddhist Dante or Milton and awaits another pen. In the remainder of this chapter, we will briefly describe the Wheel, the Spiral and the Mandala of the Five Buddhas. In the chapters which follow we will examine their various meanings. Throughout, we should not forget the purported origins of the Wheel as the Buddha's depiction of Maudgalyayana's insight. It is with inspired vision that we are dealing and we must open our Imaginations to the images as they are presented.

We have seen one version of the origin of the Wheel in the story of Maudgalyayana's journeyings in other realms of existence. Other sources tell a different story. Most of what we know about the Wheel comes from Tibetan Buddhism. Apart from one solitary example in the ancient cave temples of Ajanta, not a single picture of the Wheel has survived in India, so complete has been the Muslim and Brahminical extirpation of Buddhism in the land of its origin. But in Tibet, which inherited the rich traditions of Indian Buddhism, it is used to this day as an edifying image painted in the vestibule of many temples. A common Tibetan legend attributes its origin to the Buddha once more, but pictures him outlining the Wheel for his followers in grains of rice in a paddyfield. The details of the Wheel have, to some extent, been supplemented in Tibet, and it is on one type of Tibetan Wheel of Life that this account is based.

The Wheel consists of four concentric circles. In the central circle or hub are three animals: a cock, a snake and pig, each of which bites the tail of the one before it so that they are linked together in a circular chain. The next circle forms a thin band around the hub and is divided vertically into two segments, the left coloured white and the right, black. In the black half, naked beings tumble downwards, harried by demons, their faces contorted in agony and their arms flailing helplessly to prevent their fall. In the white section, beings are performing all kinds of meritorious actions: meditating, distributing money, venerating the Buddha. They rise upwards with joyous faces.

The next circle is placed close to the rim so that the third area occupies almost half the Wheel. It is divided into six equal segments. In the bottom segment is shown the realm of hell, containing all the tortures conventional in depictions from medieval Christendom: beings are

Fig. 2 The Wheel of Life

roasted, boiled, flayed, crushed and dissected by the pitiless demons who preside over this world of horror. The intense heat of ever-burning fire fills the hell-realm, apart from the deepest section where there is an absolute cold as in Dante's Inferno. At the centre of hell stands an enormous figure with massive limbs, glaring wrathful face, and a halo of flickering flame. This is Yama, the Judge of the Dead he holds in his hand a mirror wherein are shown the deeds of those who come before him.

40

In the left lower segment is the realm of the hungry ghosts. Smoke-coloured and insubstantial, these creatures have large bellies and pinhole mouths. Whatever they drink turns to fire, and whatever they eat, to swords in their stomachs. In the corresponding section on the right is the world of the animals, in their turn to be preyed upon by man.

The upper left segment shows the human realm in which men and women go about their daily business. On the right are the titans, or jealous gods. Fierce, ugly, powerfully built creatures for whom life is permanent warfare, they struggle against the gods who occupy the top realm for possession of the wish-fulfilling tree which grants all desires. The gods themselves live in a world of great beauty and happiness wherein all their wants are instantly satisfied.

In each of the six realms there appears a Buddha-figure, each one a different colour, holding an implement. In the hells, a dark-blue Buddha carries a pot of ointment; in the hungry-ghost realm, a red Buddha holds a jar of nectar; a light-blue Buddha, holding a book, appears to the animals; a yellow Buddha, dressed in an orange robe and holding the staff and begging bowl of a wandering monk, comes to the human world; a green Buddha in full armour, carrying a flaming sword, ministers to the titans; and a white Buddha plays upon a lute to the gods.

The outer ring of the wheel is divided into twelve segments which represent the twelve cyclic links in the chain of Conditioned Co-production as revealed in the process of human birth and death. In each segment is an image, representing a stage in that flow of conditioned factors. At the top, a blind man staggers forward, feeling his way with a stick. Then, in clockwise direction, is depicted: a potter making pots at a wheel; a monkey leaping from branch to branch in a tree; four men in a boat, one of whom is steering; an house with a door and five windows; a couple embracing; a man with an arrow in his eye; a woman offering a drink to a seated man; a woman plucking fruit from a tree; a couple in the act of sexual intercourse; a woman giving birth; and a dead body being carried to a funeral pyre. With the next link, the Wheel has turned full circle to the blind man with a stick once more.

Above the rim of the Wheel, a ferocious face appears with three fiercely glaring red eyes and a crown of skulls. This is the monster of impermanence who allows nothing conditioned to stand still. He devours the Wheel with his fangs and tears at it with strong talons.

Taken by itself, this is but one side of reality: the cyclic kind of conditionality. The Spiral is represented by the Buddhas appearing in

Fig. 3 The Wheel, the Spiral and the Mandala

each realm but this is not really an adequate apportioning of emphasis. Although it is certainly important, as it were, to know the enemy and to know the worst about our situation, we also need a strong feeling for the positive possibilities of human life if we are to have a full vision of reality. In many versions of the Tibetan Wheels of Life, there appears a Buddha above the Wheel to the right, pointing the way to Enlightenment. Here we move from the Wheel to the Spiral.

If we imagine the Wheel laid flat upon the ground, spinning so fast in the claws of the monster of impermanence that its details are lost and we see but a blurr of confusion, then we can picture the Spiral rising from its outer edge and circling round at higher and higher levels above it. The Spiral is divided into two parts at the point of Stream Entry. Below that point we see god-like beings of ever-increasing beauty and radiance, ascending the Path. Above, the beings grown in intensity of beauty, but now wisdom too shines in their eyes.

Finally the Spiral merges into the Mandala, a vast symetrically ordered circle. At the centre is the dazzling white figure of Vairochana, the Illuminator, who sits cross-legged on a white lotus-throne supported by two majestic lions. He is dressed in rich silks and jewels and turns in his hands a golden wheel with eight spokes which shines like the sun. Four other Buddhas are seated around him at the cardinal points, likewise richly adorned. The blue figure in the East is Akshobya, the Impertubable, who is seated on a throne supported by elephants. His right hand touches the ground before him and his left, resting on his lap, holds a golden thunderbolt. In the South sits the yellow Buddha, Ratnasambhava, the Jewel-Born, on a throne of horses, his right hand extended in giving and his left holding a jewel. In the West, Amitabha, Infinite Light, rests upon a peacock throne and his two hands, folded in his lap for meditation, hold a red lotus blossom. Amoghasiddhi, Unobstructed Success, occupies the Northern quarter and holds a double thunderbolt with his left hand whilst he raises his right in a gesture of confidence.

While these five figures together represent the culmination of the Path in one sense (at this level, the Wheel has been completely transcended), the Spiral process still unfolds. The figures glow and pulsate with energy, sending out dazzling beams of light. They begin to manifest from within themselves more and more figures and forms in a process of infinite creative unfoldment. Perfection improves upon perfection, without end.

4

The Roots of Evil

The motive force which drives a wheel is at its hub. Thus, at the hub of the Wheel of Life are the cock, the snake and the pig, the forces that keep it turning. They are known as the 'Three Unwholesome Roots' because from them grow all life's evils, or as the 'Three Poisons' because they corrupt us from within. The cock represents greed, the snake hatred and the pig ignorance, and it is these three which underlie all human bondage and misery.

It is appropriate that these forces are depicted by animals since they represent primitive urges beneath the supposedly civilized exterior of many men. Yet we do injustice to animals in using them as symbols of greed and hatred because animals never display these emotions, which are all too common among humans. Very few animals will, for instance, fight their own kind to the death or wantonly kill members of other species. They certainly experience hunger and desire but they rarely indulge in overeating or other neurotic behaviour – unless, interestingly enough, they have been in close contact with humans. Men, however, can carry deep and deadly hatreds which lead them to destroy other human beings, even those close to them in affection and kinship. As we know, human destructiveness can be on an immense scale. Man is also capable of intense longings which may give a whole life over to heaping up wealth or power despite terrible suffering caused to others. Human greed and hatred are of a quite different order from the hunger and aggression of the animal. They are specifically human failings and to understand their nature we must look more closely at human consciousness.

The human being is self-aware. Out of the womb of nature has emerged a separate identity, differentiated from the world around it. Initially, that differentiated selfhood is very fragile and is maintained only with some difficulty. Dawning as it does out of the dark background of nature, it is crude and rigid, closely identified with the physical body, material possessions, relationships with other people, and a fixed world-view. This insubstantial self is constantly washed away from within by the preconscious forces which swell beneath the surface of self-awareness. It is also threatened from without by the continual decay and death of the objects and people in its world. Everything from which the sense of identity is at first derived is subject to the law of impermanence and consistently fails to provide a lasting and reliable source of security. A sense of insecurity is an inevitable accompaniment of emerging self-consciousness as it is buffeted, again and again, by the transitory processes of life.

The immature self or ego tries to make itself secure by using the same instincts as those by which the animal preserves itself. Just as the animal hunts for the food which will nourish its organism, so the ego tries to possess those things it considers as securing its identity. And as the animal will attack and destroy whatever threatens its survival, so the ego seeks to destroy whatever undermines its integrity. Aided and amplified by the human power of imagination, these reactions can reach the monstrous proportions of ruthless empire-building and of mass destruction through war. Although greed and hatred are fundamentally defensive reactions, they do not always appear so. They may be the timorous and desperate impulses of those who feel that they are finally cornered by life but they may also manifest themselves with all the panache and vigour of one who believes that he is successful in the bid to secure his identity.

The strutting cock with his bright plumage represents greed. No doubt, his proverbial vanity and lust make the poor bird an appropriate symbol for this most human failing. The word 'greed' does not really do full justice to the emotion symbolized by the cock which includes the whole spectrum of unwholesome desire from vague hankerings to intense longings which allow nothing to stand in the way of their fulfilment. 'Neurotic craving' it might better be called, suggesting both its potential power and the delusion and sickness which underlie it. Neurotic craving is the longing to possess things so that one can make them part of oneself in the belief that they will help to secure one's identity. It may be *objects* that we covet in this sort of way. Craving of this kind can be observed, for instance, when we lose something and experience not merely regret or irritation at no longer being able to enjoy it but a deeper sense of loss, even a kind of panic. It is as if we have lost not merely the object but part of ourselves. It may be *ideas* to which we cling, building our security upon them. This is revealed if we feel personally undermined when those ideas are attacked or questioned. But other people provide the principal objects of craving – themselves. We crave their love and approval, their admiration, just their presence as stable factors in our universe. When this craving is connected with biological and social needs, such as sex or the support of the family, particularly unpleasant and painful situations are likely to develop.

Craving should be distinguished from healthy desire. Hunger, for instance, is not neurotic craving. One can experience an empty stomach and the desire for food in a quite straightforward way so that when one eats hunger is satisfied. No emotional disturbance or feeling of insecurity arises out of healthy hunger. Food only becomes an object of neurotic craving when the healthy desire is entrapped in a neurotic personality. Craving is to be eradicated by spiritual practice, healthy desires are not. To differentiate the one from the other we must question whether the desire has an emotionally disruptive effect and whether the satisfaction of the desire leads to its termination. Not only are there physical desires which are healthy and which should be satisfied so long as no harm comes to oneself or others but there are desires which should be actively cultivated. There is the desire for friendship, for beauty and for other ideal qualities, and there is the desire to develop as an individual. These should be strengthened as much as possible and much Buddhist practice is directed to this end. The cock represents only neurotic craving, not healthy desire nor aspiration towards an ideal.

The snake is chosen to represent hatred because of its cold blood and its poisonous bite. With its icy glance and scaly skin, rearing up, its venomous, forked tongue flashing, it seems the archetype of malevolence. Yet no snake will attack another animal except to eat it or to defend itself against what it considers a physical threat. Human hatred, however, can lead to acts of senseless cruelty against completely innocent people. At the other end of the scale, it may amount to no more than a mild dislike and a frosty manner. Whatever the degree of intensity, we hate what we feel threatens or undermines our sense of self. The animal instinct of self-preservation is now usurped to defend the weak ego. Although it may be vented on inanimate objects, hatred is nearly always directed at people. Whether they are, objectively speaking, working against us or not, we feel that their very existence threatens ours and we want them removed so that they can no longer harm us. If the threat they pose to our self-identity is deep enough we may feel that the only way we can gain security is to destroy them utterly.

There is a third way in which the immature ego tries to stabilize itself. At the centre of the Wheel is a fat, black hog, rooting around in the muck with its snout, its ears falling over its eyes so that it sees nothing but the patch of dirt before it. In the West, the pig is usually considered as the epitome of gluttony but here it becomes a symbol for delusion or ignorance. Blinkered by its ears, the pig is conscious only of what its snout is sticking into. So the deluded person is limited in his perspective on life. The limitation is not the result of plain lack of information, it is a defensive stratagem. He refuses to see anything which might threaten his identity. Security is sought in blindness. The ostrich with its head buried in the sand to avoid detection might be a better image for the ignorant man. In his delusion, he takes refuge in a narrow world and ignores everything outside it. He will not look at the basic facts of life: that everything in his world must decay and that he will, himself, inevitably die.

One can sometimes catch oneself using ignorance as a defence. A friend may draw one's attention to unpleasant truths, perhaps about one's own motives or behaviour. One comprehends what is being said but then, at the same moment, turns one's mind away from it. This self-distraction is deliberate and is a manifestation of delusion. It also displays itself in the fixed view of life adopted by many who refuse to examine or acknowledge anything which lies outside the confines of what they presently think they know.

Ignorance does not always show itself in overtly stupid or unintelligent behaviour. It can be highly sophisticated and give rise, for instance, to very complex systems of thought. For ignorance is the basic poison, the root of roots, and it is present up to the moment of Enlightenment. It is nothing less than our refusal to open ourselves to a wider sphere of reality. Whether or not we are entirely happy in our presently achieved level of consciousness, we at least have a relatively stable sense of ourselves, fragile as it may be. We know who we are, or we think we do. To move beyond ourselves as we now are to a wider dimension of consciousness is to step into the unknown and to leave behind the self as we presently know it. This is a kind of death and it is deeply threatening to the ego. So we turn away, refusing to recognise the truth that was always there but which is now forcing itself upon our attention. Sometimes, people learning to meditate will observe this reaction in themselves as they begin to touch upon a higher level of consciousness. However happy and clear that state may be, it is unfamiliar and it offers nothing through which one can identify oneself. Panicking, one seeks the safe ground of ordinary consciousness. The ignorant person is like the prisoner who prefers the confinement which he knows to the mysterious possibilities of freedom. Until we are Enlightened, we are all ignorant.

Our lives are dominated essentially by two contradictory forces: the evolutionary urge within us which drives us to achieve new levels of consciousness and the dead weight of our ignorance which pulls us back to more limited horizons. Our task, in taking up the spiritual Path, is consciously to allow the force of evolution to carry us upward and to prevent ignorance from binding us down. We are, as it were, strung between two great heavenly bodies, nature and Buddhahood, each of which exercises its own gravitational pull. The spiritual Path leads from the one to the other. In the earlier part of our spiritual career we are working all the time against the force of ignorance which is the gravitational pull of nature. The pull of Buddhahood, which is the evolutionary urge, is there within us, but it is heavily outweighed by ignorance. For any progress to take place we must make a constant effort to overcome the pull of ignorance which binds us to lower stages of being. At a certain point the two gravitational forces are evenly matched between nature and Buddhahood. Once over it, the evolutionary force is stronger than the pull of ignorance, and we enter the evolutionary stream which leads to Buddhahood. The Spiral trend works so strongly in the Stream Entrant that, although there is still ignorance in him, he continuously transcends whatever limitations he encounters at each new level and he cannot fall back. Up to that point of no return, we must unceasingly strive to overcome our own tendency to contraction and stagnation, symbolized by the pig of ignorance.

The cock, the snake and the pig circle round together, each biting the tail of the one before it. This illustrates the way in which craving, hatred and delusion are inextricably tangled together. Delusion underlies the other two and is present, to some degree, in all states short of Enlightenment. It is even found in some highly positive states in which there is neither greed nor hatred. Greed, if it is thwarted, quickly turns to hatred and most hatred contains an element of frustrated desire. Most negative mental states are made up of complex mixtures of all three. And so the three animals writhe and twist, spinning the Wheel of Life.

We seldom encounter greed, hatred and delusion in their raw forms. Such naked egoism is usually disguised and refined by the mutual accommodations of social life whose conventions cushion us against the three animals within. A polite veneer hides them from others and it may be that we are not conscious of them in ourselves. This can be observed in a person talking in a polite and friendly way, while the set of his face and the way he holds his body reveal an underlying hostility or fear of which he is not himself fully aware. Often, if our contacts with others threaten to bring such fundamental negative feelings into the open we break them off. In some people, however, the tight knot of defensive ego is relatively near the surface and it does not take much to precipitate quite extreme reactions. In healthier and more confident personalities that knot is far more deeply buried, seldom showing its naked face since the person is socially so well adapted. Nonetheless, the three animals remain the driving force. Often in the closer relationships of life that cushioning breaks down. In romance and family life, tensions and rows, impossible expectations and their inevitable disappointments, reveal the fragile ego and its desperate attempts to secure itself.

It is of great importance that we learn to recognize the cock, snake and pig within us, for by bringing them into consciousness, we can stop them dominating our lives and we can eventually eliminate them altogether. We must look with great honesty at our actions and admit what it is that really motivates us beneath our rationalizations and social face. Being with other people often helps us to do this for people are the primary targets of our emotions and close contact with them will tend to bring us up against our raw feelings. If they are not themselves trying to cultivate greater honesty, however, we may simply get very tangled with them. If they are seriously concerned to know what is in their own hearts and are trying to follow the Path of the Higher Evolution then our own efforts will be greatly enhanced. We can openly acknowledge to our friends what is going on in our minds. They will be able to give us advice and encouragement or will simply listen to us. Openly communicating our thoughts and feelings to those we trust not only gives emotional relief but helps us to perceive more clearly what we ourselves think and feel. For such trust to exist, we must feel confident that our friends share our basic desire to grow. In the end, this form of openness can only exist between two people who are both committed to the Higher Evolution and who are therefore members of the spiritual community in its only meaningful sense. One of the primary characteristics of a true Sangha, or spiritual community, is the frankness that exists between its members. They are able to admit freely to each other whatever their thoughts and emotions may be. No one pretends to be other than what he is, whether from guilt or to gain advantage over others. At the same time, since such openness takes place against the background of an higher ideal, it never becomes a mere indulgence in moods and tantrums. No one inflicts his states upon others. Each tries to know what is in his own mind, for better or worse, and he is prepared to reveal himself to his friends. Each is prepared to listen to the comments and views of those he has opened himself to and is also, of course, ready to listen when they reveal themselves.

Most people will find that all three animals are within them. One of them is, however, likely to predominate and, according to an early Buddhist system, human beings can be classified on the basis of which poison most commonly determines their behaviour. Finding out whether one is a greed-, hatred- or delusion-type can help in getting to know oneself, highly generalized though these categories may be. It is said that each type betrays his character in his every action:

In standing up he who is of greedy conduct is comfortable and polite in manner, he who is of hateful conduct is stiff in manner, he who is of deluded conduct is troubled in manner. And the same in sitting down. He who is of greedy conduct prepares his bed evenly and without haste, lies down gently and sleeps in a composed manner gathering his limbs big and small. On being awakened he does not rise abruptly but gives a reply gently as though unwillingly. He who is of hateful conduct prepares his bed hastily in any fashion and sleeps frowning with a stiffly thrown body: on being awakened he arises abruptly and gives a reply as though in anger. He who is of deluded conduct prepares an ill-formed bed and sleeps with outstretched limbs, mostly face downwards; and on being awakened he rises sluggishly uttering the sound 'humph'.*

* Visuddhimagga, III.

So says Buddhaghosa, the great fifth-century Indian Buddhist scholar, in his *Path of Purity*, and he goes on to give the characteristics of each type in working, eating, dressing and other everyday actions. He also describes the positive counterparts of greed-, hatred-, and delusion-types.

The greed type is probably the easiest to get on with since his basic purpose is to find objects which give him pleasure. He enjoys life and forms strong attachments to people. The hate-type, on the other hand, is always critical. He sees the unpleasant side of everything and it is the avoidance of pain that primarily concerns him. The delusion-type is neither one nor the other. Shambling, distracted and bewildered, he lives in a grey fog and he cannot make up his mind about anything. He suffers from chronic vagueness but will not clarify his thoughts. Most people do not fall neatly into any one of these three categories; rather, each of us combines all three in his own personal mixture of poisons.

Whether one finds this particular method useful or not, it is important that one gets to know oneself. This is not easy to do and it necessarily takes many years before one discovers what are one's real motives and inclinations, vices and virtues. One needs work that is directed to some positive end and friends who are also committed to self-knowledge and who have one's best interests at heart. If one has these then slowly one will come to understand oneself as one is and as one could be.

Greed, hatred and delusion are not the only possible motivating forces and the corresponding types are, therefore, not the only possible ones. The three poisons are essentially the defence mechanisms of an immature ego. Although some residue of greed and hatred remains until very high levels of development have been attained and ignorance is present until Enlightenment itself, a sense of personal identity can be achieved which is far more stable and mature.

The embryonic ego, in the initial stages of its separation from the sleep of nature, is very weak and feels its own vulnerability. Not only is it fragile but it is crude: it sees the whole world as existing for itself and tries to impose its demands upon its surroundings. This tyrannical project is, except in the rarest cases, quickly thwarted by resistance from the environment. Things never do quite bend to one's will or completely conform to one's desires. One is often in direct conflict with life itself. Other people are particularly intractable to our wills, for they have wills of their own. In order to deal with this basic tension in

51

life we must either erect a superstructure of personality adapted to the chances and disappointments of human life yet fundamentally rooted in greed, hatred and delusion or we must evolve a more mature sense of selfhood.

The ego matures by developing genuine confidence in its own identity. Less and less is the sense of selfhood dependent on objects and people outside and more and more is it to be found within. This more mature ego is what might be called real individuality for, up to this point, individuality has been only partly achieved. Maturation is largely the result of personal effort but it is also aided by a secure and encouraging background which imparts a sense of well-being without restricting or smothering the emergent self. Parents, teachers and friends must provide support and sympathetic guidance while acknowledging and accepting the crystallizing individuality. The person who has matured in this way has a natural and easy self-confidence. He is able to appreciate and care for himself, to love himself and wish himself well. This is no narcissistic self-obsession or egoistical self-assertion which is merely a manifestation of the immature ego. It is an healthy self-esteem which does not begrudge others valuing themselves. Many Westerners do not find it easy to love themselves since the effect of our Christian culture has, in all too many cases, left people scarred with irrational guilt and self-hatred and with the view that they are sinful and unworthy. Self-love is indispensable for further evolution, for otherwise our attempts to grow are manifestations only of self-punishment and repression. Growth can only come out of health, out of a desire to see oneself in a happier and more fulfilled state.

The self-confident, mature person is relaxed and open to new experience since his sense of himself is less easily threatened and undermined. He is, in particular, more open to other people who no longer appear as dangers to his identity or as possible objects of neurotic craving. The mature individual sees other people as people. At this crucial juncture in the Higher Evolution, one is no longer a 'self' in a world that is 'other'. One is a self interacting with other selves. One realizes that others feel in the same way that one does oneself and so one can enter sympathetically into their lives and wish them well just as one does oneself. Thus, on the basis of one's self-love, one is able to recognize that others are selves and can feel a disinterested love for them. Besides being confident, the individual is independent and self-reliant, finding security and self-assurance within himself. He is not, however, the kind of stereotyped pseudo-hero who arrogantly claims that he did things his own way and only enters into human relationships on his own egoistical terms – effectively denying the selfhood of others. This is not the individual but the individualist. The real individual is able to relate to others in friendship and cooperation. He is able to learn from them and accept their lead, if appropriate, without losing self-esteem. Greed, hatred and delusion are replaced in him by generosity, friendliness and awareness. As the cock, snake and pig are the motive force of the Wheel, so 3 generosity, friendliness and awareness lift one up the Spiral Path.

Greed is displaced by generosity. Greed is the desire to possess and is appropriate because one believes that one can fortify one's crumbling ego in that way. Individuality needs no such buttress since the individual is secure in himself. Not only is he self-confident but he is full of inner wealth which overflows to others. In contrast to the selfish, grasping attitude of the greedy he is open-handed and gives freely. Such generosity is not limited to material charity, the giving of a portion of one's goods to those in need. It is a whole attitude and approach to life. The individual is generous with his goods but also with his time and energy. He is generous in his assessment of others and in forgiving them for wronging him. Whatever he has flows out to others for, above all, it is himself that he gives. He does not give in order to get something back or to place the recipient in his debt. He gives simply out of his own inner fullness. At the same time, he does not exhaust himself through his generosity; this would only result from self-hatred. It is the super-abundance of his self-regard which enables him to see the needs of others. His generosity enables him to enter into cooperative relations with other people and to work with them in friendly association, balancing his own needs with theirs. He is not competitive and neither minds following the advice and guidance of others nor gains neurotic satisfaction from giving it. His desire is simply to share whatever he has with his companions.

Because it represents such a radical shift from the Wheel to the Spiral, the practice of generosity has assumed a special place in Buddhism. Everyone can give something and it is the minimum spiritual activity which all Buddhists can engage in. The attitude of generosity must be assiduously cultivated for, like all the positive qualities, it rarely springs up of its own accord. Whether we wholeheartedly feel like it or not, we should develop the habit of helping others and of giving to them so that we begin to establish a generous attitude. Our actions help to form our minds and by giving consistently we cultivate the feeling to give. Whenever we feel any stirring of an impulse of generosity we should follow it through, even when sober reflection later counsels against it. In this way we will gradually wean ourselves away from tight-fistedness and develop the genuine spirit of generosity.

Our friends and families, workmates and acquaintances should all be the recipients of our generosity as well as those in need whom we do not know. It is also important that we show our gratitude and generosity to those who are further along the spiritual Path than we are and who are devoted to the full-time practice of the Dharma. They are our own teachers and guides upon the Path and if we do not give to them then we have not really appreciated their worth and we cannot benefit from them. In our gratitude for the help we have ourselves received we will also want to help spread the Dharma, whether directly or indirectly. Even though generosity has to be cultivated by conscious effort, however, we should never forget that it is a generous spirit or feeling that we are trying to achieve and not a forced giving with a reluctant heart. We are endeavouring to call up in ourselves the natural generosity of the healthy and mature individual who gives out of his own inner richness.

Love replaces hatred as the inspiring force of the Spiral Path. The English word 'love' is too ambiguous to convey with any precision the emotion in question since it commonly connotes anything from a keen interest or desire for something to romantic attachment. 'Friendliness' lacks strength in modern usage as does 'loving kindness' which also has a somewhat sentimental ring. It is probably best to use a word from the canonical Buddhist languages and to incorporate it into English untranslated. The word most commonly used is *metta* in the Pali language, or *maitri* in Sanskrit. Metta is a strong, even intense, desire for the welfare of others that expresses itself in action. It is impartial and is felt regardless of whether it is returned or whether there is anything to be gained from the other person – it is no 'cupboard love'. When it is reciprocated then it flowers as friendship. Like generosity, metta is based on inner fullness. One feels such a wealth of self-metta that one can empathize with the selfhood of others and one wishes them the same welfare that one desires for oneself.

Metta must be carefully distinguished from other emotions which seem to share some of its characteristics. It is said to have both a 'far enemy' and a 'near enemy'. Hatred, being the direct opposite of metta, is the far enemy. The near enemy is a love that is really self-interested. One appears to be very concerned for the welfare of the other person but one's affection is really dependent on what one can get from him in return. In reality one is demanding a contract or bargain and one has little genuine appreciation of the other's individuality. The relationship rests, in the end, upon craving, for one wants something from the other person – acceptance, affection, approval – which one feels will help to secure one's identity. Such need-based relationships are often connected with the biological ties of kinship and sex. Families are often bound together in this sort of mutual craving and it is very common in sexual relationships. Romantic love is of this kind. What starts out as that highly idealized fascination which goes by the name of love is very often revealed as natural neurotic craving. Metta by no means includes all that is called love.

Just as generosity must be actively cultivated, so must metta. We have seen that one of the two principal meditation practices of most Buddhist schools is the 'Development of Loving Kindness' or, as we must now call it, the 'Development of Metta' – in Pali its full name is 'Mettabhavana'. This practice consists in sitting down quietly in seclusion and systematically trying to bring the feeling of metta into being. The beginner will do this perhaps once every day or two for a period of about half an hour and the more advanced may meditate several times a day for periods of an hour or more. One begins by trying to feel metta for oneself – for one cannot love others unless one loves oneself. One says over and over to oneself, 'May I be well, may I be happy, may I be free from suffering.' At first, these words may be more or less empty but, after a while, the feeling of metta will begin to flow. One lets the feeling of goodwill for oneself accumulate and then, in the second stage, allows it to spill over towards a near and dear friend, someone for whom one already feels some genuine affection. To avoid other feelings confusing the practice, it is recommended that the friend should be someone still living, of the same sex, and of approximately the same age as oneself. Again, one repeats the phrases of well-wishing. One then moves on to more difficult subjects: a mere acquaintance towards whom one feels neutral; and then an enemy – someone with whom one has some definite difficulty and towards whom one may be actively antagonistic. In the fifth and final stage one takes all four persons together – self, friend, neutral person and enemy – and one tries to feel metta for all equally. This overcomes any tendency to prefer one person to another, and therefore eliminates any hint of craving which may infect one's metta. Metta is then extended out from the spot where one is meditating to include an ever wider circle of people, until the whole world is encompassed. It is then extended to embrace not merely humans but all living creatures – the whole of evolution, we might say. From the beings on this planet metta is radiated towards all sentient creatures of whatsoever kind, wherever they may be in the entire universe. Buddhist cosmology has always envisaged that, in the infinity of space, there are many other world-systems in which the same drama of evolution is being played out as we observe on our own Earth. Within each, there are many levels and dimensions in which consciousness manifests itself. The Mettabhavana meditation culminates with one's metta pervading all these worlds and dimensions. If it is practised regularly it will noticeably improve one's attitude both to oneself and to others. Indeed, it can have the remarkable effect of dissolving old enmities as one comes to see one's adversary in the new light of one's metta.

Basic though the Mettabhavana is, it is not the only means to develop metta. One can systematically work upon one's relationships with others in all the various situations of life. The more those with whom one is in regular contact also try to do the same, the more success one is likely to have. Many people choose, for this reason, to live and work with others who share their desire to develop and Buddhists have established residential communities and 'Right Livelihood' businesses for this purpose, both in traditionally Buddhist countries and in the West. If the people one is in close contact with have no interest in working upon themselves in this way there is no sure basis for resolving the difficulties which inevitably arise in any relationship. If, on the other hand, all are committed to ascending the Spiral Path then genuine friendships can grow which transcend the overlapping of likes and dislikes in a deep sense of mutual appreciation and concern. Friends of this kind are not tied together in bonds of exclusivity as is often the case with romantic love. One's care for the welfare of one's friend does not diminsh one's concern for others and there is certainly no question of jealousy ever arising. Indeed, real friendship is not possible until there is this kind of maturity, for friendship can only develop when there is no neurotic need. The companionships of the less mature are not based on metta but on the coincidence of self-interest and need. The capacity for disinterested friendship, one of the chief joys of the Spiral Path, is the mark of mature individuality.

Delusion is replaced by awareness. No longer is there that ignorant recoil into a narrower sphere of understanding, for the individual reaches out to embrace a new and more expansive vision. He is aware, in the first place, of himself in his various aspects. He is, as it were, in full possession of his own body: he knows what his posture is, what he is doing and the direction and purpose of his movements. He is careful and dignified, never clumsy or forgetful, and he is likely to enjoy good health since he will be aware of his physical needs and will see that they are catered for in an healthy way. He is aware of his emotions. He knows whether he feels greed, hatred or delusion, or metta, generosity and clarity. He knows what he thinks: what thoughts and images are passing through his mind. And he knows where those thoughts have come from. He is able to distinguish what in his mind is simply the product of his past conditioning and what is genuinely creative. He thinks for himself, applying his mind to disentangling the various difficulties and problems which life presents to him. He is intelligent, able to rise to challenges and deal with them with imagination and resourcefulness. His mind is not passive and dull but bright and alert, interested in life and ready to read its diverse lessons and draw its conclusions. He is aware of his surroundings, both the natural environment and human culture. He sees things with the eye of aesthetic appreciation not of egoistical appropriation. He is profoundly moved by beauty in nature and in art. He is aware of other people as selves separate from him with their own individuality and he does not project on to them his own subjective desires. He is aware of their needs and is able to balance them objectively with his own. He feels metta and friendship for people and he has a natural sensitivity to what hurts or helps them. Above all he has developed the Imaginal faculty. He sees that there are higher dimensions to reality and he is aware of the whole trend of evolution. He is aware that the meaning of his life is to surpass his present limits and he knows that from where he stands the Path spirals ever upwards.

Once these three forces of generosity, metta and awareness have become the dominant motives for action, the individual has truly emerged. From the first dawning of self-consciousness to this point is a long dawn presided over by greed, hatred and delusion. In this half-light, the proto-individual with his rudimentary self-consciousness functions as a member of a group. He scarcely differentiates himself from any of its other members and derives his values and opinions from that group to which he belongs. The family, the hunting band, the tribe, the clan, the city-state, are the earliest forms of the group whose modern manifestations are the nation, religious sect, political party, social class and so forth. Group members have little identity apart from their group. Some may appear to function free of the group but they are simply its most powerful members, equally dependent upon the group for their psychological security although they are strong enough within it to follow their own fancies, even at the expense of other group members. Another type of pseudo-individual is the one who has become culturally alienated, cut off prematurely from the necessary nurturance of his group. Taking refuge in brittle self-assertion, this type remains stridently unreceptive to all influence or cooperation. This sort of individualism often results from rapid social change and the consequent breakdown of traditional cultures which, when they are stable and positive, are the necessary basis for the emergence of real individuality.

The individual has differentiated himself from the group and is no longer subject to its pressures. He feels no need to belong because his security is within himself and he therefore does not have to pay the price of conformity to the group's beliefs. But he is not hostile to the group. He appreciates the need of many people for its support and, since he is not susceptible to its influence, he does not feel threatened by it in himself. The group, however, is all too often the enemy of the individual and it may even destroy him to enforce its supremacy.

The individual has accepted responsibility for himself and for his actions. He no longer leaves his fate in the hands of fortune and he does not blame others for setbacks in his own life. He takes the initiative both as regards his own development and in the situations he encounters. He knows that his life is his own for the making and he commits himself fully to the task of the Higher Evolution.

The transition from greed, hatred and delusion to love, generosity and awareness is the transition from the Wheel to the Spiral, from the group to the individual. It is also the transition from what has been called the 'power mode' to the 'love mode'. The person whose ego is immature sees the whole world solely in terms of his own needs. He tries to dominate and impose himself, whether directly or by cunning, manipulating others to his own ends. He functions in terms of power, seeing everything, other people included, as objects for his own gratification. This is the power mode of operating. The love mode, conversely, consists in seeing others as independent selves and treating them with metta. It is on the basis of the love mode that the spiritual community exists. Its members do not come together to exploit or manipulate each other nor to gain the support and solidarity of a group. They try to relate as one individual to another, in awareness of the ideals to which all are committed, and they encourage and inspire each other's efforts. So the transition from the power mode to the love mode is the transition from the group to the spiritual community.

At this crucial transition the spiritual Path begins to unfold. Greed and hatred have less and less control over the mind and the grosser forms of delusion are purged away. A basic delusion, however, still remains; experience is still limited by the polarization of consciousness into subject and object. The two sides of the duality are now in more harmonious dialogue and the object is no longer considered by the subject as a threat or as a source of permanence. It is viewed appreciatively and, when the object is another person, communication and metta flow towards it. Nonetheless, to see things in terms of a subject and object is, from an ultimate point of view, a constriction of the perfect non-dual awareness of reality. In the end, the division into subject and object is only the way we structure our experience; it does not correspond to reality itself. Gradually, the love mode must be intensified, metta and generosity must radiate more and more powerfully, there must be a deeper and deeper awareness, individuality must become stronger, and the spiritual community must be experienced more vividly. The more one can feel metta for others, the more that tension between self and other is lessened. Yet still one's metta is based upon one's love of oneself, highly refined as that may become. At a certain point, however, metta breaks through the barrier of self and other and one feels no essential difference between oneself and the other. One identifies equally both with what used to appear as the self and with what used to appear as other. Consciousness is freed from the limitation that duality imposes and a perfectly equal metta pervades all and, with the end of self-identification, generosity becomes the outpouring of compassion. This is the point of Stream Entry and, though the Wheel and the Spiral still coexist even at this Transcendental level, the Wheel can never again be the deciding influence. Greed and hatred may sprout from time to time and a refined delusion may still persist, but love, generosity and awareness are now suffused by insight into the true nature of things. Slowly the three poisons are worn away until, with full Enlightenment, the last trace of ignorance disappears.

5

To Be Born Again

To the Enlightened mind the whole of reality is a process of becoming. So intricate is that process, so interwoven is each aspect with every other that it can never be adequately described or explained in words. Whatever we say, we can never do justice to the full complexity of things. In order to understand life and thereby shape our own actions we have to simplify that process by breaking it down into smaller systems about which we can make generalizations and formulate laws – but in simplifying in this way we inevitably falsify. This procedure is very necessary to our survival, however, and it only gives rise to problems when we think that, having comprehended the generalizations and laws with which we pattern our experience, we have understood reality. Real understanding, according to Buddhism, can only come about through the direct experience called Insight which transcends the intellect. Nonetheless, an intellectual grasp of the conditioned process can help us to orientate our lives.

We have seen that the most basic formulation of the Buddha's Insight is stated in this way:

This being, that becomes; from the arising of this, that arises; this not becoming, that does not become; from the ceasing of this, that ceases.

Every element of reality depends upon conditions without which it cannot occur. This principle governs all phenomena. Our generalizations and laws are concerned with the relationship between specific conditions and their effects within the total conditioned process. That totality can be broken down into different levels of evolutionary development. At each level a new set of laws applies.

Buddhist philosophy distinguishes five levels or orders of conditionality. There is, first of all, the physical-inorganic order whose laws are, more or less, those of physics and chemistry. The organic order is similarly the concern of biology. The lower mental order involves mental functions of a non-volitional kind, such as perception. The karmic order is the volitional level. The Dharmic is the Transcendental. Inanimate objects are subject to the laws of the physical order. Simple organisms are subject to both the physical and organic orders. Both these two orders, together with the lower mental, govern organisms with developed sense faculties. Human beings are subject to the three lowest orders together with the karmic and they may be subject, if they are approaching Stream Entry, to the Dharmic order as well.

These orders may be correlated with our previously established hierarchy of the evolution of consciousness. The physical order corresponds to the non-conscious; the organic to the lowest level of primitive sense-consciousness; the mental to sense-consciousness; the karmic to self and spiritual consciousness; and the Dharmic to Transcendental consciousness. The higher levels of consciousness, as we will see later, are not always associated with the lowest orders: self-consciousness is not always associated with the physical and organic levels, for instance. Self-consciousness in the human being, however, combines the whole evolutionary process up to and including the karmic order and has the capacity to unfold the highest levels from within itself to form a bridge stretching from the non-conscious to the super-conscious.

Inspiring as this picture of the human place in evolution may be, it also makes clear that any analysis of human behaviour is very difficult. Each of these orders, which together govern human functioning, is a complex of laws. Furthermore, each order is interwoven with all the others, acting and being acted upon by them. A human being is a nexus of all these orders and we cannot therefore arrive at easy generalizations and rapid judgements about people, even ourselves. Not only do we need a deep understanding of human nature in general but also a thorough acquaintance with the person in question to disentangle all the different conditioned processes on all the different levels. The karmic order, with which we are now concerned in this chapter, is thus but one level of conditionality within the very subtle mingling of processes which is the human being. We should beware of interpreting it too rigidly, as some modern exponents of Buddhism have done, and we should not forget that we are dealing with that elusive quantity, the human heart, and not with a mechanical robot.

The second circle of the Wheel of Life illustrates the workings of the principle of karma. It is divided into two segments, one black and one white. In the black, tormented beings tumble downwards, naked, hounded by fierce demons. In the white, smiling men and women wearing bright garments wind upwards while performing meritorious actions. The message of the image is that we inevitably reap the appropriate fruit of our karma. 'Karma' is a Sanskrit word (in Pali it is *kamma*) which means 'willed action'. The karmic order corresponds to the level of self-consciousness and is concerned with the deliberate actions of an individual, however partial or distorted his self-awareness may be and however sketchy his individuality. The law which governs the functioning of the karmic order is that *every willed action produces an effect which is, eventually, experienced by the agent, the nature of the effect being determined by the intention with which the action is performed*.

A willed or intentional action is one consciously undertaken by an individual to bring about an end which he desires. Such actions are to be distinguished from involuntary behaviour such as blinking, falling over when pushed, or inadvertently knocking over a cup when reaching for the teapot. The degree of consciousness involved in a deliberate action may, however, be relatively low. We often act in a divided state, giving only part of our attention to what we do. This may be the consequence of an habitual distractedness very common amidst the many stimuli of modern life or it may result from our unwillingness to recognize fully what we are doing. In extreme cases, this results in the sort of pathological behaviour often labelled 'Freudian'. We have a desire for something but we also have a strong feeling that we should not want that thing. So we set about expressing the desire in whatever way we can whilst, at the same time, not fully acknowledging, even to ourselves, that that is what we want. The desire has been banished to the very fringes of consciousness so that we can effectively pretend that we do not feel it. This complex state of affairs can disguise the fact that actions performed under the influence of such unwanted desires are, nonetheless, intentional, however peripheral to consciousness the wish may be. The terms 'subconscious' or 'unconscious' motivation are misleading for where there is motivation there is consciousness. Willed actions, then, range from those directed to an objective which is very clearly formulated and wholeheartedly longed for to the kind of cloudy, vague or incidental behaviour in which the agent does not allow himself to be clear about what he is doing.

Intentional action is not only bodily action. For the purposes of the principle of karma both speech and thought are actions which produce their effects upon the agent. It is the intention, the act of wanting something and forming the decision to get it, which establishes the karmic conditions. A strong intention which is thwarted by circumstances produces much the same karmic consequences as the same degree of intentionality which fulfils its objective. From the point of view of the karmic principle, consciousness is primary and the karmic status of acts of body or speech is determined by the state of mind which lies behind them.

Intentional actions produce effects which are experienced by the agent. The law of karma governs the relationship between the self-conscious subject and the world which is objective to him. The self is, as it were, in dialectical interplay with the other. The karmic order could be seen as a kind of 'feedback system' between the subject and the object which always returns to balance whenever it is disturbed. Every time the subject acts the balance is disrupted and the whole system must adapt in order to restore its equilibrium. The actions of the subject within this 'universal feedback system' modify the object which then adjusts itself to absorb the modification. This then feeds back an effect upon the subject. The kind of adjustment needed to restore the system's stasis depends upon the nature of the action which initially disturbed it and so the effects which feed back to the agent depend upon the intention with which he acted.

The effects of karma are experienced both subjectively and objectively. What we think, do or say reinforces certain trends within our own mental life and, to that extent, modifies our own consciousness. The mental images and memories which occur to us, the moods that overcome us, are shaped by what we have thought, said and done in the past. This is the subjective effect. Objectively, the effect of our past actions is to be seen in the situations we find ourselves in and the experiences which come to us. Since the karmic order is not based upon a simple mechanical causation, it is very hard to discern the way in which our past actions condition our present objective experience. What draws consciousness and experience together is a type of affinity. 'Like attracts like' and the intentions formed within consciousness attract to them the appropriate experiences. To give a simple example: when I first became interested in Buddhism, I suddenly noticed Buddhism all around me. Newspaper headlines made reference to it; Buddhist book titles jumped out at me in shop windows; I would meet people who would tell me anecdotes about Buddhism. Whether or not such phenomena were there before, my consciousness now had some connection with them and seemed almost to attract them to itself.

The nature of the effect is determined by the nature of the intention with which the action is performed. Intentions can be analysed into those that are based upon greed, hatred and delusion and on metta, generosity and awareness. Actions performed with the unwholesome motivations of greed, hatred and delusion are called 'unskilful' and those based on metta, generosity and awareness are 'skilful'. These are the basic terms of Buddhist ethics. Under the principle of karma, skilful actions produce pleasant effects and unskilful actions, unpleasant effects. The consequence of acting from unwholesome motivations is that, in the end, we suffer. When we act from a positive state of mind we are building up happiness for ourselves.

The basic principles of the law of karma are simply stated, but it is seldom possible, with any certainty, to ascribe a particular experience to the workings of karmic conditionality. It is even more difficult to connect a particular volitional action with a particular effect. In the first place, the karmic order is only one of five orders of conditionality and it may be possible to explain an effect satisfactorily within any or all of the orders. To quote a classic example: a fever might be the consequence of a sudden change in temperature and, therefore, belong to the physical order of conditionality; it might be caused by a viral infection, operating under the biological order; mental strain may have brought it on, under the lower mental order; some past unskilful action may be its cause, under the karmic order; or else it may be due to the restructuring of the whole system of body and mind as a result of insight, under the Transcendental order. The only way in which one can tell whether an experience is the result of past karma is by eliminating all other possible explanations. If none of them adequately accounts for the phenomenon in question, then karmic forces may be at work, although there can be no certainty. So, in the case of a fever, one would try to cure it by using remedies appropriate to each order of causation; only if these failed might one tentatively conclude that past actions were the cause.

The fact that there are many levels of conditionality at work in our lives makes it hard to discern when karma is operating. The complexity of human motivation further obscures the picture. For we are thinking, speaking and acting all the time, setting up trends with each act of volition which modify our experience both directly through the mind and indirectly through the environment. It is very difficult to isolate particular acts from this great current of willing. Karmic conditionality is, rather, a matter of broad tendencies and trends. All our different acts of intention mingle together, some setting up dominant themes, some merely reinforcing established patterns, some diluting the effects of others, and some cancelling others out. Different intentions are not all of the same strength and the degree of unwholesomeness and wholesomeness varies from action to action. Some karmas are said to be 'weighty', such as murder on the one hand and the experience of higher states of consciousness on the other. These have a very powerful influence on the overall pattern of karmic activity. Some actions are habitual and shape our future by inertia for, the more frequently we behave in certain ways, the more they become a permanent part of our character. Some karmas simply have a cumulative effect in conjunction with others. The 'weight' of a particular action and its relationship to the overall stream of willing determines how long it takes to mature in an effect or, indeed, whether it matures at all. We cannot, therefore, very readily ascribe a particular effect to a particular past action. The karmic level within us is like a mighty current of energy which is fed by each single thought, word and deed. It is the total momentum of this current which shapes our minds and the world we live in. By our own actions, we constantly recreate ourselves.

The operation of karma is entirely natural and in no way depends upon some superior, divine power. No external authority metes out suffering or happiness to us. Our own actions determine whether we have pleasure or pain for we attract suffering or joy by the way in which we live our lives. The momentum generated by our actions leads to suffering or pleasure under the karmic law just as a stone falls to the ground when it is released under the law of gravity of the physical order.

The Buddhist teaching on karma is in no way fatalistic. It does not teach that everything that happens to us is the result of karma for all the other orders of conditionality may be called to account. Even though all intentional acts have effects for the agent, not all the effects which one experiences are the consequence of past actions. Moreover, even when weighty unskilful karma has been performed, it is possible to counteract it with skilful actions, although they will have to be of corresponding, or even greater, intensity. The fact that our past actions have, even in a general way, shaped our present experience does not mean that we must passively accept the situation. We should do whatever we can to remove the pain and suffering which is the consequence of the other orders of conditionality and we should try to establish a more skilful pattern of behaviour which will override any negative effects of our own past deeds. The Buddhist works strenuously to remove suffering wherever he finds it, whether in himself or in others. Poverty, cultural deprivation, crippling disease may or may not be the result of karma but every effort should be made to relieve them. The charge of passivity sometimes brought against Buddhism could not be further from the truth for, above all, the Dharma stresses personal responsibility and effort as the prerequisites for any further development.

One final, minor point of possible misunderstanding needs clarification. At the outset of this discussion on karma, we saw that involuntary actions were not the subject of karmic conditionality and the example of knocking over a cup while reaching for the teapot was given. Now, one did not intend to knock over the cup and could not be accused of doing so with 'malice aforethought'. But one *can* be blamed for having carried out one's intention to pick up the teapot carelessly and without due mindfulness. To take a well-known and less trivial example, a certain monk of the Buddha's time went to visit some householders. Finding them to be out, he went into the house and seated himself on what he thought was a bench covered with a cloth. It was actually a crib containing a baby which was smothered and killed when he sat on it. The Buddha was asked if the monk had committed murder and he replied that he had not since it was not his intention to kill. He was, however, guilty of an act of gross carelessness from which he would suffer a karmic consequence. Inadvertence springs from an unwholesome mental state.

The second sphere of the Wheel of Life shows the operation of the karmic principle. In the black half, under the influence of unwholesome mental states, beings perform unskilful actions and suffer the painful consequences as they spin upon the Wheel. In the white half, under the influence of wholesome mental states, beings perform skilful actions and experience happiness and pleasure as they ascend the Spiral. This Spiral eventually leads beyond the Wheel. Once the state of Enlightenment has been reached, no more karma is produced. Even though he acts, and acts with very great and subtle effectiveness, the

Buddha's actions have no consequences for him. Dwelling as he does in non-dual awareness there is, as it were, no feedback system for him to disturb – one might say he has *become* the total system. The Buddha moves in perfect harmony with all things, unrestricted by any conditions.

Some understanding and appreciation of this principle of karmic conditionality is of the foremost importance since it underpins the ethical and spiritual life. If there were no such principle the consequences of skilful and unskilful actions would be unpredictable and unrelated to the intentions with which they were performed. It would not matter how we acted because pleasant and painful experiences would come to us in a quite arbitrary way without any meaning or discernible pattern. Sustained effort at any spiritual practice such as meditation would be worthless because we could not be certain of its positive effects. Just as the other orders such as the physical and the biological are subject to stable laws by which effect follows cause, so is the karmic. The law of karma guarantees that our actions will have appropriate consequences and therefore that we can grow. Buddhism considers scepticism on this point to be fatal, for one would be doubting that personal effort has any effect and, therefore, that there can be any Higher Evolution at all. Human beings would be merely the helpless victims of an inscrutable fate without any logic or coherence. Confirmed rejection of this principle is itself a weighty unskilful action since it negates both morality and the Spiral Path.

It is not hard, in a general way, to see that actions have consequences in accordance with the law of karma yet there are some things which happen to us which seem to frustrate all our efforts, for which no cause in our past actions can be readily discerned. Some of what happens to us seems quite arbitrary. Furthermore, each of us is born with certain advantages or disabilities. How can we bear karmic responsibility for our birth? Buddhism asserts that the law of karma does not operate within one lifetime alone because we are, in accordance with our karma, born again and again.

Before we can explore more fully the Buddhist doctrine of rebirth, we must have some picture of the cosmological background against which our many lives are lived. The Buddha denied that the cosmos was created, teaching that the cyclic process has no discernible beginning or end. Within the limitless dimensions of space, the ageless play of conditions throws up from time to time innumerable world-systems which come into being and pass away again in the course of immeasurable aeons. In some of these world-systems the conditions are established for the support of life and the long march of the lower evolution begins.

At the same time, streams of self-consciousness, under the force of their past volitions, take embodiment again and again within the various world-systems. This process, too, has no beginning. It will end only if the Higher Evolution is undertaken and Buddhahood is reached, at which point consciousness passes beyond our comprehension and there is no further rebirth within the mundane.

We have, then, two parallel processes: the evolution of lower life-forms within world-systems and the wanderings of streams of self-consciousness from birth to birth within those worlds. The continua of self-consciousness intersect the lower, biological evolution at the point where it has evolved organisms capable of expressing self-consciousness. Rebirth continues to take place within the different spheres and levels of the world-systems until Enlightenment is reached.

The organism with which consciousness associates itself and the world it inhabits reflects its own nature. Each time death occurs, that continuum of consciousness forms a new body for itself in dependence on its own past actions. For it is our own intentions and volitions which are the force that assembles, out of the raw material of the physical, biological and mental orders, a body and a personality. The kind of body we have and the kind of world we inhabit are appropriate to our own state of consciousness which fashions them in its own likeness. This stream of volitional energy, modified with each new act of body, speech, or mind, is what we fundamentally are and it moulds life, again and again, to suit its own mutations. This we have been doing since beginningless time and we will continue to be reborn in this way unless we choose to evolve to an higher level.

Not only are there innumerable world-systems capable of supporting life but each such system, according to Buddhist cosmology, contains many dimensions. Each world consists of stratified planes, paralleling the evolutionary hierarchy. The lowest group of planes is termed the sphere of sensuous desire. It is made up, first of all, of the four unpleasant and painful places of rebirth: the hell, hungry ghost, animal and titan realms. The human world and the lower heavens complete the sensuous sphere, which corresponds to the Wheel to sense and self-consciousness. The next two spheres, those of archetypal form and of no form, contain the heavens of the higher gods and correspond to what we have called spiritual and Transcendental consciousness and to the Spiral up to the point of Buddhahood. The realm of the Buddhas is outside the world-systems altogether and corresponds to the dawning of Absolute consciousness.

Within the mundane spheres – of sensuous experience, archetypal form and no form – with their many sub-planes, the drama of rebirth takes place. Unskilful actions, performed with unwholesome volitions, tend to direct consciousness towards the lower, painful realms of the sensuous sphere. Skilful deeds lead to all the other realms of the sensuous and to the spheres of form and no-form. Insight into reality, alone, leads to the highest sphere of all, the Transcendental. Until that point of Insight, one can pass up and down, around and around, within all the different worlds, in accordance with one's state of mind. No world is permanent, there is no eternal damnation or salvation. One remains in any particular state only so long as the momentum from one's previous intentions is sufficiently strong to keep one connected with that world and no counteracting tendency has been established.

The concepts of rebirth and of a multi-layered universe are both, perhaps, unfamiliar to most people today. We will examine the Buddhist teaching of multiple worlds and the mechanics of rebirth in later chapters, but we must now give some attention to the basis for the Buddhist belief in the doctrine of rebirth.

In the West, the two most commonly held views regarding death are that it is the absolute termination of consciousness or that it is succeeded by a state of eternal bliss in heaven or suffering in hell (though few will own to holding the view in such a categorical form). The materialist position that human consciousness is obliterated at death is more and more commonly considered the most reasonable alternative. It has no greater claims, however, to probability than any of the other three possible beliefs about birth and death. Indeed, it may be the least supportable of the four beliefs which are logically possible. It must be the case that there is either no life before birth nor after death, or before birth but not after death, or after death but not before birth, or both before birth and after death (this latter includes the Buddhist doctrine of rebirth). If one approaches these four positions with an open mind, as it were for the first time, there is no immediate reason to adopt any one of them, for each of them is *logically* consistent. As Voltaire has said, 'To be born many times is no more miraculous than to be born once'! The materialist claims that his view is the most reasonable because there is no evidence for any other. There is no conclusive evidence, however, that there is *no* life before birth or after death – only be the negative evidence of no evidence. One who believes firmly in the materialist view holds to it through faith no less than he considers his opponents cling to their beliefs. If there was, indeed, no evidence then, in reason, one could only be cautiously agnostic, declaring that *in the present state of knowledge* there is nothing to suggest that life extends beyond birth and death and remaining open-minded about whatever new evidence might appear.

I know of no one who believes that there is life before birth but not after death – although, in itself, it is no more or less absurd than to assert that there is life after death but not before birth. Both these positions generate problems in positing an entity with an eternal beginning and a finite end in the one case and a finite beginning and an eternal end in the other. It seems, on the face of it, far more likely that if existence succeeds death it also precedes birth and vice-versa. Certainly, those who hold either of these views will not find it hard to consider the possibility of rebirth in the Buddhist sense.

If, then, there were no evidence for rebirth we would have to remain agnostic. There is, however, quite a lot of evidence and there are other, supporting reasons for accepting at least a provisional belief in rebirth. None of this evidence or these reasons amount to full proof because, on this particular topic, conclusive proof is very difficult since many of the phenomena offered as evidence may be explained in other ways. Taken together, all the different facts build a strong case for the doctrine.

It should give us pause to think, in the first place, that belief in rebirth has been very widespread in human history. It is, by no means, a peculiarity of the great religions of India: Buddhism, Hinduism and Jainism. Many tribal peoples the world over, such as some North American Indians, Polynesians and African tribesmen, have such a belief. It has even had a distinguished history in our own Western culture. According to Greek accounts, the ancient Egyptians believed in rebirth – although this has been disputed by modern scholars. Before they were Christianized, the Celtic peoples considered that each man lived many times. Among the Greeks, the doctrine was taught by the mystery schools of Orphism and inherited by the Pythagoreans. It is probably from them that Plato derived the famous 'Myth of Ur' in *The Republic*, which gives an account of the experiences after death leading to rebirth. Many Gnostics and Neo-Platonists believed in reincarnation and, most astonishing of all, among early Christians the belief was not uncommon. Two prominent Church Fathers, Origen and Justin Martyr, are known to have taught the pre-existence of souls. Origen's doctrine of metempsychosis was not finally declared anathema until the sixth century. In the twelfth and thirteenth centuries the Cathars of southern France and Italy held reincarnation as one of their main tenets. It was to eradicate this 'heresy' that the first European crusade was launched and the 'Holy Office' or Inquisition was established. The belief continued to recur in Europe despite strong opposition from the Church, which enforced orthodoxy with violence if necessary. In this connection, it is interesting to consider that, though Buddhists have never persecuted those who disagree with them, no one has seriously challenged the teaching of rebirth from within the Buddhist tradition while many Christians have been prepared to die for this belief. More recently, various individuals – Voltaire, Benjamin Franklin, Napoleon, Henry Ford, to name a few of the more prominent – have, quite independently, declared their belief that they have lived before. This fact of widespread and recurrent belief does not, of course, prove the truth of rebirth. It should, however, be noted that many independent versions of the belief in reincarnation display strong similarities.

More concrete evidence is to be found in reports by people who claim to have been reborn. In many traditions, people have recounted their purported memories of past lives. The Buddha himself is said to have had the capacity to remember many previous lives and to have recounted them to his followers. In the Tibetan Buddhist tradition there is a detailed teaching contained in the so-called *Tibetan Book of the Dead* about the process of death and rebirth and this is said to derive from direct experience.

Historical accounts of this kind are not susceptible to any form of verification. It appears that some children, however, claim that they can remember having lived before. In the West, these are usually dismissed as fantasies or worse but, in the East, where rebirth is accepted belief, they are taken more seriously. Some modern academic researchers have carried out detailed enquiries into cases of this sort, both in the East and the West. Their findings have been quite remarkable. Children have claimed to remember a past existence in a place which they have never visited in this life. They have given details of that past which no one around them could have known and which, when checked, have been found to be extraordinarily accurate. Although the various cases come from very different cultures and backgrounds, there is, again, considerable concurrence in the broad details of the stories and certain themes are seen to recur. Much more research needs to be carried out but already the evidence is mounting that some children, at least, have lived before. Absolute proof is impossible in this field since, in the nature of things, an environment cannot be set up so rigidly controlled as to rule out all other potential sources of the information which presents itself as memories of a past life. These stories are sometimes explained away as collusion or trickery, unconscious influence from forgotten experiences, or as instances of telepathy. They do, however, constitute further suggestive evidence.

Similar cases were known in Tibet before the Chinese invasion. It was widely held that those who had developed far on the Path were able to choose where and when they would be reborn. Some Lamas – Tibetan spiritual teachers – would give indications on their deathbeds of the time and place of their own next birth and a watch would then be maintained for the fulfilment of those predictions. Children born under the appropriate circumstances would be very carefully examined to see whether they gave any signs which might suggest that they were the reincarnated Lama. Usually, neither the parents nor the child would be told what was happening at this stage so that no collusion could take place. Finally, once a child had been selected as the most likely candidate, he would be shown various articles which had belonged to the dead Lama, mixed with similar items. In many cases, it appears, the child would not only select the Lama's belongings but would show signs of recognizing his former friends and associates and some would even have strong memories of their former lives. Once a child had been acknowledged as an incarnation, he would be trained to continue his previous life's work. Sometimes, of course, this procedure was abused for the sake of the power and prestige which recognition could bring to the child's family and sometimes, no doubt, it was carried out in a naïve and superstitious manner. It is very unlikely that all or even most of those considered to be the incarnation of former teachers were really so. Nonetheless, some of these 'Tulkus' – incarnate Lamas – were very remarkable men and their selection seems to have taken place under what amounted to strict scientific control.

Further supportive evidence for rebirth is to be found in certain cases of hypnosis and of anaesthesia. Some practitioners of hypnotherapy have been able to take their patients back to their own birth and then back to what presented themselves as previous lives. Sometimes details about the past have been yielded which have been independently verified and which the subject was unlikely to have known in his present life. Under anaesthetic, many people have reported looking down at their own bodies from a point several feet away: in itself, this suggests that consciousness can exist independently of the body. There are cases of people who have been clinically dead but have then come back to life again. Their hearts have stopped beating and their respiration has ceased temporarily during an operation. They, too, have reported experiences of being out of the body but they have also related stranger experiences, very similar to those recounted by people who claim to remember what happened to them after their death in a previous life.

The doctrine that we are born many times may help to explain a number of difficult questions. For instance, some of the phenomena of spiritualism seem to be authentic and may be accounted for in these terms. Again, a newborn child is not only shaped by heredity and environment but by the momentum of consciousness carried over from a previous life. Infant prodigies can best be explained in this way. The great musical genius of the youthful Mozart, Beethoven and Handel are well known and there are, in other fields, many examples of knowledge and talent manifesting at a very early age. The Buddhist argues that these talents have already been acquired and developed in a previous life.

For the Buddhist, the truth of the teaching of rebirth does not rest upon scientific evidence. Such evidence is, of course, interesting in itself and may dispose others to give more favourable attention to the Dharma. Ultimately, the truth of the doctrine lies in experience. In the first place, it is said to be possible to remember past lives and it is a mark of the attainment of higher levels of development that one can do this. Some meditation practices are even specifically directed to developing this ability – although they are probably rarely used. One established, to begin with, a very powerful state of tranquillity and concentration and then systematically takes oneself back in memory from the moment one started meditating, recalling everything that happened until one remembers the moment of birth and then, before that, the previous life! For the Buddha, however, memory of past lives is not merely a feat of prodigious concentration, it derives from the very nature of his Enlightened mind. He has realized an awareness beyond duality and beyond time, and he has, thus, access to any point in time. It is not so much that he remembers his past existences but that he directly surveys them from a point outside time.

The truth of the doctrine of rebirth is also to be found in the higher state of meditation. Consciousness is there experienced in a far purer form which transcends physical existence. It becomes clear that the body depends upon consciousness, not consciousness on the body. One realizes that consciousness cannot be destroyed and that it is a powerful stream of energy which cannot be contained within one life.

Many Buddhists have neither the ability to remember their past lives nor have experienced those higher states where consciousness is seen to transcend the body. Their belief in rebirth rests not on their own direct evidence but, for the time being, on their respect for others. They have faith in the Buddha, in the Buddhist tradition, and in their own spiritual teachers and friends. Just as we believe in the existence of countries which we have never visited on the basis of what we are told by those we have found to be reliable in other instances, so we place our reasoned faith in those whom we find to be spiritually trustworthy. It is by no means a blind or superstitious or unquestioning faith and it can only be provisional until further experience confirms or denies it.

Although some modern, rationalizing Buddhists have tried to explain away the Buddha's teaching of rebirth so that they can make the Dharma fit in with modern, 'scientific' views, it is an integral part of Buddhism. One cannot really be a Buddhist unless one does have faith in it. This does not mean that those who find themselves unable to give it credence cannot develop as individuals or cannot make good use of Buddhist teaching and practice. Since their perspective on existence, however, will be limited to the period between a single birth and death and since their conception of consciousness will be essentially materialistic, from a Buddhist point of view their development will be restricted. Nonetheless, any development is better than none and, so long as a person retains an open mind, experience of higher levels of awareness is likely to convince him that consciousness does transcend the physical body and therefore that it may be reborn. A scepticism which arises from an honest intellect is certainly no barrier to growth. It is only rigid dogmatism and stubborn closed-mindedness that can be a permanent barrier to truth.

The principle of rebirth has application outside the round of birth and death. Coming into being and passing away is the destiny of all conditioned things. The passing of each phenomenon gives rise to a new one in dependence upon it. This is as true on the psychological plane as on the natural. Just as flowers, trees, our own bodies die in order to be reborn in new substances and organisms, so our thoughts and feelings rise and fall in an endless sequence. We are, in this sense, reborn moment by moment, recreated by our own past. Those who cannot provisionally accept the teaching of rebirth as applied to human life can see it symbolically as an underlying principle in all phenomena. And, as my own teacher has pointed out to sceptics, those who call themselves Buddhists but who do not believe that they will be reborn will have to make sure that they gain Enlightenment in this life!

Limitless time and immeasurable space are the background to the Buddhist vision of human existence. Self-consciousness flows in a powerful stream of willing, building for itself bodies and worlds which most appropriately express its own nature. If it is unwholesome in character it forms lives of pain and frustration. If it is wholesome it climbs the ladder of the Higher Evolution. It may traverse the Path in the course of countless aeons, rising slowly, life by life, or it may, with exceptional gifts and prodigious effort, pass from self-consciousness to Transcendental consciousness in a single life.

It is against these vast perspectives that we must now consider Buddhist ethics, for it is whether we act skilfully or unskilfully that determines our future rebirths in dependence on the law of karma. Within our crystallizing self-consciousness, our dawning sense of what we should and should not do is connected with our realization that our actions have an effect – both upon ourselves and upon others. We begin to realize their effect upon ourselves, through the operation of the law of karma, when we see that our own unwholesome states of mind produce further unpleasantness for us. When we indulge in negative states we feel worse and we seem to draw upon ourselves more and more difficulties and obstacles. Conversely, when we act from positive, wholesome states, we find that we feel lighter and happier, and life flows more smoothly. The more healthy-minded we are, the happier we become.

To begin with, it is seldom as straightforward as this since we may have bad karmic influences from the past still playing themselves out in our lives so that it is not so easy to see the equation between our actions and their consequences upon us. For many people, the earlier stages of their spiritual life may be a process of purgation of habits and mental currents from the past which continue to affect them even though they are no longer behaving in those old ways. Present, more wholesomely motivated activity serves only to counteract those past tendencies and it may be some time before the direct benefits are reaped. In some cases, it may even be that previous, very unskilful volitions do not allow present actions to fructify in this life if the process of purgation is not carried through deeply enough. Our skilful activity is said to 'make merit'. It stores up for us a stock of good karmic potential which we will experience in the future – even in a future rebirth. In making merit, one gathers to oneself the conditions which will assist future growth: health, well-being and good fortune.

One's first concern with ethics is likely to be self-interested but there is more to Buddhist ethics than intelligent selfishness. As we develop, a natural sensitivity to others should begin to guide our actions. The mature individual is able to empathize with the selfhood of others and he is able to feel metta and concern for them. When they suffer, he feels compassion and he seeks to do whatever he can to alleviate their pain. When they are happy he rejoices with them. He rises above the extended self-interest of family, nation or social group and feels disinterestedly for any other being. His actions are wholesomely motivated by metta and generosity. He cannot do what would harm another being and he tries, as much as he can, to help others. The ethical life, then, is based upon the love mode.

Our ethical life may start as a conscious attempt to cultivate better states of mind for ourselves but it should blossom into a natural sense of what is skilful and unskilful on the basis of our empathy with others. This natural ethical sense is what might be called conscience. It is not, however, a superego or internalized authority, ordering one what to do or not do. Rather it is the promptings of one's own awareness and metta, one's resonance with all that lives.

Buddhist morality is not at all authoritarian. No God ordains on tablets of stone what should and should not be done. Morality is not conceived of in terms of law. True ethics cannot be reduced to a system of rules, for it is not what an action is that determines its ethical status but the intention that underlies it. As we have seen, those performed on the basis of unwholesome volitions, rooted in greed, hatred and delusion, are termed unskilful and those which spring from the wholesome states of generosity, love and awareness are called skilful. That an act is said to have been done skilfully implies that it is done with intelligence and care, with a kind of practical ethical ability equivalent to the practised skill of a craftsman. To act skilfully, it is not enough blindly to follow a set of rules. One must have matured one's sensitivity to others and one's feeling for them and one must be aware of what the consequences of any action are likely to be. It is only then that one is in a position to act skilfully for the benefit both of oneself and of others.

While one is still learning to act skilfully it is hard to maintain sufficient mindfulness so that, at all times, one considers the consequences of every deed and takes into account the feelings and needs of others. One requires some sort of guideline against which one can measure one's own behaviour. This is provided by the precepts which outline the kind of behaviour which one who has developed a natural and spontaneous ethical sense does not engage in or even contemplate because no trace of animosity or egoism mars his perfect sympathy with all life. It is only the Buddhas whose actions are completely skilful because all trace of the Wheel has been eradicated from their minds. The precepts outline what the Buddhas do not do and they are for us a standard or ideal with which we can compare our own behaviour. We are still motivated to act in ways that are unskilful but we want to develop skilfulness. The precepts act as a check on our own deeds and a reminder of what skilfulness really is. We undertake the precepts as a way of training ourselves in ethics:

I undertake the training principle of refraining from harming living beings.
I undertake the training principle of refraining from taking the not-given.
I undertake the training principle of refraining from sexual misconduct.
I undertake the training principle of refraining from false speech.
I undertake the training principle of refraining from drink and drugs which cloud the mind.

The five precepts being negative in character, a further set of five precepts in positive form are sometimes given lest ethics be thought of as merely refraining from wrong-doing. Each of these positive precepts corresponds to one of the first set:

With deeds of loving kindness, I purify my body.
With open-handed generosity, I purify my body.
With stillness, simplicity and contentment, I purify my body.
With truthful communication, I purify my speech.
With mindfulness, clear and radiant, I purify my mind.

The first pair of precepts enjoin non-harm to living beings and advocate metta. This is the basis for all the other precepts since the ethical life is the life based upon the love mode of operating. It is far-reaching in its implications, ruling out all forms of violence, coercion, manipulation or exploitation. Most serious Buddhists consider that it involves vegetarianism and it certainly makes careers involving the killing or ill-treatment of animals impossible, let alone of human beings. If one accepts this precept in its full depth it means the complete eradication of the power mode of operating and the uprooting of greed, hatred and delusion. It means living in harmony with all beings. In the end, it means going beyond oneself altogether.

The remaining precepts work out in greater detail the implications of living by the love mode. To take from others what they do not give, to exploit them sexually or to lie to them is to deny their selfhood and to act violently towards them. The last precept is more specific and cautions against a loss of mindfulness through intoxication for, in getting drunk, one reverts to a lower level of consciousness and one is likely to lose awareness of what one is doing so that one may fall from the love mode.

The precepts are an aid to the cultivation of a natural moral sense. The most effective means of developing more skilful behaviour is to associate with people whose way of life and actions are already skilful. In one's fellowship with them, one will imbibe morality. When one feels respect and genuine friendship for such people, they will be guides to what is skilful until one's own conscience matures. One will feel that one does not want to let them down by acting badly – not that one is afraid of being punished by them but, such is one's respect for them, that one does not wish to belittle oneself in their eyes. They have become, as it were, the guardians of one's nascent conscience and idealism and one's sense of personal dignity will not allow one to act unworthily.

This second circle of the Wheel of Life shows us how ethics determine our future experience under the law of karma. The essential principles of the Dharma are here conceived in terms of morality. In a sense, all we really need to know is here: that we must develop wholesome mental states so that we will rise higher and higher on the Spiral of the Higher Evolution.

6
The Endless Round

Out of the all-pervading gloom, we discern a tottering shape, unsteadily groping towards us. It is an old man, bent with his years but not with their wisdom. His eyes gaze before him in the vacant stare of total blindness yet his face expresses a kind of stupid hopefulness. He thinks he has been this way before, he seems to picture to himself the landscape around him, and he moves forward eagerly. But, alas, never has he been here and the scene he imagines is quite different from reality. Over and over again, he staggers and falls. But, each time, he drags himself to his feet with renewed hope. Now, he thinks, I remember the route. And he stumbles, on and on.

Next, we see a potter turning lumps of clay on his wheel and, with deft hands, shaping vases and bowls, pots and dishes. If we look closely, we will see that many different moods flit across his face: sadness, anger, joy, guilt, conceit pursue each other, one by one. And each feeling guides his fingers. When rage inflames him, his pot is hard and awkward in shape and, when he is gripped by craving, his desires are mirrored in his creation.

A young monkey frisks in a tree, leaping from branch to branch, never still for a moment. It sees, at the top of the tree, the glint of ripe fruit and up it leaps, hands and feet clasping the tree-trunk, long tail curled and waving. It seizes the fruit, plucks it and takes an enormous bite. Its mouthful still unchewed, another fruit catches its eye, further down this time. It drops, without noticing, the fruit it has just picked, swallows whole what is in its mouth, and dashes off, down toward the new enticement. Soon, the foot of the tree is heaped with half-chewed fruit.

Four men are seated in a rowing boat. One of them has the oars and another is steering. One is the lookout and shouts out excitedly, from time to time, reporting the vague shapes he can see on the horizon. The fourth maintains a running commentary on where they are going, gives advice on how he thinks the others should be doing their jobs, and states his own preferences as to their destination. Occasionally, they quarrel and accuse each other of failing in their tasks. None of them really knows where they are going so they turn this way and that, following the whim of the moment. They do not realize that terrible dangers surround them: storms, rocks and sea monsters. They do not know that their boat is leaking and badly needs repair.

A man sits within a house which has five windows and a door. Through these apertures, he watches the world. A great concourse passes in and out at the door, consisting of many people, each dressed in his own way, carrying his shopping or his lunch, his work tools or his sports gear, some happy and smiling, some with evil intent. The man watches these many sights very carefully.

A man and a woman gaze at each other, passionately. At last, they are alone together. Their hands entwine and pull each toward the other. Clasping each other close, they kiss and lock in embrace, straining to press their two bodies into one.

A howl of pain shatters the silence and a man falls to his knees, groaning, his hands pressed to his face. At the centre of his right eye, embedded deeply in it, is an arrow.

The day has been hot and dusty and the man has been working hard in the fields. He is seated, waiting. He is tired and dirty and, above all, thirsty for he has not had anything to drink for some time. His mouth is dry and his tongue feels thick and heavy. A woman brings a glass of cool water to him, slowly and gracefully. He calls her to him, angrily, with desperate impatience.

A woman is walking in the countryside. She has not eaten for many hours and her stomach gripes with hunger. She sees apples growing in an orchard and hurries over to them. Stretching on tiptoe, she grasps a fruit and pulls it from the branch.

Lost to all but their own urgent desire, the couple melt together in the act of love. Tumbling rapturously to their release, they do not know that a new life has started in the woman's womb.

Beads of sweat cover the woman's face and her mind is swallowed in pain. Between her wide-open legs, with careful hands, a doctor gently eases the new being into the world.

Six men shoulder a large wooden coffin. Slowly, they lower it on to the ramp that leads to the fire which will consume it and the body it contains.

These twelve scenes present themselves to us like tableaux on a revolving stage, each giving way to the next in an endless round. At each turn of the Wheel, the postures are slightly different, the figures are dressed in different ways and have new features. But the twelve scenes are always the same and they always will be until we move from the Wheel to the Spiral.

Words can never capture the full richness of life. They can only be pointers or guides by means of which we leap in imagination to the reality which they attempt to express. Often we become tangled with our own language and our words enmesh us in simplistic under-standings which we cannot see since they are embedded in everyday speech. Thus, because we label objects in the world with nouns we come to think of them as unchanging entities – isolated, interacting only by a system of mechanical exchanges. We even think of ourselves in this same way. When we seek the origins of particular events, we tend to look for single causes, as if reality was a gigantic engine made up of leavers and pulleys. We search for causes which have brought about the most subtle events, just as the unwinding spring turns a clockwork motor. While such a simplified view is perfectly adequate for ordinary practical purposes, it overlooks the inexpressibly complex interlinking of all elements of our universe. Objects are not opaque and solitary units but are processes woven in with all the other processes which make up reality. It could even be said that each single event is the product of the entire cosmos.

These processes are not only interwoven in space and time, they are also, as we have seen, arranged hierarchically into orders, each level having its own laws of functioning and affecting and being affected by lower and higher orders. It is this dizzying dance of forces that our flat words try to convey. Try, of course, we must, both because words help us to reduce this cosmic complexity to a workable simplicity for the purposes of everyday functioning and because they may lead us beyond words to an experience of the ineffable richness of existence. We will only succeed in achieving this transcendent realization if we use words not as mathematical signs but as poetry to carry us to new levels of direct understanding. This is how the Buddha used language in trying to communicate his own vision of the nature of reality.

In his famous formula of Conditioned Coproduction, the Buddha showed that each thing, person or event arises out of a field of conditions without which it passes way. It *arises in dependence on* these conditions. Each single event arises in dependence on a vast network of conditions which ultimately embraces the entire universe. Not every condition has the same power of determination or is of the same importance as a conditioning factor and Buddhist philosophers have distinguished a number of different kinds of conditioned relationship: some conditions are, in Western terms, efficient causes, some provide the supportive environment in which an event can take place, some are catalysts, and others again arise simultaneously with the object they condition. The details of these and other kinds of conditions need not detain us here. The important point is that the Buddha did not see the world as a mechanical model: A causing B like billiard-balls knocking one into the other. He gave expression to his vision in terms of a very complex set of conditoned relationships between ever-changing processes. It is, as it were, an ecological view of causality rather than one based on simple mechanics. In this way, far greater justice is done to the total complexity of things and it is a shorter step from words to direct experience.

All phenomena are subject to the principle of conditionality. Whether it be a rock or a passing bad mood, each can be shown to be one link in a vast chain of conditions. We have now to explore the application of the principle of conditionality to the phenomena of human birth and death. We move to the rim of the Wheel of Life since, for purposes of exposition, it is best to deal with this outer circle before we examine the six realms. Twelve scenes are arranged around the rim, each representing one 'link' in the 'chain' of conditionality which is human life.

According to early accounts, the Buddha, sitting beneath the tree of Enlightenment, with his newfound Insight systematically stripped back the layers of conditions within human existence. He was not seeking a first cause in the metaphysical sense. Buddhism teaches that there is no discernible beginning to the conditioned process and that, therefore, there was no act of creation from which everything unrolled. Whatever condition we come to, we can always seek the conditions in dependence upon which it arose. The round of conditions wheels on endlessly and always has done. What the Buddha revealed was that the chain of conditions that makes up human life is circular, without beginning or end. That chain consists of twelve links, although that number is, in a sense, arbitrary and the process could be analysed into more or less factors. Any link can be taken as the starting point and all the others will follow from it.

The Buddha's enquiry led him through different levels of conditions which, in the twelve links, are spread out over three lives. To add to the complexity of this teaching, each condition is not necessarily of the same kind as the one which it precedes. Some factors, therefore, turn up more than once during the chain. It is, by no means, a simple series of causes – that could only lead to an infinite regress. But, despite its apparent difficulties, the basic message of the teaching of the twelve links of the chain of Conditioned Coproduction should become clear as we examine each link in detail. The chain is usually commenced at *ignorance*, for this is the condition of greatest generality which underlies all the others. Ignorance, however, arises in dependence on causes and even death gives rise to new phenomena. We have to break into this vicious circle somewhere and ignorance is, methodologically speaking, the best place.

Ignorance

This link is illustrated by the image of a blind man who blunders forward, unable to see where he is going. So, ignorance is blindness,not seeing. It is lack of insight into the reality of things, lack of imagination, lack, even, of Englightenment. Ignorance does not, however, consist merely in the fact that we do not see but that we think we do: we are ignorant of the real nature of things but we think we know. All our actions and thoughts are based upon assumptions about the meaning and purpose of life, albeit unconscious and unsystematized.

A course of radical self-questioning quickly reveals our ignorance. If we start to examine what is in our minds, trying to see how we came by what we take to be our knowledge, and questioning our own underlying assumptions, then we realize that there is very little that we really know in any strict sense. Most of what passes for our knowledge is derived from other sources. The views of those around us we absorb by a kind of osmosis – we want to belong, to be part of a wider group and so we accept the prevailing view. What the group takes to be knowledge, that we know. The facts or views held by the group may well be correct but our basis for holding them is not our own individual assessment but our primitive desire to belong. We are probably influenced in this way, to a degree we are hardly aware of, by the nation we come from, our family and social background, our education and the media we attend to.

As we have already seen in the opening chapter, not only does the group form our opinions, but our own desires determine what we believe. It is our desire to belong, to fit in, which leads us to adopt the views of family and friends. To a large extent, we believe what we want to believe and we see what we want to see. Our 'knowledge' then is rationalization, the intellectual crystallization of our basic attitudes. Our perception of the world is riddled with our subjective reactions.

Even when we begin to think a little for ourselves, leaving behind the shallow opinions of hearsay, we are only too ready to arrive at final judgements on matters about which we have little, if any, information. To give but one example from my own experience, it is surprising how swiftly intelligent and well-respected men can dismiss Buddhism as cold and nihilistic. Perhaps they have been misled by poor translations of Buddhist texts – if they have read them at all. But, as reasonable men, they should have examined the witness whose evidence they were accepting to see whether his testimony was sound. Again and again, in many fields of experience, we assume knowledge prematurely. We think that we understand other people's motives. We assume we comprehend the complex manoeuvrings of international politics. We confidently predict the outcome of events in our own lives. We may have very little experience of the phenomena in question but that does not stop us from coming to our conclusions. Even if we had information from sources which we considered yielded sound information we could still only arrive at an inference. We could not be sure of our conclusions. We do not have certainty. Almost the entire corpus of our so-called knowledge is of this kind. Naturally, we must use inductive inference to allow us to make predictions and generalizations about what we do not know using whatever evidence we may possess. We should be aware of the worth of our evidence, however, we should reason soundly in drawing our conclusions, and we should not forget that our judgements are inferences and not certain knowledge. The fact that we do not proceed in this way demonstrates, once more, the element of egoistical desire swamping our reason.

So, lost in our own ignorance, we formulate views based upon shallow evidence and our own desires. Views surround us on all sides, thrust at us by the entire culture in which we grow up and live. It is almost impossible not to be influenced unless we are exceptionally strong-minded and awake. So hemmed in are we by opinion that we cannot discriminate between what is wholesome and what is harmful. Wrong views, in the Buddhist sense, flourish like mental viruses in the weak tissue of our immature minds. They cover a vast range of attitudes from the most trivial to the most fundamental. To give but two examples: many people hold an unthinking quasi-egalitarian view and many are materialist in their outlook. The quasi-egalitarian rejects not only social distinction based upon birth but also the very idea that some people are more developed than others. This he considers 'elitist' or 'undemocratic'. The attitude behind this view might be expressed, 'I am as good as anyone else and no one is better than me.' Such people have great difficulty learning anything of importance from others and they certainly consider that looking up to them is a sign of weakness. Muddled egalitarianism of this type is very widespread in the West and gives rise to an outlook which is without any vertical dimension. All is flat and mediocre and real excellence is denied. Social hierarchy based on privilege of birth rather than individual merit must be clearly distinguished from a spiritual hierarchy based on individual attainment of higher levels of consciousness. Unless one acknowledges such a spiritual hierarchy then one cannot oneself develop through its various levels. One will feel no respect for those who have gone further than oneself and will be unable to learn from them. This hierarchy does not need to be formalized into grades and ranks (one's own experience will teach one who to respect if one is sincere) but one's perspective must include that vertical dimension if one is to grow.

While confused quasi-egalitarianism flattens everything down to the level of the 'ordinary' man, materialism effectively restricts human life to the gratification of material needs. If we believe that all phenomena, ourselves included, are but arrangements of matter and that consciousness is annihilated at death then we can place little value on the development of the mind. Philosophy, aesthetic appreciation, culture in general become, at best, mere pastimes to beguile us on the way to the grave. Morality – if it survives at all – is but a means of arranging our lives at least inconvenience to each other. Such a view sustains few values or ideals. It leaves the world meaningless and dull, productive only of a few years of purely sensuous pleasure, if we are fortunate.

Many people hold this view in the belief that it is 'scientific'. Yet, other more philosophical questions aside, before the materialistic outlook can be deemed scientifically proven, all the phenomena of mind must be satisfactorily explained in terms of physical laws. This is very far from being the case. Materialism then is but a belief and its proponents adhere to it on grounds other than rational. This view can only lead to a shallow and egoistical hedonism and is characterized by a crushing drabness of outlook.

Many other views are endemic in society at large, infecting those who are not immunized by awareness. Indeed, honest investigation may well lead one to conclude that most of one's mental contents are of this kind. There are views which cloud and confuse us about all aspects of life. According to Buddhist teaching, all these wrong views ulti-mately rest upon either of two fundamental views; eternalism or nihilism. Eternalism, put briefly, is the belief that behind all the phe-nomena of experience is a God or Absolute Being. The eternalist, therefore, thinks of life as an effort to liberate the ultimate in us, the soul, from the enslavement of the senses to union with that Absolute Being. A stern, even authoritarian ethic and a wilful asceticism are often the consequences of this way of seeing things. The eternalist lives removed from life, seeing the experiences it brings as illusory distrac-tions from the God who lies behind them. Nihilism, on the other hand, is the belief that death is the final end of life and that there is no reality beyond what we experience with our senses. Before the darkness swallows us up, all we can do is enjoy sensual pleasures, albeit quite refined ones. In one form or another, our lives are founded upon either of these two basic attitudes or else we oscillate from one to the other.

Both these views rest upon the distinction between subject and object. Eternalism is belief in an ultimate subject existing without any object and nihilism, that the object alone has any reality. Caught in the split in our consciousness, we can only think of what is ultimate by eliminating one side of the split and absolutizing the other. At less rarefied, metaphysical levels, we either overemphasize our subjective life at the expense of the world around us or we devalue our conscious-ness by overvaluing the sensuous world. These distinctions are not of merely philosophical interest, for they have psychological and ethical ramifications for everyone. The eternalist retreats from life, repres-sing the instinctual within him, and is preoccupied with his own subjective experience. The nihilist grabs at the gratification of his senses and places no importance on the cultivation of his higher faculties, except as a means to more refined sensuality.

Eternalism and nihilism underlie behaviour that is both very crude and greatly refined. Most of the great world religions are eternalist although they have followers who are highly intelligent and sensitive. In the end, both are wrong views and lead only to distortion and cramping for they rest upon that split in consciousness which is, according to Buddhism, but a stage in evolution. As self-consciousness differentiates itself out of the mass of simple sense awareness, one aspect is identified as the subject of experience and the remainder is perceived as the object. Gradually, the literalness and rigidity of the boundary between the two is relaxed and they begin to intermingle and merge as consciousness is raised. In the end, the barrier between subject and object is removed altogether and a stage of mind is experienced which is beyond duality and in which reality is seen as an endless play of conditions of inexpressible creative potentiality. There is no eternalism because within the play of conditions is to be found nothing permanent or fixed and no being which is absolute. There is no nihilism because the individual is just such a flow of states, one arising in dependence on the other and death is merely a point of transition from one stage to another.

While there remains within us yet one hair's breadth between subject and object, we are ignorant and we do not see things fully as they are – that is, as part of the vast network of processes, all inter-woven and interpenetrating, all rising in dependence on conditions. For Buddhism this is knowledge. When one has a direct experience of reality as the rise and fall of conditioned processes then one has cer-tainty. And knowledge, here, is one and the same as compassion, for every element of reality is loved as if it were oneself – indeed, since no distinction now exists between self and other, it could be said that one is identical with the whole of reality.

Ignorance is our basic condition and we should face up to it. We should accept that even our mundane knowledge is intelligent guess-work. All we can be certain of, at this moment, is that we are having certain experiences whose exact nature eludes us for the present. Every-thing else is assumption and estimate. Such honest scepticism is the beginning of knowledge. This point was made by Socrates when, on being pronounced the wisest man in Greece by the Delphic oracle, he declared that if he was wisest it was because he alone knew that he knew nothing whereas other men claimed to know. Once we are aware of our ignorance, we can begin systematically to cultivate wisdom.

Until ignorance has been replaced by wissdom, we need some intellectual guidelines. It is not enough to eradicate wrong views, we must cultivate right views. Right views are intellectual understandings which help us to grow. They provide us with the basis on which we can arrive at vision and wisdom. Fundamentally, right view consists in seeing that, between eternalism and nihilism is a 'middle way' which is the perception of things as arising in dependence on conditions. Right view is this same Conditioned Coproduction that we are now studying. It reveals, above all, a Path which we can follow, eventually crowning our efforts with wisdom.

While we are ignorant, however, we cannot help but act in an ignorant way. So, in dependence on ignorance, there arises *volitional activity*.

Volitional Activities

The next image, moving in a clockwise direction round the rim of the Wheel, is a potter shaping pots on his wheel. How each pot turns out depends upon the potter. What he has decided the pot is to be used for, his skill and experience, his aesthetic sense, even his mood at the time of manufacture, all determine what shape he will form from the lump of clay before him. The volitional activities are, like the potter, formative forces which shape our own future. They are the sum total of all our willing, whether the intentions manifest themselves in overt action or in speech or remain as desires in our hearts. Although some volitions may be very powerful and have a dominant influence, it is the accumulated momentum of all our wishes which determines the flow of our lives. As a rope is plaited from many tiny hairs, no one of which reaches for more than a fraction of its full length, so the direction and tendency of our being is shaped by the countless acts of volition which we make in the course of every day of our existence.

Our volitions are formative forces. Not only do they form our words and deeds through the action of the brain and nervous system, but they imprint themselves directly on the world around us. Thought, desire and consciousness are energies just as are radiation or electricity within the physical order. A thought has a direction, an inherent momentum which discharges itself upon the world. With every mental image, every longing, every coherent idea, we are radiating a very subtle, but extremely powerful, field of energy which influences our environment. When our thoughts are concentrated and intense enough, that influence may even be measurable. The phenomena of parapsychology – telepathy clairaudience, psychokinesis, etc. – are all evidence of the direct action of the mind and some of them have been demonstrated under laboratory conditions. According to Buddhist tradition, such powers can either be systematically cultivated – although this is considered to be something of a sidetrack – or they arise spontaneously as one cultivates higher stages of consciousness. As one's mind becomes more and more unified and powerful, so the field of its influence becomes stronger. Sometimes, such powers arise as 'gifts' in people who have no apparent spiritual commitment. This is often explained as the consequence of actions performed in past lives.

The volitional activities are a kind of force-field or blueprint, on the level of the karmic order, which moulds the lower order – the mental, biological and physical – and expressing through them its own character. The impulses that move us manifest themselves concretely, not only in our actions but in our bodies and the worlds we inhabit. This is, in essence, what our lives are: the embodiment of our volitions in a world of experience.

The blueprint is a very complex one. It encodes all the greed, hatred and delusion whereby we seek to build a false security for our fragile egos, but it also contains the outline of far deeper and more creative urges. The evolutionary thrust, the pull of Buddhahood, is present in the most egoistical and twisted personality. Consciousness, at whatever stage, contains within it a momentum to attain higher levels. Just as the seed contains the flower and inexorably unfolds from within itself so even rudimentary sense consciousness contains the full flower of Transcendental consciousness and rises up towards it. Primitive consciousness prefigures full consciousness and has a latent tendency to develop. It is this propensity of consciousness to unfold itself which powers the whole evolutionary process. Consciousness, as it becomes more complex, moulds for itself organisms through which it can express each new level. The same process can be looked at the other way around, from the biological point of view, in which evolution is seen as the development of more complex organisms which permit the expression of higher levels of consciousness.

This reciprocal process continues until self-consciousness is achieved. At this point, the vertical momentum of evolution is intersected by the oscillations of individualized consciousness as it wanders through the rounds of birth and death. Being self-aware, we have the power to interrupt the evolutionary current by trying to stabilize our rudimentary selfhood using the devices of greed, hatred and delusion. We also have the power to continue evolution by actively cooperating with the force of our own unfolding consciousness. Impulses expressive both of the evolutionary urge and of our ignorance are part of the blueprint of our volitional activities and pattern matter as they discharge themselves. We are made up of these conflicting tendencies and our lives give full expression to them. Which one predominates is a matter for each of us to determine.

It is the formative blueprint of the volitional activities which carries over from the past life to shape the new one, forming matter into a body. The most comprehensive traditions and what evidence there is from modern research suggest that there is an interval between one life and the next, known as the 'intermediate state'. According to the *Bardo Thödol*, the so-called *Tibetan Book of the Dead*, which gives a detailed account of the experiences of death and rebirth, the intermediate state lasts for forty-nine days – but this is clearly symbolic. The length of time probably varies, depending on the volitional activities of the person who has died.

As death approaches, so says the *Book of the Dead*, consciousness gradually recedes from the physical body. This is spoken of as the dissolution of one element into another: earth dissolves into water, water into fire, etc. Just as when we go to sleep our hold on the world around us slips away, bit by bit, so the physical world slowly recedes from us as we die. Each of the senses becomes weaker and weaker until we are left in a state of pure consciousness without any objective grounding. Nothing remains whereby we can identify ourselves and so we experience our ego-hood being swallowed up in the undifferentiated infinitude of pure consciousness. Without the bases upon which we usually ground ourselves, we are brought face to face with reality. With nothing to limit or restrict it, the pure, non-dual awareness inherent within our self-consciousness is released.

The moment the experience of the 'clear light of reality' dawns

91

upon us we recoil from it and scramble for the sure ground of ego-identity. Consciousness is still connected, though more and more loosely, with the body even after the heart has stopped beating. So, recoiling from the overwhelming vastness of pure awareness, we find ourselves again at the scene of our death. But we can no longer communicate with those around us. Consciousness is not situated in the body any more, and we find that we are witnessing our own funeral from within a 'mind-made' body. This body, although it has the appearance of a physical body to us, does not interact with the old world except insofar as we perceive, very vividly, what is happening there. Since it is, as it were, the direct emanation of our volitional activities, it moves as swiftly as our thoughts. As soon as some place comes to mind, we are there; as soon as we remember an old friend, we stand before him.

So we find that we can no longer connect with our old life and that none of the people we spent our time with are even aware that we are still in their midst. Unable to ground ourselves in the old life, we continually oscillate between the experience of reality latent within our minds and the pull towards ego-hood. We cannot bear the brilliance of pure consciousness and yet the intermediate state offers us nothing firm upon which we can build an identity. We are lost in a storm of visions which are the productions of our own volitional activities. Now the visions unfold the deepest potential within us, now they represent to us our own greed, hatred and delusion. In this intermediate state, we live out all the tendencies within us. Gradually, the fluctuations stabilize and the overall drift of our character asserts itself. We long to possess a body again which will crystallize our identity and we are drawn to a world which matches our own volitional blueprint.

According to the Tibetan tradition, death offers a unique opportunity to gain liberation or, at least, to attain a deeper understanding, for with the safe and familiar removed from consciousness we are faced directly with reality. Even if we cannot come to terms with this experience, we have the chance to see our own motivations and functioning more clearly, no longer hidden by the comfort of familiarity. We have the opportunity to make major changes in our consciousness since the fixed, habitual routine of our world has gone. Although death is the greatest of such periods of transition, it is not the only one. At death, we are removed from our old lives quite literally, but experiences of failure or loss of loved ones or extreme disruption through war or disaster are little deaths within life in which 'the bottom drops out of our world' and we are left 'floating in a vacuum'. Often these are times of mingled hope and anguish. The pain of loss and insecurity is balanced by an awareness of new horizons opening up and of freedom from old, restricting routines. Usually, of course, we settle back into our old ways but, sometimes, major breakthoughs can be made after such experiences. Meditation, too, is an intermediate state since we are deliberately withdrawn from the sure ground of the senses. Dreams, even life itself, are considered to be intermediate states for, all phenomena being impermanent, we can rely on no conditioned state for security.

From the *Book of the Dead* it is clear that contact can be maintained with the dead person up to the time when they are reborn. They, at least, can hear us even if we cannot hear them. It is said that we can help them considerably by directing positive feelings towards them and even, if they are Buddhists, by reading to them from the *Book of the Dead* which guides the dead person through the different experiences between death and rebirth and teaches how to deal with them. The art of helping people to die in such a way that they enter the intermediate state in a clear and confident condition is well studied in the Tibetan tradition of Buddhism. Our attitude and behaviour can have a strong influence upon our dead friends and can help them to face the bewildering experiences of death with courage and awareness. This will, in its turn, enable them to be reborn under circumstances favourable to their future development.

It is the volitional activities which drive us through the intermediate state, determining the sequence and intensity of the visions and the world into which we will be reborn. By that process of attraction of mental state for like experience, which is the mechanism of the karmic order, the pattern of volitional activities leads consciousness to the appropriate world where rebirth is to take place. As we will see in detail in the following chapters, the human world is not the only one in which rebirth may take place. In some worlds, rebirth is by parturition as amongst humans, but in others it is apparitional – one appears, instantaneously, as a fully mature inhabitant of that realm.

If one is to be reborn into the human world one finds oneself wandering over the earth, seeking a body. One is attracted to a particular couple who suit one's karmic propensities. It seems that rebirth, very often, takes place within the same locality which one previously inhabited and even in the same family since one will seek the familiar and bonds of strong feeling, whether of craving or hatred, will bind one to well-remembered places and faces. One sees the chosen couple in the act of copulation and, if one is to be reborn as a man, one feels a strong attraction for the woman, and for the man if one's karmic tendencies will find best expression as a woman. One tries to take the place of the future parent of the same sex towards whom one, apparently, feels intense jealousy. At the moment when sperm and ovum meet within the womb, the full force of one's volitional energy concentrates upon that point of fusion and a living cell comes into being. So great is the shock of the condensing of one's volitions upon one tiny cell that, at that moment, one faints away. Some highly developed beings are able to maintain consciousness as they enter the womb, some can even leave the womb fully mindful, but for most the moment of conjunction of sperm, ovum and volitional activities is the moment when one is dipped in the waters of Lethe and memory of everything that went before is erased. Some children, however, as we have seen, do retain some memory of their previous life and, also, whether spontaneously or by systematic effort, memory of past existences may return to beings who are advanced upon the Path.

At the moment when that junction of the father's sperm, the mother's ovum and the consciousness to be reborn takes place, there arises, in dependence on the volitional activities, *sentience*, the first tiny flash of consciousness in the single cell of the embryo.

Sentience

The third link is represented by a monkey in a tree, restlessly jumping from branch to branch as his eye is caught now by one fruit, now by another. The monkey represents the very primitive spark of sense-consciousness which is the first moment in the mental life of the new being.

Traditional expositions of the twelve links are at pains to insist that there is, in fact, nothing which is reborn. There is no 'soul' which drops the shell of one body and takes on a new one, like a hand taking off one glove and putting on another. This would be eternalism. At the same time, the new life is not completely different from the old one. We would not be able to speak of rebirth at all if that were the case –

this view would be nihilism. The new life is said to be 'neither the same as nor different from' the old one. This is not nearly as mysterious as it seems. The two lives are two different phases of one continuous process consisting of a flow of conditions. The old life establishes the conditions in dependence on which the new one arises. When a wave passes across the sea, there is no single drop of water which travels along with it from start to finish – the water particles do not move along but only up and down. Nonetheless, we speak of one wave, for there is a continuity of causation between the wave at its origin and at the point where it breaks upon the shore. In fact, everything conditioned is like that: a process consisting of conditions arising in dependence one upon the other. Thus sentience arises in dependence on the volitional activities established in the previous life.

Conception is the point at which biological evolution is intersected by the continuum of self-consciousness. The father's sperm and the mother's ovum contribute the material base, but this is not sufficient for life to start. There must be the blueprint generated in a previous life which can manifest itself through that particular genetic combination. There must be a pattern of volitional activities which, as it were, fits the sperm and ovum and which can unfold itself through the developing embryo. Without both the genetic and the karmic factors, no conception can take place.

This first flash of sentience, rudimentary as it is, contains, in condensed form, the entire momentum from the past existence. Just as the first single cell of the embryo contains the genetic code in its DNA which will determine the general characteristics of the mature body, so the preliminary consciousness carries the seed of the adult personality. Sentience is the point at which the volitional activities begin to ground themselves in a new identity. In studies of rebirth, some physical characteristics and deformities seem to be the consequence of actions performed in the past life. It is traditionally held that karma determines whether one is good-looking or ugly, strong or weak, and the like. So complex is human motivation, however, and so hard is it to discern the workings of karmic conditionality that we should beware of ascribing every physical debility to past actions. Yet, the physical form is strongly influenced by the pattern encoded in sentience. The energies latent in acts of volition begin to discharge themselves by moulding the physical body. They have, as it were, seized upon a material configuration which is of sufficient organic complexity and which corresponds

95

to them and this they begin to shape. Thus, the karmic order of conditionality patterns the physical, biological and mental orders without in any way disrupting their laws.

Though the link of memory between one life and the next is usually lost, the broad characteristics of personality pass over – for personality is the general outline of our volitions. Carried in that seed of consciousness are the reactions of greed, hatred and delusion and whatever there might be of love, generosity and awareness. The embryo is no *tabula rasa*, a blank sheet formed simply from its environment. We come into life with dispositions and tendencies which emerge more clearly as we mature. It is for this reason that children often display marked preferences and repulsions which they did not, apparently, learn from their parents. Indeed, it has often been remarked how quickly a little personality appears in an infant, well before it has had time to be shaped by its surroundings. Exceptional talent and genius, even, when displayed very young, is to be explained as the continuation of trends established in the past. Our attitudes and responses go very deep in us. We can never fully disentangle all the factors that have made us what we are since some of them go back over many lives. A certain amount of self-analysis may help us to understand what we feel more clearly but we cannot always determine why we feel it. We carry into life with us a residue of hatred and craving and of love and generosity. These will assert themselves no matter what our upbringing is in the present life. Neither our parents nor our social environment can be made to bear more than a part of the blame for how we are. Most of it we must shoulder for ourselves.

Life begins at the point when sperm, ovum and volitional activities merge. It follows, then, that any termination of an embryo's development destroys life. When this is done intentionally, it is a form of murder. Since self-consciousness does not begin to emerge – or, rather, re-emerge – until the first years of a baby's life – it is not, perhaps, so obvious that abortion is murder. In the first place, however, Buddhism teaches that the harming of any living being, at whatsoever stage of evolution it may be, is unskilful and should be avoided. Moreover, since the sentience in the womb will, in the normal course of development, become the full self-consciousness of an human being, the unskilfulness is all the greater. From the point of view of the teaching of rebirth, one must also take into account the disruption to the being whose life would be cut short. Having just experienced the trauma of death and the terrifying uncertainty of the intermediate state, at last he has found a point upon which his energies can focus. When the consciousness is abruptly cut loose again, the effect may well be to accentuate feelings of fear and insecurity which will make an unfavourable rebirth more likely. When considering whether or not to have an abortion, all of this should be taken into account. The effects upon the woman herself should also be considered for, very often, deep feelings of guilt and regret persist for many years and there may well be other karmic consequences. If a woman goes against her natural maternal instincts in this way, she will, inevitably, be affected.

In this light, it is clear that abortion should be avoided. Most contraception, however, interrupts no life-continuum since sentience does not arise until sperm and ovum actually meet. It is not, therefore, in itself, unskilful.

Sentience is the germ in dependence on which the whole *psychophysical organism* unfolds.

The Psychophysical Organism

This link is depicted by four men sitting in a boat which one of them is steering. This represents all the different bodily and mental processes of which the mature human being is compounded as consciousness gradually objectifies itself. This psychophysical organism is, traditionally, divided into five 'heaps' or categories of interrelated functions, represented by the four men plus the boat. Every element of our being can be assigned to one or other of these heaps. They are: form, feeling, recognition, motivation and consciousness. This classification is not so much a philosophical analysis of human personality as a kind of meditation upon everything which makes up our experience, every aspect of which can be assigned to one or other of these five heaps. Having broken experience, both inner and outer, into its constituent elements in this way, we can examine each part more closely. What we find is that every one of them is transient. Every aspect of us is a process arising in dependence on conditions and we are the sum total of all of them, woven together into a dynamic and complex whole. We realize that we must not identify ourselves in a rigid way with the body, personality or any particular state of being. This, in its turn, helps us to see that we can develop. Every one of these processes can be made to function at higher levels.

Our analysis begins with *form*. This is a difficult concept in Buddhist thought, quite different from our ordinary understanding of matter. Buddhism does not accept uncritically the 'commonsense' view of matter as something solid, 'out there', independent of human perception. As in everything else, it requires us to come back to what we really know. All that we can with any certainty claim to know is that we are having certain experiences. We seem to occupy a world of objects which we perceive through the senses. But in reality we do not *experience* objects or a world, we experience sensations. The assembling of those sensations into the world we preceive is an addition to our basic experience. Something of this distinction can be seen if we analyse a situation such as sitting in front of a fire. We feel the heat on our legs, hear the crackling in our ears, see the flickering with our eyes and smell the pungent fumes with our nose. All of these sensations present themselves to us as the coordinated perception of sitting in front of a fire. If we deliberately let go of the assembled picture we can feel each of these impressions as raw sensation, playing upon its own sense organ, independent of the others. This is our basic experience and it is all that is given to us. Everything else we add on.

Buddhism's approach, here, is strictly empirical. It invites us to strip away the layers of our ignorant assumptions by becoming aware of what our immediate experience is before we work it up into objects. What we are left with is the experience of different kinds of sensation, as if of resistance. When we touch something hard, we have the experience of being resisted, pushed back at. This sensation of resistance is a manifestation of form. Such resistance is of four different kinds, referred to as earth, water, fire and air. These are, however, not physical elements; the terms are symbolic. Earth is what gives rise to the sensation of a solid impediment to our senses; water is everything that gives the sensation of pliability with cohesion; fire is the experience of radiance and heat; and air is that which moves freely, barely resisting our senses at all. These four elements are the bases of all our perception and it is from this bare data that we derive the objective world as we perceive it. Form, then, does not correspond to matter at all. In the basic experience of sensation there is no reference to an external object, since form is just these elementary resistances from which the physical world and our own bodies are made up. At every moment, they pass across our minds in very complex patterns, an endless flow of sensations each of which arises and passes away, instant by instant.

Form is the objective element in our experience which is illuminated by *consciousness*. There is a seeming difficulty in considering consciousness as part of the fourth link which arises in dependence on the spark of consciousness which is the third. The fourth link, however, represents the fully developed psychophysical system which evolves out of the seminal flash of sentience. Consciousness means, in this context, the faculty of discriminative awareness. The sensations of resistance called form are distinguished and attended to in an act of awareness. Consciousness is never still, constantly changing with the ever-flowing stimuli. We must not allow our words to mislead us into thinking of consciousness as a single, substantial entity, for it is like everything else, a process whose different phases arise in dependence on conditions and pass away again.

The sensations which have been presented to consciousness are compared with past sensory data and are fitted into a pattern of perception which is our world. *Recognition* is the process of assimilating sensations and recognizing them as particular objects with certain properties and relations. One can observe this process in action when, for instance, there is an object in the distance which one cannot properly make out. It may be a goat, grazing amongst the trees, or it may be a rock – or perhaps it is something else again. While one looks, trying to see what it is, it actually is a goat for a while, then it is a rock as one interprets the sensations now this way, now that. Recognition is the point in the perceptual process where we split our experience into a subject and an object, an inner personal world of mind and an outer objective world of things. Both subject and object are interpretation, neither being given in the raw data of our experience. Our perception is composed of a never-ending series of such judgements, each of which is an interpretation of our sensation in the light of our own past perception, experience, and view of life. We are constantly readjusting our picture of life as we try to fit new data into our overall view of ourselves and the world.

Having assembled various sensations into one object and having assigned that object a place in our scheme of things, we have certain *feelings* about it. These may be direct physical pleasures or pains or they may be of a more mental kind based upon anticipation or memory. Some objects, of course, barely arouse our feelings at all and have little or no hedonic tone. All the time, we are making evaluations as new experiences come to us and as our own inner states shift and change.

Finally, *motivation* is our active response to things. After evaluating the interpretation of the sensations we have sensed, volitions arise. We want to possess those things we judge pleasant and to reject or destroy those which we see as painful. Motivation includes the whole complex world of our emotions which are as much ever-changing processes as any of the constituents of the other heaps.

If we examine carefully the different phenomena of our experience we find them all to be conditioned processes. Most cells in our bodies are completely renewed at least every seven years and our mental states are far more fleeting. It is this complex of bodily and mental processes which now unfolds in dependence on the potent seed of primary consciousness. The pattern of the five heaps of form, consciousness, recognition, feeling and motivation contained in the blueprint of sentience gradually unfolds itself in the womb. The energies of volition fuse with physical and biological energies to form the human being.

The psychophysical organism is, at this point in the chain, considered as a potentiality but it begins to function actively, opening up to the world around it. In dependence on the psychophysical organism, the *six senses* arise.

The Six Senses

This link is represented by a house with five windows and a door. The senses are the 'portals' whereby we gain our impressions of the world. Each of the senses is the manifestation of our desire to experience things in that particular way. We get, in fact, the sort of sensations we want and deserve.

The six sense organs are the five outer organs of eye, ear, nose, tongue and body together with the mind. Just as the eye sees sights and the tongue tastes flavours, so the mind has its own data. Memories, anticipations, fantasies, thoughts are all objects of the mind considered as a sense. It is both imagination as the mere capacity to produce images and as the Imaginal faculty, able to perceive higher dimensions of reality. The worlds to which the physical senses give us access are, as we will see, the lowest. It is through the door of the mind that we have access to the higher worlds which are no less real than the physical. The faculty for perceiving them is cultivated through meditation. Like any other sense organ, it develops in response to our volitions about it.

If we want to perceive higher 'worlds' then we will do so as our organs of mental perception become more acute.

At this stage in the cycle of conditionality, the links are all the passive resultants of previous volitional activity. The body and the senses are the inevitable consequence of what we have done in the past. This means that they are not themselves volitional and, therefore, that no ethical evaluation applies to them. The body and the senses are innocent and cannot be considered either skilful or unskilful. Simply to see things, of whatever kind, cannot be wrong. Problems only arise when we start to react mentally to what we perceive. We need therefore to be very much aware of what we take in through the senses. In the traditional phrase, we must 'guard the doors of the senses'. We must try to prevent ourselves from attaching unwholesome volitions to whatever we let into the mind through the senses. This may require us to restrict ourselves from experiencing those sensations which are likely to trigger in us reactions which we cannot control, at least until we are strong enough to perceive them without generating negative volitions.

The senses are the apertures through which the external world is perceived and so, in dependence on them, arises *sensuous impression* or contact.

Sensuous impression

A couple embracing depicts the contact of the sense organs with their objects. With this link, the psychophysical organism begins to interact with the world.

When we were examining the five heaps which make up human experience, we saw that form does not correspond to matter in the ordinary sense. Form is the sensation of resistance, either earth, water, fire or air. By interpreting these sensations we arrive at our picture of the world. What then are we contacting with our sense organs? We should beware of the fascinations of philosophical speculation on this, as on all topics, and adhere to the empirical traditions of Buddhism. All we can know, at this stage, is that we have certain sensations and that much of our image of the world is actually assumption, worked up from the raw data of these sensations. By and large our world picture holds true for operational purposes: it usually allows us to operate effectively – although we do make terrible mistakes from time to time.

If we accept it as a kind of working diagram which we adjust and improve as our understanding increases, then no difficulties need arise. If we forget the raw data of our senses and become attached to our own mental constructions then we run into problems. For then we see things very rigidly and we mistake our own mental picture for reality itself. We are therefore closed to other worlds of experience and to the possiblity of seeing things as they really are.

We can only remain agnostic about what it is that our senses contact. What we call the contact of our senses with an object is no more than the experience of resistance. The concept of resistance, of course, implies something which resists and something which is resisted. There is no way in which we can express that experience without implicit reference to a subject and an object but the basic data yields us but one fact, that there is resistance, without reference to resister or resisted. Perhaps, since we are constrained both by our language and by our own level of consciousness to think that there is something independent of our perception which we are contacting, it is best to imagine that the four elements which resist our senses are actually more like spirits than matter. The world that we are in contact with is not made up of dead atomic building blocks but of a living energy which animates every object. It is thus that our ancestors saw the world when they imagined tree sprites and river gods, spirits that inhabited every part of nature. We cannot recapture the innocence of that perception but we can learn to see things as vital, animated by forces which are identical with the quickness in our own consciousness. We can free ourselves of the sterile materialistic view of nature and recapture the experience of its wonder and power.

The particular experiences of resistance that we have come to us as the consequence of our volitional activity; just as our psychophysical organism arises, by way of the initial sentience, from our past volitions, so the kind of sensations we feel are determined by the kind of body and senses we have. From this point of view it can be said that, not only do we create ourselves, but we create our world.

We have our sensations which we interpret and place within our total view of things. This then gives rise to our evaluation of our perceptions and so, in dependence on sensuous impression, arises *feeling*.

Feeling

To illustrate this link, a man is shown with an arrow sunk deep in his eye. The arrow represents sense data impinging upon the sense organs, in this case, the eye. In a very vivid way, the image suggests the strong feelings which our sensory experience evokes – although only painful feeling is here implied, both painful and pleasant are intended. We are not like television cameras, impartially scanning the environment, for what we perceive has an effect upon us and gives rise to very strong feelings.

Feelings are either pleasant or painful or are so low in hedonic tone as to be neutral. Pleasure and pain are experienced on a number of different levels ranging from direct physical sensations to the loftiest bliss of liberation from the Wheel. According to Buddhist psychology, the experience of direct pain is confined to a relatively small area of the total possibilities of conscious experience. These are, however, the areas in which we habitually dwell!

At the lowest level, feeling is a response to the five physical senses. In the grossest forms, a release of accumulated instinctual tension is experienced as pleasure and the frustration of physical energies or the damaging of the body is experienced as pain. A more refined form of sensuous feeling is to be found in our enjoyment of beauty and dislike of ugliness. Many of our evaluations are not directly sensuous but psychological in character; they include feelings of insecurity and security, of triumph and failure, and those deriving from our expectation of pleasure or pain to come, or from the reliving of past experiences. Feeling includes more generalized moods of well-being and elation, of depression and hopelessness and other such responses to our total experience. Our immediate likes or dislikes of other people are also aspects of feeling.

So far, all the kinds of feeling we have examined are based upon the physical senses, whether directly through the five senses or through our mental consideration of sensuous experience. They therefore belong to the sphere of sensuous desire, the lowest of the three mundane levels of existence. In the higher spheres, there is no pain at all of the sensuous or mental kinds. Pain is restricted entirely to the sensuous sphere. In the sphere of archetypal form, there is a subtle experience unmediated by the five senses. It is the Imaginal faculty which witnesses its visions and mingles with its archetypes. There is very great beauty, but beauty is no longer limited by the imperfections of the physical form. It is an ideal beauty but not an abstract beauty for it is vividly envisioned and arouses intense feelings of pleasure, far greater than any earthly rapture. In the sphere of formlessness, we go still further to contact, not the outward form of beauty, however refined and exalted, but Beauty herself. It is a world of pure qualities whose essences are conveyed directly to the sublimated Imagination. Here there is a delight of an even more powerful kind, surpassing the ecstasy of the visionary dimension.

Yet all the way from gross physical feeling through to the heights of pleasure in the formless sphere, there is a basic underlying tension: the tension between subject and object. As we burst through boundary after boundary, the tension diminishes and we experience the increasing harmony of self and other as mounting pleasure. But the tension remains, however subtle. There is a final pain and a final pleasure: the pain of consciousness divided and the bliss which comes from breaking, totally and for ever, the distinction between subject and object and experiencing the non-dual awareness of Enlightenment. This is what could be called 'absolute pleasure' and is the perpetual experience of the Buddhas.

It should by now be clear that Buddhism does not condemn pleasure. The pursuit of the Higher Evolution is accompanied by ever-increasing happiness and joy. Furthermore, a certain amount of pleasurable experience seems to be essential to human well-being, otherwise all but the strongest lose heart and their vitality drains away. Persistent pain tends to colour one's whole mental outlook, causing a mood of depression and hopelessness unless some deeper sense of meaning has been contacted. A moderate amount of pleasure stimulates and helps to create a mood of confidence and well-being which is an essential basis for further growth. In this respect, we probably do not appreciate the extent to which our surroundings influence us. Every sensory impression leaves some mark upon us, whether pleasant or painful, unless we have the indifference of the bored, the withdrawn or the saturated. The ugliness, dirt and noise of many parts of big cities must powerfully affect their citizens. Often, as a desperate substitute for the simple pleasures of natural surroundings, modern man seeks very strong sensations in loud music, garish colours, highly flavoured foods and intoxicating substances. It is as if only these can reach his jaded feelings, worn down by ugliness and deadened with overstimulation. A beautiful and harmonious environment can, in itself, have a tonic effect upon a weary mind.

Pleasure and pain only become a problem if we relate to them neurotically, and make the pursuit of pleasure and the avoidance of pain our only guiding principles. Sensuous pleasure and pain arise in dependence on our sense organs and their contact with the world. They are, as it were, byproducts of our lives; and pleasure cannot be healthily taken as an end in itself. If it is then we simply become entrapped once more in the turnings of the Wheel. While we live our lives, pleasure may come to us and we can accept it and enjoy it to the full, relinquishing it without regret when it passes. As far as possible, we should open ourselves to the enjoyment of the more refined pleasures, since these will lift our consciousness. Pain indicates that there is something wrong either with our bodies or in our attitude to life. We should do whatever we can to remove the cause of pain in either case. If it cannot be alleviated then we must bear it with fortitude. Neither pleasure nor pain should be allowed to overwhelm us so that we lose our awareness and become lost in a new cycle of reaction.

This link of feeling marks a crucial transition in the whole chain of conditionality. It is a point to which we will be returning in a later chapter of this book, for it is after feeling that volition once more enters the succession of conditions. Once the volitional activities in the past life have been set up, they form sentience, the psychophysical organism, the six senses, sensuous impression and feeling, none of which have volition connected with them. The body, the senses, the objects we perceived and the feelings they give rise to are all the passive resultants of our past intentions. But then a new phase of willing in the present life begins. That volitional activity may be skilful or it may be unskilful and so this transition between feeling and the next link is the point at which we either renew the cyclic motion of the Wheel or begin the steady ascent of the Spiral. It is the Wheel with which we are concerned, for the time being, and so we must spin on through its remaining links. Later, we will return and complete the ascent of the Path.

If we react to feeling, we long to continue the pleasurable experiences and we reject the painful. With no regard to the overall direction or purpose of our lives and with no thought but for immediate gratification, we crave and we hate. So, in dependence on feeling, there arises *craving*.

Craving

This next link is illustrated by a seated man being offered a drink by a woman who stands before him. The word here translated as 'craving' literally means 'thirst'. Of course, thirst is properly but a physical sensation arising out of the body's need for water – it is not craving at all but an healthy need. The image of thirst is used because it suggests the immediacy and strength of neurotic craving. The fact that it is a woman offering a drink to a man may be intended also to bring to mind the intensity of sexual desire.

We have already seen that craving is the longing to enjoy things, events or people because we believe that their possession will make our egos more secure. More particularly, we want those things which we think will give us pleasure and therefore affirm and strengthen our self-sense and we want to be rid of those things which we judge will cause us pain, checking and crushing us. So we crave and hate in dependence on feeling.

There are said to be three basic forms of craving. Firstly, and most simply, there is *Craving for sense objects*. Any of the sense faculties, whether the five physical senses or the mind, can provide objects for our neurotic longing. *Craving for existence* is the deep-seated urge to exist in a fixed state of being, particularly in one of the worlds of heavenly delight, and it is connected with the wrong view of eternalism: that there is a soul within us which is eternal and that there is an absolute being or God. It is our desire to maintain our ego-identity and it is the basic force which keeps most of us alive – the will to live, as it has been called. *Craving for non-existence* is connected with the wrong view of nihilism which considers that there is no consciousness after death. One who craves non-existence longs to pass into the complete oblivion which he believes follows death. In its absolute form, this is perhaps a very rare condition which results from craving so severely frustrated that all belief in the possibility of satisfaction is reliquished. Human hope has its limits and a point is reached where one just gives up the will to live, whether in this life or in any other, because one does not believe that one can ever satisfy one's craving. Although craving of this type is seldom encountered in such an extreme form, it is an element in many people's make-up. It is manifested as the lassitude of despair, the desire for a quiet life, the longing for narcosis or anaesthesia. Perhaps it lies behind some forms of drug addiction. It is the unwillingness to face up to the responsibilities of individual identity, the attempt to find refuge in regression to the group or in unconsciousness or in any state of existence in which no demands are made upon one as an individual. Each of these three kinds of craving – for sensuous objects, for existence, for non-existence – arises out of feeling and, together, they are the basic force that propels us through life, around and around the Wheel. Hatred is not mentioned here, since craving is treated as the primary unwholesome volition and hatred is considered as frustrated craving.

Craving does not long remain a purely mental phenomenon. We act upon it, seizing the objects of our desires. Thus, in dependence upon craving, *grasping* arises.

Grasping

A woman plucking fruit from a tree is the image for this link. Craving has taken effect in concrete action. The objects of grasping are said to be of four kinds. First of all, we grasp after *sense pleasures*. Our longing for them turns into attachment and we live our lives for their sake. But it is not only objects of sensuous experience to which we become attached, we are also bound to our *views and opinions*. The way we look at the world, our beliefs and prejudices, are objects to which we cling, making them part of our identity. It is for this reason that people are seldom able to hold a friendly conversation on matters about which they disagree. To question or deny someone's views is to question or deny him. Religious or political dogmas are often the objects of such attachment and so spark off persecution and 'holy war'. All wrong views are rationalizations of our basic attitudes and are manifestations of the ignorance which underlies the whole cyclic chain of conditionality. We compound our ignorance by grasping after more ignorance.

So important is the cognitive element in conditioning our lives that the remaining two forms of grasping are also connected with views. The first is attachment to *external observances and ethical rules as ends in themselves*. This is manifested when we assume that merely to do something without the corresponding mental attitude is sufficient to gain the benefits we expect and desire. For instance, we know that the regular practice of meditation helps us to gain higher states of consciousness. But we will not experience those benefits if all we do is sit down for a period every day in the correct posture for meditation. We must be making an active attempt to concentrate and refine our minds. Again, merely to 'obey' the precepts, as if they were commandments, will not help us to develop the natural ethical sense which is the mark of a mature individual. We tend to cling to routines and patterns of behaviour, little personal rituals which are familiar and therefore seem to provide comfort and security. Even what we consider to be our spiritual life and practice can all too easily become an empty habit which we perform with faithful regularity but without any real effort or meaning. Worse still, we come to think that just to do the practice, to perform the ritual, to keep the rules, itself guarantees us, as it were magically, spiritual progress or at least material well-being. This is the world of superstition and hypocrisy to which so much religion is prone. It should be stressed, however, that regular spiritual practice, a skilful routine and ethical observance are all essential in following the Path. They only constitute objects of grasping if we treat them superficially and do not use them to bring about changes in our consciousness but as talismans, the possession of which will give us good luck.

Lastly, there is attachment to *belief in a permanent, unchanging self.* The ultimate objective of the immature ego is to stabilize itself eternally. It comes to believe that this is possible, that beneath the everchanging circumstances of life there is a core which remains untouched. It is clinging to this idea of an 'absolute ego' which prevents us, in the first place, from developing our consciousness and, ultimately, from leaving the ego behind altogether.

By clinging to sense pleasures, opinions, rules and routines, and ego identity, we condemn ourselves to the Wheel and a new round of birth and death. So in dependence upon grasping, *becoming* arises.

Becoming

The image for becoming is a man and a woman performing the sexual act, initiating a new life. This link sums up the whole Wheel of Life, for the Wheel is one continuous process of becoming. The word here translated as 'becoming' is the same word in Pali and Sanskrit as is translated as 'life' in 'the Wheel of Life'.

Becoming has two aspects: one active and volitional part and the other the passive resultant of the active phase. The motion of the Wheel consists in the movement from volition to its consequences as the potential energy of volition fulfils itself in states of being and concrete experiences. With this link, we rise to the most general view of the conditioned process. Set up by our clinging and grasping in this life, we establish tendencies which discharge themselves in our rebirth in a new life on the plane of existence which corresponds to our own volitions. Thus, in dependence on becoming, arises *birth*.

Birth

This link is represented by the very explicit image of a woman giving birth to a child. Once more, the kinetic momentum of our volitions has resulted in a new life in whichever of the many planes of existence corresponds to our pattern of willing. This new life is, itself, the condition in dependence upon which arises *death and decay*.

Death and Decay

The final link is portrayed by a corpse being carried towards the cremation pyre. Whatever is born is bound to experience the attacks of sickness, the waning of physical powers in old age, the pain of separation and loss, and finally death. Once birth has taken place a process has been set in motion which must end in death, for birth and death are two sides of one process of becoming. The inherent decay in all conditioned things leads to 'sorrow, lamentation, pain, grief and despair, in short, this whole mass of suffering', as the text has it, which is the lot of those who cling to the Wheel. We are born because we cling, but from what we cling to we must be parted.

The twelve links in the chain of cyclic conditionality show how the ignorance which lies in the depths of our hearts guides all our actions; how the total pattern of our mental volitions forms for us a mind and body in a new life which is in contact with its appropriate world; how that contact gives rise to our pleasure and pain, likes and dislikes. We see, at this point, that we have a choice: whether to continue to spin on the Wheel or to start to ascend the Spiral. If we merely crave the pleasurable and hate the painful then we form for ourselves the volitional momentum that carries us again into a new birth with its own share of pain and its inevitable death. It is, indeed, a vicious circle, without end. Whatever pain we feel, whatever frustration or imperfection we see in life, it is our own desires that have in the final analysis created them.

The message of the chain is simple; however, its exposition is very subtle and complex. The whole chain is spread over three lives: ignorance and the volitional activities belong to the past life; sentience, the psychophysical organism, the six senses, sensuous impression, feeling, craving, grasping and becoming, all belong to the present life; birth and death and decay belong to the life to come. The twelve links can also be analysed into those that are active volitional forces which have a formative effect and those which are passive resultants, following inevitably from volitional activities. All conditioned processes can be divided in this way into a causal phase, during which the conditions are established, and a resultant phase when the effects of the conditions come to fruition. Within the karmic order, it is volitions which establish the causal phase. So, ignorance and volitional activities are the causal phase in the past life; sentience, the psychophysical organism, the six senses, sensuous impression and feeling are the resultant phase in the present life; craving, grasping and becoming are the causal phase in the present life; and birth and death and decay are the resultant phase in the life to come. All of these divisions are shown in Fig. 4.

It will be noticed that the causal phases in the past life and in the present are the same process but looked at from slightly different points of view. In the past life it is seen at its most general: as a formative force. In the present life, we are shown in greater detail how that pattern of volitional energy comes into being. Similarly, the resultant phase in the present life is the same as that in the life to come but is examined in much closer detail. The same movement from resultant phase to causal phase is present in each life and each life can be considered as, itself, either a past, present or future life since they are part of an endless chain. So each life contains both the causal phase of the past and of the present and the resultant phase of the present and of the future. Each life can, therefore, be considered as containing thirty-six links. The links can also be seen as all being present at every moment of our lives as we create our own future out of our acts of will, again and again. Each link can be seen as acting simultaneously with all the others. The chain is a very subtle, dynamic process, not a rigid mechanical routine.

We should not allow ourselves to become lost in the complexity of the chain but try to feel and picture the forces that the links represent: the forces of human desire based upon ignorance forging for us, again

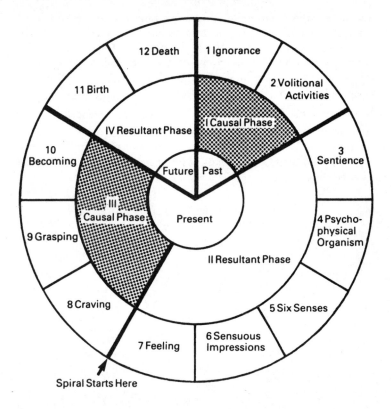

Fig. 4 The Twelve Links

and again, worlds of inevitable decay which restrict and confine our consciousness. We then react to the worlds we have ourselves constructed and the chain turns once more. It is this process that has brought about the life we live at this very moment.

Perhaps more dangerous than to become swamped in the complexities of the chain is to think, too readily, that we understand it. On a well-known occasion, the Buddha's friend and personal attendant, Ananda, commented to him on the straightforwardness and clarity of the teaching and the ease with which it could be comprehended. The Buddha rebuked him, saying:

111

Say not so, Ananda! Say not so! Deep indeed is this Causal Law, and deep it appears to be. It is by not knowing, by not understanding, by not penetrating this doctrine, that this world of men has become entangled like a ball of twine, become covered with mildew, become like munja grass and rushes, and unable to pass beyond the doom of the Waste, the Way of Woe, the Fall and Ceaseless Round [of rebirth].*

In the end, the teaching points to an experience beyond intellectual apprehension. It is meant to turn us away from our craving, to lead us on to the Spiral Path, and to induce in us that vision of reality as a network of conditions, a vast nexus of interpenetrating forces of infinite creative potentiality.

* SamyuttaNikaya, XII, 6, 60.

7
Worlds of Woe

The third circle of the Wheel of Life, between that of karma and that of the twelve links, shows the six realms of conditioned existence. The lower five realms – those of the hell-beings, hungry ghosts, animals, titans and humans – are all contained in the sphere of sensuous desire. The sixth, the realm of the gods, is stratified into many layers which extend from the peak of the sensuous sphere through the sphere of archetypal form and culminate in the formless. Each of these three spheres contains a number of sub-spheres so that existence as a whole is made up of many different worlds of which the six realms are the generic types. These worlds are not spatially distributed – although countless other world-systems than our own are said to exist in all the regions of space (a world-system is a kind of 'island universe' made up of all the different planes and sub-planes from the hells to the highest heaven). It is not possible to reach the other planes within our own world-system by spacecraft, however sophisticated, for worlds, in the sense of planes within a world-system, exist in different dimensions. Access to them can only be gained by a modification of consciousness.

A world is the objective counterpart of the self. When we crystallize our individuality from the undifferentiated field of sense-conscious-ness, we divide what is self from what is other. The other is the world. The world is what is experienced and the self is what experiences. The world is everything 'out there', the self is everything 'in here'. The nature of the perceiving subject determines the nature of the perceived object. In the first place, the actual perception we have of the sensible world is an interpretation of the raw data of sensuous impressions. We sense shapes and colours and we assemble them into visible objects on the basis of our past experiences of similar kinds and of what we have learnt from the culture in which we have been raised. Our own predilections and prejudices, interests and viewpoints all modify our

113

interpretations and therefore the world that we actually perceive. Not only is what we make of the data of sense experience determined by the kind of consciousness we have but so are the impressions themselves. Our own past volitional activities establish the type of experiential field we will encounter. Our karmic pattern attracts to itself matching impressions. Our own character leads us to be reborn in a world which corresponds to it.

This concept of reality as having many dimensions to which varying states of consciousness give access may be unfamiliar, yet it is a commonplace insight that there are great differences in the way in which people perceive the world. Climate and geography, political and economic structures, history, culture and language, even genetic factors perhaps mark off the outlooks of various nations and peoples to such an extent that they effectively live in different worlds. Even within a single country we speak of worlds: the underworld, the theatre world, the world of high finance. People from these separate worlds can sometimes barely comprehend each other at all. Again, people have very dissimilar temperaments and dispositions and see the same surroundings in quite different ways. In this sense every one of us is unique, each with our own experiences, history and viewpoint. It could be said that each of us has his own world though there may be considerable overlap between our separate worlds.

Even within the life of a single individual, mental states may be experienced which are so unlike each other that what is perceived may amount to different worlds. Fluctuations of mood can alter the appearance of things to a very great extent, even though a sufficiently strong common thread may run through them all for us not to think of them as different worlds. Yet in moments of very intense experience, as for instance under poetic inspiration or deeply moved by art, nature or our human communication, we speak of being transported, uplifted, taken out of ourselves and we see the world transfigured or as if renewed. Sometimes, so great can be the difference between such moments and normal consciousness that people talk of dwelling for a while in another world. No doubt, at the other end of the scale, moments of depression and despair can be equally transporting, although it is to hell that one may then be taken. Some people have greater fluidity of consciousness than others and are gifted (sometimes perhaps cursed) with the facility of slipping into quite different visionary or prophetic worlds. Drug-induced experiences, harmful as they may often be, are a further illustration of consciousness gaining access to radically different ways of seeing things. Experiences of any of these kinds – ecstatic, prophetic or psychedelic – are not uncommon and many people will acknowledge, by their own witness or by acquaintance with others, that the range of possible states of mind is far wider than we usually allow.

Most people are not perhaps familiar with visionary or inspired states in any depth. There is, however, a state in which everyone dwells quite regularly and which carries them to other worlds: dreaming. Although dreams are usually, if not always, assembled from the data of waking life, the dream world obeys its own dream logic. Often, we dismiss dreams as irrelevant, a kind of mental filing system best left to itself, or else we consider them as providing important messages about our unconscious functioning which, should we decode them, will benefit us in everyday life. We identify almost entirely with the waking state and place value on dreams, if we value them at all, only in relation to it. While it is undoubtedly true that dreams have the function of sorting out daytime experience and that they may help us to understand ourselves better, we are severely undervaluing dreams if that is all we make of them. The dream world is no less a reality than the waking state and should be enjoyed and valued as such. The worlds to which we are carried in sleep are as much 'out there' as the world which surrounds us now – even though they may change within an instant or be two contradictory things at the same time. Even on those occasions when we are aware within a dream that we are dreaming, all of our impressions are as cogent and convincing as waking sensations. From the point of view of our experience within each world, we cannot say that one or the other is more real. We are usually totally convinced by the dream world while we are in it, and it is only later, from the prejudiced viewpoint of the waking state, that we relegate dreams to the status of psychological by-products.

It is, then, Buddhism's contention that modifications in our consciousness give us access to different worlds of which there are as many as there are possibilities of consciousness. Some of them differ far more radically from normal human consciousness than do either the worlds of inspiration or depression or those of dreams. All of them are, nonetheless, objective realities, experienced as 'out there', for a world is simply whatever we experience. Although each world is equally real to those who inhabit it, worlds are ordered hierarchically in accordance with the refinement of the consciousness which they reflect. The higher the state of consciousness, the more pure and beautiful will be the world. In so far as the higher worlds are more subtle refractions of the subject/object dichotomy, they are closer to the ultimate nature of things.

These many worlds are inhabited by those whose volitional patterns correspond to them. The higher godlike realms of the sphere of archetypal form and formlessness may also be visited by those who practise meditation at all deeply because the states of consciousness enjoyed in meditation correspond to these worlds. Until physical death, however, a return is always made to the human state. Certain highly gifted individuals, like Maudgalyayana whom we have already encountered, have access to all the different planes and can visit any of the worlds at will.

All worlds do not function according to the same laws. In dreams, for instance, what we perceive is far more malleable and the environment and the sequence of events may change with extreme rapidity. Similarly, in the mind-made body between death and rebirth what one experiences changes with the speed of thought. In other worlds, like our own, there is greater stability in what we perceive and the core of experience persists despite our own mental fluctuations. We could say that some worlds have a more stable objective content and that other worlds are perceived as more immediately influenced by subjective factors. Thus in some worlds birth takes place by parturition, whilst in others we appear instantaneously, fully mature, by a process known as 'apparitional birth', in the same way as we simply find ourselves within a dream. Whether the worlds are constructed of more cohesive and stable processes or are closely influenced by alterations in subjective mood and outlook, they are all worlds.

A world is the field of experience of the subject. But a world usually contains other beings who are themselves experiencing subjects. There are worlds of common experience which all inhabit who share similar patterns of volition. The personal worlds of each are never identical (identity of the object would entail identity of the subject) but they intersect to a greater or lesser extent. Perhaps this provides us with our most useful meaning of the word 'world': a world is the area of coincidence of experience of two or more perceiving subjects. To the extent that we share with others a world in which our personal experience overlaps with theirs, we can interact with them. The fact that there are other beings within our world with whom we can interact helps to reinforce the solidity of our world. We are educated into seeing things in a particular way when we communicate with them. The inhabitants of each world have bodies which are the appropriate manifestation of their consciousness. In some, the bodies are solid and heavy, as stable as the objects around them. In others, they are not made of solid matter at all but consist of a luminous, subtle substance. In the hells, the body is indestructible until the full force of the karmic pattern which keeps it in being is spent, even though it is subject to continuous dismemberment and destruction.

This Buddhist vision of a multi-layered universe is not one which fits well with modern opinions. Many other cultures, however, have traditions concerning non-human beings, often with quite elaborate systems of classification. If one accepts the two premises that consciousness survives after death and that the world is the counterpart of consciousness it is easy to see that there must be many other worlds when one considers the extent to which people's states of mind vary one from another. Little convincing proof can be offered for their existence beyond the testimony of those who claim to have explored reality in its heights and depths. For those who cannot suspend disbelief, although they will not be able to appreciate the full extent of the Buddhist vision, there is a principle underlying this teaching which is equally relevant to the human world of our common experience. Different people are in very different mental states and what they see is, to a large extent, a projection of their own minds and not something inherent in the objects of sense. It is in this more restricted sense that there can also be said to be different worlds corresponding to different psychological states. The six realms which we will now be examining can be understood either as objective dimensions of experience into which we may literally be reborn or as symbols for psychological states experienced by human beings.

The concept of projection may help us to understand the six realms better. Projection is the psychological mechanism whereby we attribute to our surroundings and to other people feelings and thoughts which are our own. We throw on to the world what is actually in us. In extreme cases of mental disturbance, for instance, the world is so overlaid with projected subjective content that it becomes a completely different world from the one which others occupy. The most innocent scene can be filled with horrible demons and frightful dangers and a friendly greeting may hold hidden menace. But projection is a common fact of most people's lives. They see not only what their senses present to them but aspects of themselves. Nowhere is this more evident than in our dealings with other people. We attribute to them our own motives or see in them highly idealized qualities which they do not really possess. Since in our human world the objective element is relatively stable and enduring it is easier to discern the discrepency between projection and reality, although we by no means always do so. There are other worlds, according to Buddhist teaching, however, where objective content is more directly determined by subjective state. We are able, so to speak, to indulge in an hallucination in which we live and interact with other beings who have a corresponding hallucination.

Karmic conditionality itself is a process of projection, for we are constantly creating a world for ourselves which is the projection of our own volitions. But at a more immediate, psychological level, there are two main varieties of projection. Firstly, we project when we interpret the data of our sense impressions in terms of our own mental states – we fail properly to distinguish the subject from the object. The person whose mind is dominated by fear sees the innocent stranger as intent on attacking him. The cheat assumes that everyone else is trying to cheat him. A variant of this type of projection is found in cases where people have strong feelings which, for one reason or another, they cannot admit, even to themselves. Since those feelings are energies which must find some expression, they are attributed to other people in whom they are often sternly disapproved of. Most people have a darker side to their personality, made up of those aspects which they do not approve of or of which they are afraid. This 'shadow', as the psychologist C.G. Jung called it, is then projected on to others.

The second type of projection comes about not through the projection of our negative qualities, real or imagined, but through our own unrealized potential. When self-consciousness first differentiates itself from its surroundings it does so in a quite crude and rigid way. The resultant ego is narrow and lopsided since it contains only some aspects of individuality. What we conceive of as ourselves is but a small portion of the total possible energies of personality. Those aspects of a mature individuality which have not yet emerged into the full light of consciousness are projected on to others in idealized form. Thus, if we lack confidence and self-assurance we look to others as sources of reassurance and security. If we have developed the intellect at the expense of the emotions then we see in someone else the warmth and spontaneity which we do not have. This type of projection often occurs in sexual relationships when we 'fall in love'. It is also present in hero worship where the object of the projection – sporting champion, entertainment star, even political figure – is seen as possessing almost superhuman characteristics. These are really latent qualities which those who project could realize within themselves if they became fully self-aware. This type of projection is the result of alienation from the full energies of personality. The cultivation of a mature ego is the first task of the Higher Evolution, and so alienation must be overcome by what has been called *horizontal integration*: the drawing together in consciousness of all the energies of the mature personality. Only when we have withdrawn all these projections and integrated them into consciousness can we be said to be fully and truly human.

Projection of inner qualities goes beyond the horizontal plane, for rudimentary self-consciousness is not only alienated from the characteristics of full individuality but also from the whole range of consciousness, up to and including Transcendental awareness. Self-consciousness contains the Transcendental within it in the form of the evolutionary urge to attain higher levels. Latent spiritual and Transcendental qualities also manifest in projection, now of a vertical kind. The whole spiritual Path leading to Buddhahood could be seen as a process of *vertical integration* of our projected higher potential.

Projection often has very unfortunate consequences but it can provide us with a means whereby we contact and integrate those unrealized qualities within us. While they are unconscious we have no knowledge of them at all. If we recognize our projections as projections then we have made them conscious, although we are still separated from them. It is then possible gradually to withdraw the projection back into ourselves. Usually, of course, we fail to realize that we are projecting and we remain tangled up with the object. When that object is a person, we may well be in trouble for they will have designs and purposes of their own. We may, for instance, feel weak and impotent and will therefore project our own potential power on to some authority figure who may abuse the trust we place in him.

If we are going to take advantage of projection as a means of recapturing qualities from which we are alienated then we must beware of allowing our projection to become caught up in real events. Otherwise, we may find that, even if we withdraw the projection, we are ensnared in its consequences whether we like it or not. Art has often provided the kind of neutral ground where the full passions may be expressed without the danger of entanglement. The artist uses his medium to give full shape to the ideal qualities he feels within himself. In the act of giving them expression, they become part of his own being. Buddhism provides a number of means for the vertical projection of the qualities within us, notably the worship of the Buddha image which is a representation of our own Transcendental nature. If no such process takes place there is nothing for the full force of our emotions to engage with and our development remains an abstract and bloodless ideal without any ardour to nourish it.

We will now examine, one by one, the six worlds and the beings who inhabit them. We will start, in this chapter, with the unhappy places of rebirth where suffering predominates. These are the projection of an immature consciousness dominated by greed, hatred and delusion. They represent, from an evolutionary point of view, blind alleys up which a distorted and unhealthy mind may go, producing for itself the concrete realization of its own nature.

The Realm of Hell

Pictures of hell in Buddhist tradition show strong similarities to the medieval Christian Inferno and the painful afterworlds of many other cultures. It is shown as a place of intense pain and torment where its victims are subjected to the most excruciating tortures, inflicted on them by the presiding demons. Flames engulf the whole realm which is unbearably hot although, in the bottom reaches, there are regions of bitter cold which yield the worst sufferings of all. Hell consists of sub-planes, each of which specializes in a particular kind of pain appropriate to a certain kind of unskilful action. In popular Buddhism these are, all too often, described in considerable detail. There is, for instance, the hell of filth where the corruptors of the innocent wallow in slime whilst they are devoured by monstrous maggots. Murderers and torturers are spitted upon sharp spikes and their guts are pecked by birds with steel beaks. Perhaps we should beware of the literalism of such accounts which sometimes amount to little more than crude superstition. Although Buddhism has never descended to hellfire preaching, the image of hell has sometimes been drawn in rather sharp detail. Such an emphasis may have a salutary effect, making some people consider the consequences of their actions more carefully, yet it may simply induce feelings of irrational fear and guilt. While for Buddhism the existence of hellish states is a plain fact which cannot be avoided, the image of hell should never be used to manipulate or to induce unwholesome mental states of gloom and despair such as affect many people who have been brought up within those churches where hell is emphasized, even to the very young, in all its ghastly detail. A genuine moral sense comes from self-confidence and maturity, not from terror.

Hell is probably not as orderly as it is often presented in Buddhist tradition, with a particular torment allotted to each unskilful deed. Perhaps we should not take the traditional depictions too literally. The basic features of hell are constant suffering and relentless pain inflicted by furious and vengeful beings. This kind of experience is to be met with even on earth and there are people who habitually see the world in this way. Everyone around them seems to be trying to do them down and they feel under constant threat. Their primary motivation is to eliminate or evade this menace and they are in a state of covert or open enmity with almost everyone they encounter. They suffer agonies of insecurity and feel the pain and humiliation of every imagined wrong or slight. They see this torment as if it were inflicted upon them by their enemies who, they feel, are constantly trying to undermine them. In many cases, because of the way they behave towards others, they bring into being the enemies they at first only imagine. Such people are dominated by the root mental state of hatred and they see the whole world through the mist of their projected feelings. They lived in an hell on earth and they make every situation a place of torment for themselves. The hell of the Wheel of Life is but that same mental state made manifest in all its painful detail after death. No doubt, hell has been modernized to suit more sophisticated minds, but it will still be a world of torment which is the objectification of a hate-filled mind.

We have already seen that hatred is the attempt to secure the ego-identity by excluding those objects which are considered to be threats. Human hatred is quite different from the aggression of an animal. When an animal does inflict harm it is to preserve its immediate survival and cannot be called hatred. Hatred is fed by the imagination and is the desire to cause another person pain and suffering, even to destroy them, because they pose a threat to us which is not merely physical but which strikes at the roots of our selfhood. Whether they have actually done something to us or we only imagine that they have, we feel weakened in our very being. The only way we can reassert our own identity is to retaliate. We may start off by reacting resentfully to someone over particular incidents but, sooner or later, a permanent attitude of hatred may develop. We no longer simply want to get our own back over those incidents – that is not enough any more. Regardless now of what the other person may do or say, we feel that we would like to see them suffer and we may be prepared to inflict pain on them ourselves.

In some cases, hatred hardens into an habitual mood as if the person carries within himself a permanent store of undischarged resentment, dammed up from the past. Not related to particular people or events, it has become a permanent attitude which always seeks some outlet. Grumbling and complaining, backbiting and gossip are all ways in which such residual bad feeling is vented – and it can be much more vicious than that. So common is this underlying negativity that most human groups have an established enemy or 'out group' against whom the feeling can be discharged. Everyone in the group is united in their hatred of a particular person or class of persons. In families and other small groups one person may become the scapegoat and bear the burden of the residual hatred of the others. Similarly, many people find that there is always one person who seems to undermine or annoy them. When the enemy of the moment is removed, however, a new one soon arises, as if they must always have someone to dislike, regardless of personal qualities.

The elimination of hatred from our minds is no easy task. By being mindful we can gradually restrict its expression and can check habitual negative states. By living happier, more fulfilled lives with friends with whom we share good feeling, we will feel confident and contented and therefore less prone to hatred. By actively practising the Mettabhavana, we will gradually bring into being, more of the time, the love which drives out hatred. Yet we must beware that, in trying to get rid of hatred, we do not simply lose vitality. Because Buddhism is a non-violent teaching, it is sometimes thought that any vigorous words or deeds or any disagreements are incompatible with the Dharma. On the contrary, drive and energy, even a kind of anger, are essential to human growth. We need that sort of force to break through the many barriers, both internal and external, which we encounter in the course of our lives. This aggressive quality is never directed to hurting others, however, but to breaking through to new levels of clarity and truth. For instance, in friendship we must be prepared to speak our minds frankly, even with a certain heat, if we feel our friend is wrong or that something stands between us and him. This 'positive anger' arises from the frustration of healthy energies which then accumulate and burst forth, sometimes in a hot and emphatic way. Naturally, with more skill and maturity, we will learn to express this positive drive in a less spectacular fashion. The point, here, is that the principle of non-hatred does not mean that we must always be very meek and gentle in a rather bloodless way.

Spiritual life requires our full vigour and even a kind of destructiveness. We have to destroy everything within us which sweeps us back to lower forms of consciousness. The forces of greed, hatred and delusion, the pull of the lower evolution, the inertia of ignorance: all these must be resisted and overcome. Not only are these forces within us, they are also in the world around. Here, of course, we must beware, because it is in people that they are embodied. Our battle against the forces of ignorance must never be a battle against people, for that is completely contrary to the whole spirit of the Dharma. In the whole history of Buddhism, no war has been fought in its name and persecution has been completely foreign to it. Buddhism teaches that evil must be combated by non-violent means. We must battle against everything which drags men down, using criticism, exhortation, influence and whatever methods are ethically sound and cause no harm to others.

The need for a skilful cutting-edge to our spiritual life gives us the opportunity to sublimate the hatred within us. We can put it to use. In the words of one Buddhist sage, we must use hatred to destroy hatred. Although the truths we have to speak may be uncomfortable to some people, our aim should never be to hurt them, and we should avoid any action likely to cause violence to others, whether directly or indirectly. Yet we can be hot and sharp against what limits and binds men, restricting them to lower states of mind. In this way, we can skilfully vent and tame the destructive force of our own, latent hatred while it still remains, at the same time as we actively work against the forces of darkness in the world.

If we do not learn to sublimate the hatred within us it will continue to exercise a controlling influence on our lives. If we allow it to dominate us it can make a hell for us, both here and now and in the states beyond death.

The fiery heat of the hells corresponds to the passionate intensity of hatred. The frozen hells are reserved for those in whom hatred has passed beyond the volcanic eruptions of ordinary passion and has become cold malice – the enjoyment in inflicting pain and suffering on others regardless of whether the victim is innocent of harming us. This is probably the most unskilful state into which one can fall since all feeling for others is completely dead. The frozen hells are therefore at the very bottom of the whole system of worlds.

Although the traditional Buddhist depictions of hell bear a close resemblance to those of Christianity, the concept of hell differs from its Christian counterpart in two important respects: hell is not a punishment and it is not everlasting. Each of the worlds is the objectification of an individual's own mind in accordance with the natural workings of the principle of karma. No one judges, no one condemns. The figure of the Lord of Death in Buddhist mythology is the personification of death itself and the mirror which he holds up is our own conscience – our sensitivity to the feelings of others – which we often suppress but which stands revealed at death. (According to some traditions, the Lord of Death is Avalokiteshvara, the Transcendental Being who embodies the Compassionate aspect of Buddhahood. This signifies the fact that even death, which most people see as the great catastrophe, when looked at in its true light, reveals the real nature of things. If only we would face up to death fully we would see not the red-glaring eyes of an horrifying monster, but the compassionate smile of Avalokiteshvara.) Many people who have been close to death report having witnessed their lives passing before their eyes. In a similar way, at death one sees the deeds of one's past life reflected in the Lord of Death's mirror.

The momentum which one has oneself set up determines the kind of world into which one will be reborn. Buddhism contains no conception of creator or divine judge – these figures it regards as nothing more than the projections of our own hopes and fears, based upon our need for a reassuring father-figure who orders the cosmos. The universe is made up of processes which contain within themselves the laws governing their own functioning. The principle of karma is the law inherent in individualized consciousness and determines the effects of its own volitions that it will experience.

Every process is impermanent and a particular state continues only so long as the conditions which have brought it into being are still present. Volitions based in hatred bring the experience of hell into being. When they are exhausted or counteracted by skilful volitions, then one will disappear from hell and reappear in some other state which suits one's new karmic configuration. One will remain in the state of torment so long as there are undischarged karmic energies to keep one there. Tradition has it that a life in hell may extend over many aeons – perhaps this corresponds to the well-known experience of time dragging when we are suffering.

The Realm of the Hungry Ghosts

A desolate landscape stretches as far as the eye can see, a cold desert of rock and sand. A few leafless trees are the only protection against the biting wind and a tiny, pale sun sheds a piteous warmth. A great river of brackish water flows slowly through the vast plain.

Groups of ungainly creatures huddle together for warmth beneath the skeletal trees. Their distended bodies are the colour of smoke and they appear insubstantial as if they are made of mist. Their arms and legs are spindly and frail and their heads are carried on long, thin necks, while their bellies are bloated, sagging masses which their legs can barely support. Tiny mouths, no thicker than a needle, are topped by round, staring eyes, filled with pain and longing.

An unquenchable thirst and perpetual hunger obsess these pathetic creatures. They stagger on their feeble limbs to the river's edge but, as soon as their mouths approach the water, it recedes from them. Even those who stand in the stream's midst cannot get a drop into their mouths. The tortures of Tantalus are theirs. Those few who, by chance, manage to swallow some meagre mouthfuls soon regret it, for the water turns to liquid fire in their guts. One or two sparse fruits grow on the trees but these, too, evade the reach of any creature who, maddened with hunger, drags his enormous belly up among the branches. Any which are eaten turn to swords and daggers, piercing and slicing inside the stomach.

Driven by their overwhelming hunger and thirst, the hungry ghosts live out their lives for no other purpose than food and drink. Their weak limbs and pinhole mouths make it almost impossible for them to gain any sustenance. And whatever they do manage to get into their mouths causes them more pain than the torment of desire that drove them to it. And so they live until the avarice and greed which brought them to this world is spent.

The world of the hungry ghost is a king of hell, constituted not so much of physical torture – although some of that there is – as of the pain of unsatisfied desire. Just as hell is the objectification of hatred, so this realm is the reflection of a mind in which craving predominates. In our human world, there are people who are so possessed by greed and longing that they live only to gather things to themselves. Even if they get what they want it gives them little pleasure. No matter what they possess, they always feel that there is something missing. The realm of the hungry ghosts is built from this attitude.

Craving is the longing to possess things in the belief that they will make the ego more secure. Underlying it is a feeling of inner emptiness and insubstantiality. The immature ego is weak and incomplete and does not have a very strong experience of itself, leaving an uncomfortable feeling of vacancy and poverty. To feel real and substantial, the ego craves certain experiences, for experience absorbs consciousness, giving an illusion of inner fullness and distracting momentarily from the lack within.

The failure fully to experience oneself which underlies craving results from a psychological warping as individualized consciousness emerges. In one way or another, emotion comes to be minimized or excluded from self-awareness. Sometimes, this is the consequence of repression as when someone refuses to allow certain feelings into full consciousness because they have learnt that they are 'wrong'. Certain sorts of Christian upbringing, for instance, can imbue a sense of guilt about the body and its sensations, particularly those of sex, and so some who have succumbed to this kind of conditioning refuse to acknowledge what they feel. Emotion comes, therefore, to be pushed out of awareness leaving an inner blankness. Others, again, may have suffered so much unhappiness and pain, at some point in their lives, that they numb themselves to emotion. A development which is one-sidedly intellectual can have the same effect. In these ways, the person is left without much emotional life and he longs for some solid experience which will make him *feel*. The inner richness which he lacks is, then, projected on to the world outside him. He imagines that, by possessing certain objects, by having certain experiences, or by being in certain kinds of relationships he will gain the fulfilment he longs for. Pleasurable sensations may accompany the acquisition of what he desires which may temporarily overlay the feeling of emptiness; but, sooner or later, it returns and a new cycle of craving begins.

The human hungry ghost is the miser who lives for his money, the collector who is never content with what he has but must have more, or the addict. The drug addict is, perhaps, the archetype of the hungry ghost, barely alive to the world and concentrated solely upon the next dose – whose effects will soon fade away, leaving him longing for another. The hungry ghost is the addict, for addiction is a state of mind and one can be addicted to anything which one sees as a source of palliation for that restless inner longing. Whatever the object of addiction, it cannot give one satisfaction because what one longs for is an inner fullness, not the object itself. As soon as the brief respite, the 'Drug' brings begins to fade, one must have more.

Addiction can have many objects, but among the most frequent are other people. The addicted person is neurotically dependent on others, seeking from them the emotional nourishment which should be found within himself. This dependence is infantile and repetitive in character, for even if he is given the kind of attention he craves, he soon wants more. Reassurance, approval, attention, security, all may be sought in neurotic relationships. The unnatural attachment between parents and a grown-up child who is kept in a state of prolonged infancy is a not uncommon example of neurotic dependence. It is to be seen with especial frequency in sexual relationships. Bound together not by mutual respect and cooperation in raising a family, the partners in addiction are tied by their neurotic needs and each seeks in the other the satisfaction of his own inner emptiness. When they cannot find what they seek instead of learning their lesson, they often blame each other for not giving it, adding resentment to craving. Some psychologists have suggested that this form of addictive relationship is becoming more common. They consider it to be an aspect of the 'me-generation', the children of the post-war period in whom affluence has encouraged appetite and whom rapid social change has made restless and insecure. Immature and self-centred, such people seek to perpetuate with their sexual partner their infantile relationship with their mothers. It is a most unhappy and ugly phenomenon: two weak people, like shadows, trying to get something from each other which the other, too, lacks.

The circumstances of modern life, perhaps, encourage the attitude of neurotic craving because, in many ways, feeling is undervalued. The ease and speed of communications have made people highly mobile, reducing stability and continuity. They do not have much opportunity to form deep connections with the people and places around them and therefore lack the satisfying depth of feeling which a more firmly rooted background can give. Again, modern life offers so many sensations and distractions that people are encouraged to fritter away their emotional resources. The result is an hollowness of feeling which breeds a neurotic quest for experience.

Neurotic desire must be clearly distinguished from healthy need. The desires of the body are not, in themselves, cravings. Hunger and thirst are objective needs which arise from lack of nourishment and dehydration and, when we eat and drink, they are satiated. As anyone who has undergone a fast will know, one can remain perfectly happy even though deprived of food and feeling hungry. The case of sex is rather more complicated because a number of different elements are bound up in it. The immediate biological urge of sex, however, is not dissimilar to hunger and thirst, deriving from our physiological constitution. If we are able to satisfy these desires in a straightforward way which causes no harm to others then they are not neurotic. Unfortunately, food and sex are quite frequently distorted and abused and thus become the objects of neurotic craving. In these kinds of cases, there is a neurotic attempt to fill an inner lack by perverting desires which are not, themselves, unhealthy.

Healthy needs extend beyond the physiological plane. We have social needs which are not neurotic. We need, for instance, acknowledgement – to be seen and recognized by others. It is very hard to live in contact with other people if they never show any sign of having seen us as separate individuals. This need for acknowledgement of one's selfhood by others is quite different from the neurotic need for attention. The latter cannot be satisfied: the more attention one gives, the more will be devoured without any diminution in craving. Like a vampire or leech, the neurotic sucks energy from those who allow him to fasten on to them. Someone who is given the human acknowledgement he needs very quickly becomes brighter and more cheerful.

Though the neurotic may indulge in sensual pleasure, he does not get much enjoyment from them. The emotional poverty of the neurotic prevents this, for the capacity to enjoy things comes from inner richness. Enjoyment is the contact between the object and one's own healthy emotions. When one is most contented one is able to enjoy the beauties of the senses. One is, then, satisfied with very simple pleasures and does not crave the sensory saturation that neurosis so often demands. Since spiritual growth is a growth of inner fullness, it is marked by an increasing capacity for enjoyment.

There is one final form of healthy desire to be distinguished from the neurotic form: the attraction to spiritual ideals and to the people who embody them. That desire to evolve, to reach beyond our present level of consciousness must be stimulated and intensified. Sometimes people do have a neurotic, appropriative attitude to what they consider to be the Higher Evolution. They see the spiritual life as a means of gaining power, or as an escape from themselves and their personal responsibilities. But the urge to develop is not narrow and personal, it is selfless and expansive. This desire is latent within everyone, covered over, more or less, by greed, hatred and delusion. It is only by following it through that one will find the store of inner wealth which will finally dispel all craving.

The Realm of the Animals

In the realm of the animals, life is the life of the body. All endeavour is directed to the satisfaction of physical desires and the business of self-preservation. This world is the objectification of the ignorant refusal to see beyond the needs of the body. The animals of the field and jungle are not ignorant in this sense since, being without self-consciousness, they are not responsible for the limitation of their understanding. Their ignorance is the ignorance of nature, not of individuals. The human animal, however, wilfully narrows his horizons and refuses to look at the meaning and purpose of life.

The animal-like human is not neurotic like the hungry ghost, and no bottomless hunger drives him. His bodily needs for nourishment, sleep and sex are healthy and he gets satisfaction and enjoyment from them. But their fulfilment becomes his sole end. For him, human life has no other significance. Although he is ignorant in that he fails to see any higher human destiny, he is not necessarily stupid in a practical sense. He may live a very sophisticated life, fulfilling a complex job and surrounded by elaborate technology. He may have a very well-developed practical intelligence. But he has no ideals and there is nothing beyond himself and his group for which he lives.

The animal lives without vision and without culture – in the senses of interests and pursuits through which he can cultivate his mind. Much of modern society is of this kind. Although there has never before been such an highly ordered civilization with such advanced technical capacities, remarkably few people have any broad perspective on life and there is no widely held common vision. In most other civilizations of the past, religion has been at the heart of all public acts and has provided the assumptions on which life was built. No longer is this the case: Christianity in the West and other religious traditions elsewhere are decaying before the onslaught of consumerism – which might be called the 'philosophy' of the animal. In some way, this decay of old values is no bad thing since much that was rotten or inappropriate is also cleared away. But many people now live in a world of drastically restricted horizons and can only lose themselves in the animal-like pursuit of bodily gratification.

Whether human beings can literally be reborn as cats or horses, even as flies or fish, is a matter of dispute in Buddhist circles. The Buddha seems to have taught that they could (although, in one scripture, he speaks of rebirth as an animal as being the outcome of a systematic and sustained effort to act like an animal). On the face of it, it would seem unlikely that a human being could so utterly douse his self-consciousness as to be reborn an animal. Perhaps, however, if one does persistently deny all creative tendencies within oneself and disregard the higher possibilities of human life, then one's consciousness may gradually atrophy with neglect so that one is nothing but an animal. It is certainly possible to regress permanently from an adult to an infantile state, so it may well be possible to regress even more drastically to a preceding stage of evolution.

Whether or not humans can be reborn as animals, there are animal-like human beings. There are areas of the planet where the level of culture is very low indeed and there is little understanding of man's potential. Neither the arts nor an higher philosophy lifts the gaze beyond the shallow concerns of everyday survival. Such areas are not only to be found among 'primitive' peoples at the edges of the civilized world, they are to be found in the midst of many of our great cities. To be reborn into such societies is to be born an animal.

The Realm of the Titans

Knowing only war, the titans live all their days in armour and rest with their weapons beside them, ready for battle. Each of these jealous gods cuts a ferocious figure, towering thickset and powerful, his skin a forbidding dark blue or green. His face is horribly ugly, knotted in a mask of fury, with bulging eyes and snarling lips. Again and again, in seried ranks, these giants rush upon the gods of the sensuous realm and try to grab from them their happiness and delight. They try to capture the heavenly tree which fulfils all wishes and, in their foolish envy, they begin to hack it down. But the gods rout them and they fall back in disarray. They immediately start to fight among themselves, each trying to gain for himself greater power in the ordered hierarchy of their armies.

The titanesses are one of the principle causes of dissension among the menfolk. They are no less jealous and acquisitive but they win their wars not by force of arms but by enchantment. For each titaness is as voluptuous and bewitching as any film starlet and knows how to captivate and charm her chosen victim. Like the Sirens, Lorelei and Lamia, she destroys those who fall into her power.

The inhabitants of this world seem to be descended, mythologically speaking, from one group of those gods who took part in the battle for heavenly supremacy recorded in the legends of Greece, Iran and India. For this reason, I have called them by their Greek name although they should not be equated too closely with Atlas, Prometheus, Hyperion, etc. They are variously referred to as anti-gods, jealous gods or angry gods, for they are godlike in their power and vigour although not at all in happiness and pleasure since they are driven by the misery of envy. Their longing to possess does not come from desire or greed, like the hungry ghosts. They want things because they begrudge others whatever possessions, achievements or qualities they may have. The success of others makes them feel belittled, for their self-sense rests upon feeling themselves to be the centre of the universe, like a babe-in-arms. Whatever others gain, they cannot have, and this deprivation fills them with fury. The deep discontentment which others' good fortune breeds in them leads them to struggle vigorously, even violently, to grab it for themselves. In the myth they make war on the lower gods for possession of the wish-fulfilling tree, which instantly grants all desires. The gods have gained this wondrous tree as a result of their good deeds done in the past. The jealous gods want to seize it without having laid the foundations for its enjoyment. Thus they try to cut it down to carry it off, severing the fruits of the tree from the roots that nourish them – killing the goose that lays the golden egg.

The male titan is highly competitive and tries to outdo others in every way so that he can maintain that sense of being the most important person in the world which is so essential to his identity. He always tries to be cleverer than others, or stronger, or richer, or more experienced, and so forth. Whatever they do, he must go one better. Such people are not uncommon in the worlds of politics or business – and in many other walks of life. Although they are always trying to prove their superiority, titans are very conscious of hierarchy and tend to form ordered power structures. They are able to relate to others only on the basis of dominance or submission, not as equals, and, where they can, they will dominate. Only where they feel that domination is not possible will they submit. The ranks into which they arrange themselves make for a very effective cooperation against a common competitor. But, as in any military dictatorship, each member is watching for others to weaken so that he can seize their power for himself. The hierarchy is not based upon respect and honour but on fear and ambition. Backstabbing and conspiracy constantly undermine the stability of the social structure and new leaders are, all the time, pushing themselves forward.

The male titans compete through brute force or cunning. The females are equally competitive but they use their 'feminine wiles' to get their way. They manipulate their prey through their emotions and use sexual fascination to bait their traps. The titan seeks to reduce the world to his ordering and tries to turn it into a masculine hierarchy centring on himself, the Cosmic King. The titaness tries to form a vast family with herself as its Great Mother with everyone, male and female, brought back to a state of infantile dependence upon her.

These male and female titans represent the extremes of sexual polarization. Differentiation into sexes is a feature of all the worlds of the sensuous sphere, excepting those animals which are hermaphrodite or parthenogenetic. The higher gods are not divided into sexes but are androgynous. Dominating all the lower forms of self-consciousness, the split into male and female is an important factor in evolution and we must now examine it in some depth. Amongst the titans, the polarity is highly exaggerated and is the consequence of a considerable distortion of self-consciousness.

In the growing infant, consciousness is very closely bound up with the body which powerfully conditions the emergent personality. One of the strongest of these bodily determinants is sex. Sexual differentiation is not reflected in the genital organs alone but in dissimilarities of shape, strength and adaptation to certain movements. The differences based upon reproductive function extend far beyond the distinction between the one who fertilizes and the one who carries the ova, and it includes adaptation to different kinds of behaviour such as childrearing or hunting. This very sensitive issue is complicated by the vast range of human types and by the fact that conditioning of a social kind is imposed upon that originating in physiology. Although it is almost impossible to tell where biological conditioning ends and social conditioning begins, however, it cannot sensibly be disputed that our sex is a basic factor in forming our consciousness, independent of any social determinants. Men and women, in so far as they remain biologically based, have quite different psychologies. This fact is abundantly obvious in animals which have little or no social conditioning and is only obscured in humans, if it is obscured at all, by the fact that human consciousness begins to transcend the animal.

The female is much more closely connected with childbirth than is the male. Her monthly periods are part of a constant cycle of preparation for fertilization and, when she does become pregnant, she must carry the child within her for nine months. Her body is smaller and plumper, generally, and is adapted to the tasks both of bearing and nurturing children. Her basic instincts and psychology follow this adaptation. The biological impact on the male of his immediate reproductive function is relatively short-lived, albeit very powerful. His direct physical involvement in childbirth is limited to the sexual act and babies and childrearing are correspondingly less binding on his mind. He is stronger and faster and better suited to tasks which involve force and agility. His freedom from the all-absorbing process of pregnancy and childrearing leaves him more adventurous and better able to take initiative.

The masculine and feminine psychological characteristics which develop out of biological maleness and femaleness might be generalized as initiative and nurturance. Inevitably, in view of the complex nature of human conditioning, there are all sorts of exceptions and cautions to be appended to this broad generalization. But, as a broad generalization, it is true and useful. Most men are inclined to be more active and goal-oriented than most women, more keen to have the initiative and questing for new ways of understanding and doing things. It is for this reason that by far the greatest number of artists, thinkers and leaders have been men. Most women are more concerned with family and home and are inclined to find fulfilment in the nurturance of children. Some men are more feminine in their outlook and some women more masculine; some men are more masculine than others, some women more feminine. Nonetheless, the basic pattern of biological determination of personality, outlined here, is valid.

From the point of view of the doctrine of rebirth, it should not be forgotten that consciousness determines physical form. The physical body may condition, to some extent, the consciousness which is bound up with it in this life, but that body is itself the objectification of the pattern of volitional activities established in a previous life. Men and women are born male or female because that form is the most appropriate concrete expression of their consciousness. Biological gender is determined by past consciousness and helps to shape the new personality. Maleness and femaleness are not accidental or arbitrary phenomena. They stem from the desires and interests we had in the past. Not only may we be reborn into any of the three spheres or six realms of existence but we may be born male or female, or neither (in the sense of being asexual), or both (in the sense of being androgynous). Just as the world we are born into is determined by our volitional activity, so is our sex.

The titans and titanesses and their human counterparts are at the extremes of sexual polarity. Neither extreme is redeemed by any of the qualities of its opposite. Indeed, femininity in a man or masculinity in a woman would be considered shameful. Exaggeratedly one-sided and alienated from the complementary characteristics, the male titans are all brawn and aggression, establishing the dominance of their egos through their masculine drive and initiative. The females use their feminine emotionality and their sexual attraction to weave their own brand of control, a kind of perverted motherliness. Identified almost entirely with their own gender and using its characteristics only to defend their distorted self-sense, the titans represent another of the evolutionary cul-de-sacs in which consciousness can wander.

Because the male and female titans are so much identified with their own biological sex, they have no experience of the psychological qualities associated with the opposite sex. Yet those qualities are latent within them. The psychologically masculine have within themselves the potential for femininity and, likewise, the feminine conceal the masculine in themselves. If these qualities are not experienced consciously they are projected. This is the main component in 'falling in love' in which the object of adoration is seen as the embodiment of unrealized inner qualities. The more extreme the polarization between those attributes which are expressed in consciousness and those which are not, the more intense the pangs of love and the more complicated the relationship which ensues – for the loved one is seldom the paragon that he or she first appears to be and at the same time may have his or her own projections. The titans flounder helplessly in the toils of their own projected expectations but continue to seek outside them the masculinity or femininity which is, in reality, their own.

Human consciousness is, initially, conditioned by biological form, yet it need not remain so. The psychological characteristics which first emerge on the basis of bodily gender can be rounded out by the process of horizontal integration to include all aspects of a full individuality. The mature and healthy ego unites both qualities of masculinity and femininity. On the one hand the individual is able to take the lead, is resourceful and positively assertive, and has drive and energy; and, at the same time, is sensitive to others, careful of their needs, sympathetic to their sufferings and receptive to their words. Both the masculine and the feminine modes are represented in his or her behaviour so that the individual seems to be neither merely a man nor a woman but both and more. Male and female biological character is transcended in the individual who integrates both masculinity and femininity in one fully mature personality.

The integration of both psychosexual poles is no easy task, reinforced as their separation is by the insistent demands of the body and by the full pressure of social conditioning. In some ways, the modern concern with 'sexual politics' has complicated the matter still further since many theorists in this field underplay the importance of biology as a determining factor. It is sometimes even suggested that the psychological differences between men and women are purely socially determined. This cannot but encourage the tendency to alienation from basic feelings so common among modern Westerners. Human growth always begins with self-awareness and we must know our basic temperament and inclinations. In order to develop, we must take the raw material of our crude selfhood and gradually shape it into something finer and more complete. Thus, we must start with our biological nature and sublimate that, rounding it out with its complementary qualities. A creative outlet must be found for the masculine drives: work that challenges and calls up initiative and ingenuity, companions to enccurage and stimulate, even a certain amount of healthy competitiveness, always based on friendship and the desire to reach higher rather than merely to win. The feminine impulses to care, to respect and to serve need healthy expression. Neither function is at all dishonourable and the more masculine and the more feminine, whether men or women in either case, should be encouraged to fulfil in a skilful way their basic psychological character. At the same time, unrealized qualities should be contacted and integrated into one harmonious whole.

Both men and women are capable of achieving the androgynous state and of passing far beyond it to Enlightenment itself. The Buddha was surrounded by men *and* women who had attained Transcendencal Insight. This noble band, however, included far more men than women; down the ages and in different cultures, the finest achievements of Buddhism have been accomplished by men. This is not due to ancient Indian masculine prejudice but reflects the basic nature of men and women. The overriding interest of most women is in children and families, and their psychological character is mainly supportive and nurturent. Whilst these qualities are the germ of a more mature femininity, there is a lack of the masculine drive which is essential if there is to be any *movement* towards a further, more integrated state. The Higher Evolution must be consciously undertaken with deliberate effort. It takes, in other words, the masculine spirit to start the process of integrating masculine with feminine. Most women lack this in sufficient strength to have any urge to outgrow their present level. More exclusively dominated by the bilogical demands of the lower evolution and without the same restless drive which a man can harness to his own development, most women are not able or willing to commit themselves to the task of the Higher Evolution. The fact that most women are far more preoccupied with what is essentially the concern of the lower evolution – the reproduction of the species – has led Buddhists to consider rebirth as a woman to be much less favourable than that as a man. No attitude of contempt or oppression is engendered by this consideration. It is no more than a recognition of the observable facts of the spiritual life. Perhaps the chief danger is that it may be allowed to harden into a rigid generalization which is applied without reference to the various natures of particular individuals. Not all men, by any means, are attracted to the spiritual life in its full sense, although the proportion is far higher than women, and some women, of course, are so attracted. Those of either sex who do want to make the necessary efforts should be given all encouragement.

Normal social conditions tend to reinforce sexual polarization. In our own culture this is particularly evident in the glorification of romantic love – which is, as we have seen, the projection of one's own unrealized qualities on to another person. The isolation of the family unit and the common insistence that personal fulfilment is to be found in marriage do not encourage the development of a balanced individuality. In the nuclear family, men and women are thrust into a proximity for which history has few precedents and which breeds psychological dependence and tends to perpetuate psychosexual extremes. Very different social institutions are required if men and women are to become mature individuals. Buddhism has traditionally considered that the evolutionary interests of men and women are best served if they spend much of their time apart. For this reason, Buddhist communities are usually for men and women separately. To begin with, without the powerful element of biological attraction, a principal distraction is removed. Although sex in itself is not unskilful, the subtle sexual byplay which is almost inevitable in a mixed atmosphere is an annoying diversion when one is trying to concentrate on other things. But, more deeply, where those concerned have not reached the stage of integrated individuality, there is always a tendency to polarization and projection – to falling in love. While this may, initially, be a harmless and enjoyable pastime, it can lead to entanglements and complications. Not least of these is the likelihood of a family. For a woman, having children may represent a healthy expression of her biological nature but for any man whose principal interests lie elsewhere it is likely to ensnare him in the lower evolution. Though it is certainly possible to grow within the context of a family, its demands and pressures are such that it is a far less advantageous situation than a single-sex community.

Not all will, of course, choose to live in the intensive and dedicated environment of a community. Many will, for instance, choose to live in a family of one kind or another. In any event, there needs to be a social system in which the feminine are encouraged to serve and support some skilful end beyond their own family and the masculine are able to use their energies for the good of others. Both must be able to pass beyond their initial biological determination to an integrated individuality in which masculinity and femininity are merged. If this does not happen then biological maleness and femaleness may dominate consciousness and, if allowed to become accentuated and distorted, will result in rebirth among the titans.

8
Men and Gods

The Human World

The human realm is the world of everyday experience. It contains the whole animal side of man's life: his birth, mating and death, his quest for food and shelter, and his struggle with the forces of nature. In it are all his technical productions: mighty cities, roads and communications systems, and complex agricultural and industrial developments. Included too are the social organizations he has evolved for himself: tribes, city states, kingdoms, empires and nations. It is the world of man's cultural achievements: his languages, learning and scientific knowledge, his arts and crafts. Finally, rooted in, but towering above, the human realm, are the highest attainments of the human race: the great works of art and philosophy, the universal religions and, above all, the true individuals who lead mankind beyond itself.

In the previous chapter, we examined the worlds of misery created by immature and distorted self-consciousness. In each, the burden of suffering is so great that there is not much energy available for developing higher modes of awareness. The agonized inhabitants of these realms can do little more than wait until they are no longer the victims of their own past unskilfulness and until all their unwholesome volitions are exhausted. We must now concern ourselves with the two realms of happiness within the sensuous sphere which represent the healthy development of embryonic individuality from the first dawning of self-consciousness to its maturity on the threshold of new levels of spiritual awareness: the worlds of men and gods.

A human rebirth is considered the most favourable at the outset of one's spiritual life because it contains a balance of pleasure and pain. Constant pain, as experienced in the four lower realms, is demoralizing and numbs initiative. Persistent pleasure and success tends to breed complacency. Human life, containing both pleasure and pain, confronts us with the limitations of lower states of existence while allowing us the freedom actively to evolve our own consciousnesses. The human world is thus an axial point in the whole system of worlds: in it the lower evolution becomes the Higher Evolution. Since human life gives us such rare opportunities for growth, Buddhism teaches that it is very precious indeed. We may not be born in such favourable circumstances again for many lifetimes, so we should take full advantage of them. We should not waste our life frivolously squandering it in careless living because we have failed to grasp its true significance.

Communication is the principal feature of the human realm. Communication, here, means more than mere flashing of signals and exchanging information. Many animals have ways of signalling to each other and, no doubt, the hell beings are able to howl their pain and fury to their fellow sufferers, the hungry ghosts to whimper their longings, and the titans to give commands and utter their battle-cry. But each of these is solely concerned with himself, he has no feeling for, or real awareness of, those to whom he passes on his messages. Communication, in this special sense, involves a mutual recognition of individuality. Each party to the exchange is able to see the other, free from projections, as a separate person and is able to enter sympathetically into his world. Each knows that the other is an experiencing subject and feels metta for him and appreciation of his special viewpoint. Where the animal looks to others only as a source of herd-security, the hungry ghost as an object of longing, the hell demon as threatening aggressors and the titan as rivals, the human being is able to see others as individuals. He is not only able to exchange with them facts about the world (although he has raised this capacity to a high level of exactitude and universality) but to convey and recognize inner qualities such as love, courage, beauty, honesty and understanding.

The human capacity for communication, in both its superficial and deeper senses, makes possible the cooperation which brings about civilization and culture. This marks an enormous acceleration of the evolutionary process, for through culture is handed on to the future the stored experience of the past. The achievements, both technical and moral, of dead generations are retained in the various systems of transmission of a particular civilization. Epic poems, preserved in oral traditions, books, music and works of art, all hand on to us what our ancestors learnt. The newborn human infant need not recapitulate for himself, by trial and error, the entire course of human civilization. He can learn from the past and launch himself from the highest achievements of his forefathers. Of course, the collective memory embodied in these systems is selective and open to tampering, as recurrent book burnings demonstrate. Nonetheless, in our own age as never before, a wealth of material is open to us. Scientific data is stored in computer banks to which access can be gained from all over the world. The greatest of world literature has been translated into all the major world languages. Works of art can be seen in public galleries or enjoyed in inexpensive reproductions. The best of music is played by great performers in most major cities. With all this available to us in our human world, we may, if we choose to, deepen and extend our knowledge of physical nature and soar with the loftiest flights of the Imagination.

The human world comprises a number of different levels, corresponding to degrees of maturity both in the individual and in human culture. From the birth of a human being and the first emergence of true *Homo Sapiens* to mature individuality and the highest peaks of civilization as man merges with the gods is a long slow path. It has taken many millennia for man to achieve even his present limited level. Several different stages could be distinguished through which healthy self-consciousness passes in its transition from the animals to the gods. For present purposes, we may divide that long passage into two and examine proto-man and the positive group, on the one hand, and the committed individual and the spiritual community, on the other.

The dividing line between these two levels of humanity is the act of commitment to the Higher Evolution. We will be examining this crucial step in more detail in the next chapter but, for the present, it is taken when an individual feels sufficiently drawn to the Ideal of Enlightenment to place its pursuit at the centre of his life. One who has 'Gone for Refuge to the Three Jewels of Buddha, Dharma and Sangha', as this act of commitment is known in the traditional language, has set his feet upon the Spiral Path. It is in the human realm that the Spiral really begins and so our examination of the second level of humanity belongs mainly to the next chapter. It could be said that the only true human being is the committed individual – the one who is inspired by the ideal of self-transcendence – for the development of mature individuality depends upon being able to look beyond one's own self-interest. There is a line of healthy development up to that point, however, which does not involve the distortions of immature self-consciousness which breed the hungry ghost, demon, titan or animal.

It is this process of development that I have described as the stage of proto-man and the positive group.

To the extent that there is not full individuality, there is group membership. If one has not fully differentiated one's own thoughts and feelings from the views and attitudes of the society in which one lives, if one has not become aware of the conditioning which has shaped one's mind, and if one has not taken full responsibility for all one's deeds, then one will still be a group member. One will be shaped more by the pressures and views of those who surround one than by one's own individual awareness. Just as a child is formed by parents, teachers and other social influences and cannot really be said to have an independent point of view or be accounted morally responsible, so most humans can barely be distinguished from the social group to which they belong. A child inevitably depends upon its parents for moral values and social education – this is, of course, normal and healthy. In the same way, many people need the support and security of the group and its norms until their own individuality has matured. The way in which the child matures depends, to a large extent, on the adults in his life; the way in which the proto-human matures depends on the group to which he belongs. We must, therefore, distinguish between different types of group.

Groups may be analysed in terms of six worlds. Whole societies, whole nations, may be broadly characterized as hungry ghost-like, or titanic, or demonic or bestial if, respectively, craving, envy, hatred or ignorance are the predominant forces of the culture. The proto-human also lives in a group but this time the group is of a positive kind. All the influences in society tend towards the production of positive emotions and wholesome states of mind.

In the first place, the positive group is, what one might call, healthily pagan. The human is the axis of the Wheel and the Spiral, the point of intersection of the lower with the Higher Evolution. He possesses a body which is the product of the long process of biological development and he has self-consciousness which is capable of unfolding into Buddhahood. He denies either aspect of himself at his peril. The pagan, in this sense, recognizes the natural forces both within him and around him and allows them their appropriate expressions but he does not let them dominate or distort his mind. He does not despise or hate the body, for such an attitude breeds repression and leads to the tortures of those hungry ghosts who cannot admit to what they long for and can only crave some unsatisfying substitute. At the same time, the healthy pagan does not allow instinctual demands entirely to dominate his self-consciousness. If this were to happen he would be living only to eat, sleep and copulate as does the animal.

Sex is the most commonly abused of the natural instincts because of its overriding power. Within the positive group, sex is not regarded as 'dirty' or sinful. It is considered normal and healthy to have sexual feelings and the pleasures of sex are openly acknowledged. It is, however, not overestimated or raised to an all-consuming obsession. At the same time, its very strong and even disruptive force is recognized, for it can tear apart stable family life and undermine community harmony. A framework of custom and eitquette ensures that, while there is no repression, there is no enticement to excess or indulgence. This will be manifest in ordinary relations between the sexes which will be decent and decorous. In this way, the sexual instinct has a healthy outlet and outside this it does not plague the mind. In some of the most successful pagan cultures of the past, such as that of ancient Greece, sex was surrounded by few taboos, apart from those of incest. Homosexuality was often regarded as honourable, even noble, not just tolerated as the necessary aberration of a twisted few. In the first place, it allowed a sexual outlet for the unmarried without the responsibilities which pregnancy would entail. It was also considered to strengthen the bonds of friendship between men – for it is was men who most commonly practised homosexuality – without sexual polarization arising. For some men and women, homosexuality may provide a way in which they can keep free of the ties of family life so that they can devote themselves full-time to the following of the Spiral Path without having to give up sex altogether.

The men and women in the positive group have a wholesome attitude to the body in all respects. The pagan satisfies his bodily needs in a straightforward way and he ensures that he is fit and physically healthy. He neither despises and tortures his body nor indulges it. It is his vehicle for self-expression and the medium through which he acts. In the human body, he has the possibility of growth and so he guards and nourishes his body with pride and care. His soundness of mental attitude manifests itself in the elegant and pleasing way he dresses and adorns himself. Neither trying to attract attention to himself by excessive display nor expressing self-hatred and neglect through untidy or unattractive clothing, he shows in his appearance a proper self-love. In the same way, he is in harmony with the natural world around him. He appreciates deeply the vitality in all things and responds immediately to beauty and sublimity in his environment. He is careful not to waste or exploit the earth's natural resources.

The positive group imparts to its members a sense of self-confidence and assurance. Each feels that he is valued and has no sense of self-hatred or unworthiness. He trusts his own culture and those that bring it to him and has none of the suspiciousness and rebelliousness which many modern Westerners feel towards the civilization which has bred them. He respects and loves the traditions of his group and preserves them with pride. He is able to believe in his culture and so to believe in himself. He can, therefore, cooperate in a friendly spirit with other group members in communal economic, political and social affairs. The collective energies of the group are harnessed to positive ends: social enterprises which bring benefits to its members whether in material prosperity or in beauty and learning. No group enemy channels surplus aggression, for all the community's vigour is used in a skilful way.

The traditions of the positive group are manifested, first of all, in manners and customs which guarantee harmonious and sensitive relationships between people. Each newborn child learns, from its parents' own behaviour, that one should act in a polite and friendly manner towards others and, for instance, that guests should be treated kindly. Social relations are, therefore, characterized by consideration and care. The tradition will cover the minutest of matters so that each person knows what behaviour most fittingly expresses that friendly sensitivity in each situation. It also imparts a more basic code of ethics concerning abstention from murder, theft, sexual violence, etc. Since even this model society is still a group whose members have not yet developed a natural ethical sense then that moral code must be sanctioned by a system of justice which punishes those who transgress and rewards those who fulfil its injunctions. Each person will know what is his duty as a citizen and what it is that he must and may not do. He will feel full confidence that the laws of his group are just and he believes in the fittingness of the retribution which follows an offence.

All the influences of such a positive tradition are upward. Cities are built so that they are beautiful to look at and graceful to live in, learning and the arts are encouraged and, pervading all the acts of public life, is a sense of idealism. Decisions are taken not on the basis of sectional interests, each jockeying for position and power, but through a common regard for certain values which transcend narrow personal wishes. The whole of society is raised up by a vision of a higher kind of life which all, at least to some extent, honour and respect. Without that leaven of a higher set of values, the group can only fall back upon the interests of its members. Since these are bound to conflict sooner or later, the fabric of society will be rent by conflict and the positive group will become a negative one: either demonic, titanic, bestial or hungry ghost-like. Without some generally accepted ideal, there can be no positive group.

An ideal cannot be manufactured, a vision cannot be artificially constructed on abstract principles. A vision must be a living experience, vividly felt, washing aside all egoistic aspiration and dead values. A vision needs a visionary. There must be people within the group who have gone beyond the group. There must be individuals who see the ideals clearly and who sufficiently embody them so that they may hand on the higher vision from which the culture of the positive group springs. The group must gather itself around people who are individuals enough to have had their own experience of a higher level of consciousness. The positive group needs leaders who are individuals with their own direct experience of truth. Only if the members of the group respect and are receptive to the wise in their midst will the sort of inspired culture, outlined above, come into being.

It is probably clear by now that Buddhism is not inherently democratic, much as many modern apologists would like it so. It is not, of course, aristocratic, in the usual sense of the term, nor totalitarian. It does not advocate the subordination of one part of the population to the egoistic wishes of another. Its 'political ideology' stems from its belief that human life has a purpose: to evolve as individuals to the goal of Buddhahood. It shows that different people are at different levels of development and, from common observation, it is but a few who are relatively highly evolved. If decisions are based upon the opinions of the majority inevitably they are going to be founded on the lowest level of understanding. What most people want is likely to be what they consider to be in the interests of their own limited egos, not of some higher code of values. At the same time, Buddhism is not anti-democratic – it is certainly the case that the Western-style parliamentary democracies of the present are the least offensive form of government to anyone who wishes to grow since they impose little conformity of ideas. No particular form of government was, in fact, advocated by the Buddha. Whoever does exercise power, however they derive it, is simply urged to govern in accordance with moral principles and not with personal interest at heart. If those who govern have regard to the welfare of all the people, see that justice is impartially administered and ethically based, and encourage higher culture in general and the spiritual life in particular, honouring those who have given themselves to it fully, then it is of secondary importance how their power is derived – so long as it comes without harm to others; revolution, except in the most extreme cases, cannot usually be justified because of the disruption of the continuity of tradition and the violence it entails. It could be said that the principal issue of politics is not constitutional but moral and even spiritual. Without true moral and spiritual leadership, there can be no positive group.

The positive group is thus a network of people who have yet to achieve full ethical individuality and who have not committed themselves to the realization of the Transcendental ideal. They have no moral sense or spiritual vision of their own. Left to themselves, they can only fall back on their own limited self-interest. They are, however, able to respond to the ethical guidance and reflected vision which is part of their cultural heritage. This allows them to act skilfully and encourages them to look beyond themselves. The worth of that tradition is guaranteed by the creative individuals who generated it in the past and their successors who now sustain it with their own renewed vision. The positive group, in this way, encourages a happy, vigorous and friendly life devoted to ends greater than the individual. Above all, it urges and educates all those who wish to go beyond the group to experience for themselves the Transcendental reality which is the positive group's ultimate basis.

All those who have felt that impulsion to achieve a higher level of consciousness are eligible as members of the spiritual community. If the members of the Sangha consider that their request is sincere and that they are able to carry out the commitment which they wish to make then they will be accepted regardless of their background or previous experience. Although the new member of the spiritual community or Order may not be anywhere near Stream Entry and may still have greed, hatred and delusion swirling within him, he has decided that he wants to function in a quite new way. He wants to live ethically, not from fear of punishment or love of reward but because he has some foreshadowing of the sensitivity and metta to all creatures that is the real basis of morality. He wishes to develop higher states of consciousness and, in the end, Transcendental Insight. He wants to develop friendships with others which are based, not on overlapping self-interest, but on mutual love and concern. He has some glimpse of the vision which inspires the spiritual community and he is prepared to open himself fully to its influence. He allows himself to become a participant in the culture and tradition of the spiritual community which is at the basis of the culture and tradition of the positive group.

The spiritual community is the fulfilment of the human life and is its ultimate meaning. The positive group is kept in being by the Sangha but it also provides a bridge over which those who wish may cross to the spiritual community itself. In a sense, it is only then that one is a full human being.

The Heavens of the Gods

Above the human world stretches plane upon plane of heavenly worlds, each one of greater subtlety and happiness than the one which precedes it. The lower of these god-worlds are still within the sphere of sensuous experience but the higher are within the dimensions of archetypal form and of formless quality. Although the heavens collectively correspond to the ascending Spiral of the Higher Evolution, we will be examining those of the sensuous sphere in this present chapter.

The Pali and Sanskrit words which are usually translated as 'god' come from a root meaning 'to shine'. The gods are the 'shining' or 'radiant' ones who live in unalloyed happiness and pleasure. It is traditionally recognized that such beings are heavenly and are also to be found on earth. There are heaven worlds into which one may be born as a god but it is also possible to live on this earth as if one were a god. Kings and princes seemed, in earlier times, to live a divine life, full of wealth and power, able to satisfy every desire. We have our own rich and powerful, today, who move in a sphere of opulence far removed from the ordinary man. (That many of them are notoriously unhappy is a sign, perhaps, that they are actually titans who have grabbed at riches and not gods who have attracted riches to them by their virtuous deeds!) Another sort of god-on-earth is the one who has spiritual attainment. The Stream Entrant and those beyond him are respondent with their Transcendental knowledge and shine with the ideal qualities which they embody. They experience continuously the bliss of non-duality and they walk, like heroes, in full confidence and power. The world of the gods, properly speaking, however, is an objective dimension of existence into which any self-conscious entity may find himself reborn.

God realms of the sensuous sphere, according to tradition, consist of six levels. The beings of the lowest are said to be able to interact with the human plane and are the benign spirits of folk-lore: fairies, dryads, nereids and other nature spirits. Above these are beings of greater power and splendour who correspond, roughly, to the Greek Olympians – although they are of more blameless life. The highest planes are, respectively, occupied by the Contented Gods, the Gods who Delight in their own Creations, and the Gods who Delight in the Creations of Others. Each divine being has a physical body of a subtle substance which is not perceived by the ordinary human eye. They are very beautiful of form and noble of aspect. Everything they wish for presents itself immediately before them and they experience constant sensuous delight and satisfaction. The higher the realm, the more refined and satisfying are its pleasures. The gods of each world form a highly civilized society which is usually depicted as a royal court presided over by the king or chief god. They pass their time together in the enjoyment of beauty.

These gods of the sensuous realm are sexually differentiated, although at each level the difference becomes smaller. They do engage in sexual activity but, as the polarity between male and female relaxes, sex becomes more and more subtle. At the lowest levels, sexual gratification is by copulation, as among humans. Higher up, it is achieved by holding hands and then, progressively, by a smile, by prolonged gazing and, finally, by a mere glance. At this highest level, masculinity and femininity are so closely united that if the eyes of a male meet even momentarily those of a female it relieves the tension which one-sidedness brings and gives all the pleasure of sexual release. Each rank of god is thus more highly integrated than the one below and ascent through their levels marks the progressive overcoming of sexual polarization.

Since they share the same sphere of sensuous experience, albeit at the most rarefied levels, the gods are not so far removed from the human dimension that they are unable to interact with it. It is said that gods like to visit places of great natural beauty and are attracted to people who are happy and positive. They particularly like to be around those who are spiritually developed and are often said to shed as benevolent influence over them, like guardian angels. It is also claimed that humans can develop the faculty of seeing and communicating with these divine beings. Buddhism is not alone in this belief, for many other traditions tell of sages who are able to speak to the beings of higher dimensions. Since these gods are the embodiment of a higher level of consciousness, only those who have raised their own human minds to that same degree can contact them.

These gods, and those of the higher realms too, are all impermanent. Life for them is immeasurably long – the higher the realm, the longer the life – but they all must die when the pattern of volitions which made them gods has been exhausted. There are no immortal beings in Buddhist cosmology, extraordinarily long-lived as some gods are said to be. The gods are conditioned like any other inhabitant of the Wheel or Spiral. Not one of the gods is a creator, for the conditioned process has no beginning and was not created. Buddhism considers the idea of a single god who presides over the universe, whether the concept is presented in its crudest, anthropomorphic form or in highly abstract, philosophical theories, to be extremely dangerous from an ethical and spiritual point of view. A god-centred universe is conceived of as containing an ultimate authority and thus may encourage moral irresponsibility since the god's commands are to be obeyed regardless of personal feeling. It also places a limit on human development since there is always an irreducible dichotomy between creature and god. For Buddhists, there is no limit to the evolution of consciousness and all dualities can be transcended. The gods, however refined their level, are always inferior to the Buddha since they still stand within the conditioned process and are caught in the framework of subject and object.

The god realms of the sensuous sphere are the objectification of an ethical consciousness. Those beings who usually function skilfully and who have achieved a natural moral sense act from increasingly wholesome volitions. In traditional terms, they 'make merit', that is, they accumulate a stock of positive volitional potentialities which will eventually fructify in pleasurable consequences. These they will experience in this life, if they have not set up too much countervailing negative momentum in past lives, or in a future rebirth in a heaven world. If one can see that others have feelings like one's own and can feel sympathy for them then one will act ethically and will begin to accrue merit. This merit may be experienced quite quickly as life becomes more pleasant and smooth and opportunities seem to present themselves more and more readily. To an even greater extent, the consequences of merit will be found in the worlds of the gods which are altogether more beautiful than earth and lack most of its unpleasant features. The karmic results of skilful action are an increased feeling of well-being and ease and a more pleasurable sensuous experience.

That a more skilful way of life is likely to be accompanied by greater sensuous pleasure is an indication of the identity of ethical and aesthetic awareness, 'goodness' and beauty. One whose mind is dominated by negative mental states will scarcely be able to appreciate the more refined delights of the senses. His pleasure will, for the most part, be found in the release of pent-up tension, not in the enjoyment of proportion or harmony. The contemplation of sensuous beauty in its fullness is reserved to those with an easy conscience whose wholesome mental states have some correspondence with the pleasing forms they perceive. The cultivation of the aesthetic sense must go hand in hand with the development of morality otherwise it will degenerate into mere connoisseurship – extensive technical knowledge without real appreciation – or into sensualism. The gods of the sensuous sphere are those who, by their goodness, are able to appreciate beauty.

The pleasures of the god realm hold out a danger. So enjoyable is it to live in the unalloyed delight of the senses that the god may lose his awareness of who he is. It is as a result of his mindfulness and his skilful actions, his moral efforts in the past, that he enjoys now the bliss of the senses. But unless he continues to make an effort and maintains his self-awareness, he will gradually sink back to a lower stage of evolution or, at best, settle down where he is. For most of us, this welcome danger lies in the future but it holds a message for us, nonetheless. When we are happy and enjoying ourselves we tend to lose self-awareness and slip into unskilful behaviour. It is not that we should avoid happiness or that the gods should avoid the pleasures of their realm, but we should strive at all times to maintain consciousness of ourselves as developing individuals under the most pleasurable and the most painful experiences alike. It is all too easy for the god to slip into the forgetful rapture of the moment, giving no thought of climbing higher. It is easy, in the spiritual life, for complacency to set in.

9

The Mundane Path

The human world and the lower heavens are the bottom steps of the Spiral Path, which we must now pursue. We will be examining each step of that Path by means of another chain of twelve links which is the Spiral counterpart of the cyclic chain at the rim of the Wheel. This time, the links do not form a circle but carry one upwards in a progressive order. This evolutionary chain of conditioned coproduction leads away from the Wheel, breaking the endless circularity of its turnings. Each link in the Spiral provides the conditions for the arising of the succeeding link, which is at an higher level, surpassing it in happiness, clarity and love. All of these twelve links, from the lowest to the peak of Enlightenment itself, may be experienced in human life. The states of mind to which they correspond may also, at death, give rise to rebirth in worlds of ever greater beauty and purity. We will be exploring these steps on the spiritual Path both in terms of subjective, inner experience and of the objective worlds which are their concrete expression.

The twelve links in the chain of progressive conditionality start with the experience of *imperfection*. In dependence on imperfection, there arises *faith*, on faith, *delight*, on delight, *ecstasy*, and then, each unfolding out of the one before, *peace, bliss, absorption, knowledge* and *vision of things as they really are, disentanglement, dispassion, liberation* and *recognition that the poisonous mental floods have been destroyed*. The first seven links, from imperfection to absorption, are the mundane Path since no Insight into reality has, as yet, arisen and whatever gains have been made can be lost. 'Knowledge and vision of things as they really are' is the point of Insight and, therefore, of Stream Entry. From here on, the links constitute the Transcendental Path. We will be following the mundane Path in this chapter and the Transcendental in the next.

The Path arises out of the Wheel for, endless as the cycle of links is, there is a point at which a gap opens up and we can escape. We have seen, in chapter 6, that each link of the cyclic chain can be assigned to one of two phases. There is an active, *causal* phase which is established by our own volitions. The *resultant* phase follows inevitably from the momentum inherent in the causal phase. We have now a body, sense organs and sense experience because of what we willed in the past; our present volitions are not responsible for our present experience. The whole cyclic chain consists of action and reaction between these two phases. In the twelve cyclic links, there are three points of transition between the two phases: where the causal phase in the past life gives way to the resultant phase in the present; where the resultant phase gives way to the causal, both in the present life; and where that causal phase gives way to the resultant phase in the life to come (see p. 111). The result follows from the cause without possibility of variation: having been given the impulsion of the volitions, the Wheel must spin until its potential energy has been fully discharged. Once the resultant process has unwound to its limit, however, further reaction is not inevitable. Only renewed unwholesome volition gives the Wheel another spin. The gap between resultant phase and causal phase, both in the present life, is the point on the Wheel where change is possible. That gap is between the link of feeling and the link of craving. Pleasant and painful experiences come to us as the consequence of our psycho-physical make-up. Usually, on the basis of those feelings, we crave what is pleasurable – or seems so – and try to cling to it and we hate what seems painful and try to repel or destroy it. In this way, the causal phase is set up again.

Feeling, then, is the last link in the resultant process after which we begin a new round of volition which either sends us spinning upon the Wheel again or sets our feet upon the Spiral. But there are different levels of feeling and if we are not deeply aware of our feelings we continue to react with unhealthy volitions. Often our reactions are based upon relatively superficial likes and dislikes, even on immediate physical sensations of pleasure and pain. At a somewhat deeper level, our ability to imagine what is not immediately present to us gives rise to expectations and anticipations, hopes and fears. If we become dissatisfied at this level, it is because we want and expect more gratification from life and we are disappointed. We hope for better and we believe that we could be fully and perfectly satisfied if only we could achieve the right combination of circumstances. This attitude leads us to further craving and hatred as we throw all our energies into creating the ideal circumstances for our own limited individuality.

Imperfection

As we spin upon the Wheel, however, another kind of feeling may grow in us. Although we may be, in the more superficial sense, quite happy and may experience an abundance of pleasure of a sensuous or psychological kind, a deeper frustration begins to emerge. We begin to see that, in its very nature, worldly life is imperfect. It does, of course, offer very real pleasures but they are always limited. Something always mars or spoils them and they always come to an end. Whatever in the world we look to for any lasting security and happiness, shows itself to be vulnerable. There is nothing we can fully rely upon: the happiest life contains some experience of pain and decay. We are never able to reach our fullest limit in enjoyment of any pleasure; something inside us remains unfulfilled, some constriction holds us back from complete happiness. Even, it is said, the most refined happiness of the highest god realm contains some faint trace of that constriction.

This growing sense of the imperfection of everything the world has to offer is not simply the disappointment which arises from frustrated ambition nor is it the reaction of a weakling who considers himself to be cheated by life. He who feels this kind of frustration no longer expects to find perfection in worldly things. He has some faint intimation, some groping intuition, that real fulfilment is possible although he does not know where to find it. Everything that he now does seems empty and meaningless although he may have no problems in his relations with other people or in his work and he may be physically and psychologically perfectly healthy. He knows that there is more to life than he now realizes, and he is searching for its deeper meaning.

This feeling of imperfection is the natural expression of a consciousness which wishes to develop. The evolutionary tendency inherent in all consciousness exerts its influence upon us. Our self-awareness is the seed of Transcendental consciousness and cannot be long contained within the restricted circumference of the Wheel without our feeling cramped and confined. The nature of consciousness is to expand and, if that nature is not fulfilled, then frustration and pain arise. The repression

of this, the most fundamental of urges, has far more drastic consequences than the repression of the instincts for it can leave us sour and
embittered for a lifetime if we do not fulfil it. Many people feel this
sense of imperfection or frustration; some simply lose it in the mael-
strom of their own reactive impulses, others again are swept away by
the pressures of the group in which they live which forces them to fulfil
its conventional expectations, some begin their quest but are discour-
aged, sooner or later, by lack of any clear guidance or support and by
the confusion of possibilities that confronts them. That call is not easily
distinguished from all the other desires and longings that seethe within
us and it is harder still to find our way forward without any help or
encouragement. It is not surprising that very many people who do
experience at some time that sense of imperfection simply give up and
carry on around the Wheel. Prevailing social attitudes and institutions
scarcely encourage them to do otherwise. Yet that feeling of frustration
with mundane life is not something to be drowned or cured. It should
be honoured and cherished for it is the entry to the Path of the Higher
Evolution.

Some who experience the imperfection of a limited life do go in
quest of something more real. If they are fortunate, they encounter an
embodiment of the ideal which gives them a glimpse, at last, of what
they seek. It may be that a statue of the Buddha, if it is of high artistic
merit, conveys to them the peace of the Enlightened state together
with its deep understanding and strong sympathy for all living beings.
Again, a book may succeed in communicating to them the truth for
which they long. Or they may meet someone who impresses them
with the human qualities which he has developed. In these and other
ways, out of that noble sense of frustration, there emerges a new and
real hope. In dependence on imperfection, arises *faith*.

Faith

In Buddhism, faith is a multi-faceted term of far broader significance
than the English word conventionally conveys. It is not unreasoning
belief but the wholehearted response of the total being to the Ideal. It is
the surge of the Imaginal faculty beyond one's immediate experience to
touch, and ultimately to grasp, the highest truth. Once faith has
arisen, one knows what it is that one must do.

In the first place, faith is a direct, intuitive response. The force of evolution coiled within us is released by something which embodies the possibility of complete fulfilment and perfection. Whether it is a work of art, a person, or a book, the Ideal which it manifests corresponds to something in us. The Transcendental consciousness latent within our own self-consciousness vibrates in sympathy with the Transcendental reality mirrored in the object that fires our faith. Like is attracted to like and we are irresistibly drawn by what we feel reflects our own deepest nature. At first, faith may be rather vague and confused but it is, nonetheless, a very powerful emotion which lifts us up towards the Goal.

When it reaches its maturity, faith includes clarity of mind. The Ideals in which one develops faith – in Buddhism these are the Buddha, Dharma and Sangha – are understood rationally. One has an accurate intellectual comprehension of the Dharma and one is able to investigate it with the intellect as well as to respond to it emotionally. No blind belief is required at all and an open-minded enquiry into the rational consistency of the Buddha's claim to Enlightenment may be necessary before faith can come to fruition. Faith must have sharpness and definition so that one has a clear apprehension of the Ideal to which one is responding with that powerful intuitive attraction. If there is not this more cognitive aspect to faith one can be very easily led astray. Faith may be confused with other, less healthy emotions so that, for instance, one's neurotic need for security may lead one to place faith in a guru who likes to have authority over others for his own neurotic reasons.

As faith is strengthened and sharpened by the unleashing of the emotions and the assessment of the intellect, it is further confirmed by experience. When faith is applied by following the Path, one will find that it is justified as one gains the benefits of the Dharma and sees by one's own direct insight some of the truths which are laid before one. Faith becomes yet more intense, being based now not only on emotional response and intellectual conviction but on the steady rock of confidence born of experience.

Faith is the first step on the spiritual Path, the counterpart of craving which is the first step in a renewed round of the Wheel. That step away from the Wheel is not one which is taken all at once. Every second of our lives, pleasant, painful or neutral feelings are being presented to us and we have the choice of reacting with craving or responding with faith. If we crave then we deny our own higher

155

destiny and identify ourselves completely with our present level of experience. Our deepest longings are invested in mundane pleasures. If we feel faith then we see that pleasurable and painful sensations arise from conditions, and our hearts are fixed on a happiness which is beyond conditions. We are thus able to respond to the feelings which arise during the course of our lives in a healthy way – enjoying the pleasurable, trying to remove the painful where possible, but never intoxicated or overwhelmed by them because, for us, they do not contain the full meaning of life.

Gradually, we learn to recognize the conditioned nature of our feelings and to discriminate between our reactions of craving or hatred and our healthy responses of faith and metta. More and more of our energies are placed upon the Spiral until, with full Enlightenment, there is nothing of the Wheel in us at all. It is in the choice between craving and faith that the Higher Evolution consists. While we have yet to reach the point of Stream Entry, when the Spiral unfolds spontaneously, all our efforts must be directed to discriminating the healthy from the unhealthy impulses within us. Unremitting mindfulness must be brought to bear on our mental processes so that we see clearly where they tend and are able to act as skilfully as we can. Our initial efforts only prevent the committing of the more obviously unskilful actions but, in time, our powers of self-awareness will increase and we will be able to watch the ebb and flow of wholesome and unwholesome mental states within our minds before they ever reach the threshold of overt behaviour. In this way, the cyclic tendencies within us will gradually be starved and the Spiral will flourish.

This effort of mindfulness and mental discrimination is one of the active consequences of arisen faith. Faith is not merely an appreciation of the Ideal but a desire to move towards it. Not only do we see the correspondence between Buddhahood and our own deepest nature but we want to make it a living reality – we want actively to develop our own consciousness. So we begin to practise, applying the teachings of Buddhism to our own lives and thus shifting ourselves from the Wheel to the Spiral. At first, this will require that we consider the morality of our behaviour as we try to make our actions expressive of our new-found vision. We will try to order our lives so that we are guided by the Ideals to which we have responded with faith. Faith, then, gives rise to ethics.

The active aspect of faith, the desire to realize the Ideals in one's own life, is called Going for Refuge to the Three Jewels: the act of commitment to the Buddha, Dharma and Sangha. It is the expression of Going for Refuge and its acceptance by one's teacher and spiritual friends which formally constitutes one a member of the Sangha – the spiritual community.

With faith, one has taken a leap beyond one's old self and has opened up to a wider sphere of consciousness. One acknowledges something beyond oneself and one is no longer so tightly self-centred. One feels uplifted and inspired and a new mood of generosity possesses one. Because one is no longer so bound up with oneself, one wishes to share. One feels such inner wealth that it overflows to others and one has a strong sense of gratitude to one's teachers and spiritual friends. They have kept the Buddha's message alive and have enabled one to find this Path which is the fulfilment of all one's aspirations and which allays the emptiness and frustration of imperfection. The Ideals themselves and those who embody them fill one with strong feelings of reverence and respect. One wants to express one's devotion to them and to honour them for their many wondrous qualities.

The cultivation and expression of these devotional feelings is of great importance. If they find no expression, like any impulse, they will wither and die. The more richly they are voiced, the more strongly will they rise, strengthening our faith. It is for this reason that, in every Buddhist tradition, there are images of the Buddha before which people bow and make offerings or perform ceremonies with chanting and ritual. Often the shrines and the halls where they are situated, as well as the words and actions of the ceremonies, are very beautiful and deeply stirring, even if one does not know the precise significance of each sound and gesture. In this way, the emotions are drawn behind one's efforts to grow, providing the motive power which will move one forward. A theoretical grasp of the Dharma's formulations is not enough, one must be emotionally involved. We must want to move forward and our emotions must be harnessed otherwise they will simply fasten themselves to the objects of craving. Faith and devotion are the emotional aspects of the Higher Evolution and we must take active steps to develop and extend them. Without devotional practices of some kind, it is likely that Buddhism will remain merely an intellectual pastime.

Faith then is the first step on the Path. It is the point where we contact the Ideal and commit ourselves to realizing it. We are carried beyond our own narrow self-interest and start to live more skilfully, to be more open-handed, and to feel gratitude towards teachers and friends on the Path and devotion for the Three Jewels and their embodiments. This corresponds to the second level of the human world where the individual has separated himself from the group and joins the spiritual community. The true human being is characterized by his faith in Transcendental Ideals.

Although faith is the first step on the Path, it is not abandoned in the transition to the next. It develops and is strengthened more and more throughout the Spiral, underlying each succeeding link.

Faith followed through in active commitment begins to transform the individual. His whole way of life is changed, his perspective on the world is different, his states of mind are on a new and higher plane and he begins to experience a quite new sense of exultation and pleasure. In dependence on faith, *delight* arises.

Delight

Because one is living in a skilful way, in fulfilment of one's faith, a sense of well-being and harmony arises – this is delight. One feels then the inner satisfaction of knowing that there is nothing with which one can reproach oneself. One's conscience is clear and one feels fully at peace with oneself. The fact that one is putting one's aspiration into practice means that one has none of that sense of self-disgust and disappointment that comes from failing to live up to one's ideals.

Not only does one feel happy with oneself but one also feels at ease with others for there is nothing with which they can reproach one. Often our social difficulties arise because of our defensiveness against the blame of others but, in the stage of delight, there is no corner of inconsistency by means of which others can manipulate us. We feel psychologically secure and confident.

If we do not experience this sort of innocence then our minds will be clouded and distracted with guilt and self-reproach. Furthermore, we will always be vulnerable to those who wish to exploit our weakness and we will feel uneasy in meeting people. Such guilt may be rational or irrational. If it is irrational one has the neurotic feeling that one has done something wrong – whether one actually has or not. As a result of his upbringing the irrationally guilty person has learnt to think of himself as fundamentally sinful and he has a permanent, underlying sense of guilt and fear of punishment. This is a thoroughly unskilful state and must be corrected as soon as possible and replaced by self-love and confidence. Rational guilt, on the other hand, is quite healthy and is our remorse at our own genuinely unskilful behaviour. We have done wrong and we feel sorry for it; however, it is not skilful to remain too long in this state of remorse. We must, of course, face up to our own shortcomings and unskilfulness but we should aim to resolve the feelings of guilt which arise, as quickly as possible. Very great importance is attached, in Buddhism, to the eradication of guilt. First of all, it is important to acknowledge what we have done. This is best done by openly confessing it to a teacher or spiritual friend who is able to appreciate that our action was really unskilful but who will remain positive in his basic attitude towards us. By making it open in this way, and by expressing our regret for what was done, our conscience may be clean once more. Sometimes, however, either because of the magnitude of the fault or because our conscience is very tender, confession may not cleanse our hearts and we may still feel guilty. Then devotional practices of various kinds are recommended which stimulate feelings of faith and will eventually induce a more positive state of mind. Of course, a crucial part of confession and of the devotional ceremony is a firm commitment to avoid such behaviour in the future.

Delight is the perfect absence of any moral conflict or guilt. Not only is there a subjective feeling of happiness and ease but objectively one will experience the karmic fruits of one's skilful actions. One's merits will bring their benefits. On death, one in whom this stage predominates will be reborn in the heaven worlds of the sensuous sphere and will enjoy the subtle sensuous delights which they afford.

The pursuit of the Spiral Path bring joys from the start but they swell ever greater the higher one climbs. An integrated ethical life forms the basis for a deeper psychical integration in which all the conflicting energies are harmonized and unified in an experience of overwhelming happiness and pleasure. In dependence on delight, arises *ecstasy*.

Ecstasy

With this link we step, for the first time, beyond the sphere of sensuous desire into the realm of archetypal form. The succeeding three links take us through all the archetypal levels together with those of the formless realm. Both these are the spheres of meditation; the states of mind which constitute them are quite different to those of ordinary consciousness. Our language is strained to its limits in trying to convey something of these sublime heights. Nonetheless, these states are quite within the reach of anyone who applies himself systematically to the practice of meditation.

Meditation has two primary, related effects when one first engages upon it: it integrates all the energies of the psyche and it leads to more and more positive emotion. The stage of ecstasy comes about as all psychological conflict and tension is resolved and the subconscious impulses are released and absorbed into full consciousness. This gives rise to intensely pleasurable physical sensations and an even more light and zestful joy than was known in the stage of delight. Much of the time we are mentally divided and our energies are scattered over a number of different interests and preoccupations which are not formed into one harmonious pattern. To further complicate the matter, we are often not fully aware of, or are confused about, our own motivations. It is as if we are not one single person but an assembly of different personalities, some of which may be in direct conflict with one another. We are seldom able to call upon our full emotional and mental resources for any task. For most, if not all, of the time we operate with a fraction of our total potential and we do not experience the richness of a life lived wholeheartedly. It is a striking fact that many of the great artists and inspired figures of the past seem to have enjoyed super-abundant energy and to have been capable of an eagerness and enthusiasm which most of us lost in childhood.

In order to bring about the horizontal integration of all these sub-personalities within us, we must apply mindfulness and self-reflection, getting to know ourselves more deeply and fully. Meditation, positive work which is 'Right Livelihood', spiritual friendship all help in this key task of drawing together the fragments of the personality into one balanced individuality. But, above all, it is the possession of a vision and the devotion to its realization which pulls our energies together. Just as all the struggling factions in a nation are united by the common desire to prevail against an aggressor, so we need something beyond our own selves to which we can be dedicated. If such a goal is to bring every aspect of being into harmony it cannot afford to be one-sided or contain any trace of unwholesomeness. That Ideal is Human Enlightenment. At the stage of ecstasy, our faith in the Three Jewels and our active pursuit of a skilful way of life bear fruit in the resolution of all conflicts and tensions and the release of subconscious energies into the strengthening current of faith. It is only a high purpose which can mobilize the full force of the human heart.

Conflicts and tensions are not merely mental events, they find expression in the very posture of our bodies. The anxious man hunches his shoulders against the blows of fate, the angry man clenches his teeth and holds himself ready for attack. Our predominant emotions permanently shape our muscles into what the psychologist, Wilhelm Reich, called 'character armour'. As psychological tension is resolved in the integrated state, this rigidity begins to break down and nervous energy locked in the musculature is able to flow more freely. The melting of these blockages and the resulting release of physical vitality is experienced in sensations of actual bodily pleasure. The extent to which the rapture is felt depends upon the amount of previous inhibition and tension – it may be very strong indeed. Buddhist psychological analysis enumerates five levels of ecstasy. First, there is the 'lesser thrill' which is strong enough only to raise the hairs of the body. Then comes the 'momentary rapture' which shoots intense but brief currents through the frame, like flashes of lightning. The 'flooding rapture' washes through the body, ebbing and flowing like the waves of the sea beating upon the shore. 'Transporting rapture' is said to be so powerful that the body may actually levitate! The 'all-pervading rapture' brings the process to its culmination and is likened to a balloon, full of air, for the sensations of ecstasy have become so pervasive and enduring that they fill the entire system.

These progressive levels of ecstasy are but more intense forms of the kinds of physical manifestations which powerful emotion often excites. When we are very deeply stirred by something – art or nature, acts of heroism, or our communication with another person – tears may start in our eyes or we may find ourselves shaking uncontrollably. These are not signs of weakness or lack of self-control, but evidence that something has moved us so profoundly that the emotions cannot be contained within the boundaries of normal expression and seek some more immediate discharge. Such rushes of emotion are not uncommon in meditation and people may find themselves weeping, shaking or laughing quite involuntarily. These may all be manifestations of ecstasy and they are characterized not only by sensations of physical release and pleasure but by very strong feelings of happiness. All one's psychological energies flow more and more powerfully behind one's faith and one feels complete and whole, deeply satisfied that one is engaged in the best and noblest task that a human can undertake.

The deeper the ecstasy becomes, the more the purely mental experience predominates and so, in dependence upon ecstasy, there arises *peace*.

Peace

Sooner or later the process of horizontal integration is completed and all the energy locked in tension and subconscious conflict is released. The experience of physical ecstasy therefore subsides and the exhilarating joy becomes steadier. The fact that there is no longer the thrilling pleasure of rapture does not mean that the ensuing state is less happy, rather is it even more so, but the happiness is of a more refined nature, passing beyond the body which can no longer contain it. At this stage, awareness of the body recedes altogether and the world of sensuous experience is left entirely behind. One dwells in a state of complete ease and tranquillity. The mind is light and clear, very receptive and pliant without rigidity or prejudice. No tremor of negative emotion disturbs the profound and invigorating calm in which one is immersed.

In this state of deep peace, the emotions flow more and more powerfully in one swelling flood yet, at the same time, they grow ever more subtle and delicate. So, in dependence on peace, bliss arises.

Bliss

Having used up all the available superlatives for happiness and positivity, it is hard to describe a state which is happier and more positive still – and we are only halfway up the Spiral chain. But this is what bliss is: the happiness of peace raised to a yet higher degree. The process of vertical integration is now drawing up energies from a far deeper level, energies of inspiration and creativity which enhance the powerful current of emotion which, since it first bubbled up from the spring of faith, has gathered into a mighty force which sweeps all before it in one gigantic tide of happiness. All the other positive emotions are present too: an all-embracing metta, radiating to all creatures; a sympathetic compassion for all who suffer; a rejoicing in the happiness and virtue of others; gratitude and devotion to those more developed. No element of personal prejudice or predilection mars the perfect equanimity of this love.

Vertical integration continues until all the forces of mundane consciousness are flowing together so that, in dependence on bliss, arises absorption.

Absorption

Nothing is excluded from consciousness. The total energies of the whole being are united in full awareness and are brought to bear upon a single point. Everything is focused, in perfect equipoise, at the highest level of refinement. The mind is exalted and enjoys sublime happiness. It is fresh and zestful, sharp and clear, concentrated in pure awareness. Subject and object are now so fine and vibrate so closely together that it is hard to distinguish one from the other. The mind has been brought to its very peak of mundane excellence. It is from this point that the great leap takes place into the Transcendental for, in dependence on absorption, there arises *knowledge and vision of things as they really are*.

The link of absorption represents the culmination of that stage of the Path which is primarily concerned with meditation. As we noted in Chapter 2, the Path has three principle phases: morality, meditation and Wisdom. Faith and delight are connected primarily with the stage of morality; ecstasy, peace, bliss and absorption, with meditation, and the remainder of the chain with the cultivation of Transcendental Wisdom. Since the practice of meditation is one of the central methods of the Higher Evolution, we will now examine it in a little more detail.

The purpose of methods of meditation is to help us to develop systematically the higher states of consciousness. Their aim is to bring about that highest link of the mundane Path: absorption. There are other meditation techniques which are directed to the cultivation of Insight but we will not be concerned with these since they imply that absorption has already been achieved. The logic of our chain of Spiral Evolution seems to tell us that we should only start practising meditation when we have perfected the phase of morality comprising the first three links of imperfection, faith and delight.

In fact, human development is never so neat and orderly as such a formula suggests. We are not so much at one particular stage on the Path as spread out over an whole area of it. Our predominant experience, for instance, may be one of imperfection but we have periods of faith, even of delight, and there may be brief moments when we feel the first thrillings of ecstasy. We cannot really go very much further than the link that is, as it were, our base and we must beware of trying to run before we can walk but the attempt to bring into being a stage a little higher than the one we are now on will help us to consolidate the lower levels. We must, however, put our main efforts into perfecting the lower levels otherwise our practice of the higher ones will be useless. So, even though some practice of meditation may be beneficial before morality has been made firm, unless we try to make our lives more ethically sound, meditation will not get us very far. Many people who are at the stage of 'looking for something' may try meditation. It will certainly help many in their quest although, sooner or later, they must develop faith and commit themselves otherwise they can go no further.

The two basic techniques of meditation common to many schools of Buddhism are concerned with the cultivation of positive emotion on the one hand and concentration on the other. Positive emotion will, of course, be reached through concentration and concentration through positive emotion – we have seen that the higher mental states are characterized both by happiness and integration. There is some danger, however, that we will develop in a one-sided way unless we attend to both: concentration may become rather dry and even alienated from feeling and feeling may be too vague and imprecise with a tendency to distraction. Although each implies a slightly different line of development, the general principles for both techniques are the same.

When one first sits down to meditate, although all the external conditions may be ideal, it is soon apparent that there are inner forces which are going to make it very difficult to carry out the simple process of counting the breath. These mental tendencies are known as the 'hindrances' because they prevent one from becoming concentrated on the object of meditation. The hindrances are five in number and the first is *sensuous craving*. Much of one's mental activity is devoted to fantasy about various things. When one first tries to meditate, it can be quite a shock to become aware of the persistent tendency of one's mind to dwell on certain longings and preoccupations. These fantasies may be quite pleasant but they stop one from letting go of sensuous experience altogether and entering the higher dimension of archetypal form. *Hatred*, the second hindrance, similarly absorbs one in thinking of the evils of one's supposed enemies and in dwelling upon the revenge one is going to mete out to them. *Sloth and torpor* are the states of dullness and lethargy which afflict many when they try to meditate. They fall into a drowsy reverie and may even go to sleep. This state is usually induced by mental conflict going on beneath the surface of consciousness, starving the mind of energy. *Restlessness and anxiety* cause our minds to flit from topic to topic so that we never settle down to meditate at all. The last hindrance, *doubt*, is the chronic inability to commit ourselves, to anything – even to the meditation for the one session. We are unwilling to push everything aside and put ourselves wholeheartedly into following the technique.

These five – craving, hatred, sloth and torpor, restlessness and anxiety, and doubt – must all be temporarily laid aside so that we can concentrate on the breath. While we are doing the practice, we keep on returning to the breath no matter what happens. As soon as we notice that we have wandered under the influence of one or other of the hindrances, we bring ourselves back to watching the breath. The more skilful our lives are and the happier we are, the easier it will be for us to rid ourselves of the hindrances.

If we are able to avoid too much distraction by the hindrances then we will be able to carry out the meditation practice. If we are doing the 'Mindfulness of Breathing' exercise mentioned in Chapter 2, at first, we focus upon the breath very much as we would upon any object, watching it and trying to feel it as fully as we can. After a while, the whole experience becomes more subtle. The breath is no longer a gross physical sensation to us, it seems very light and delicate, even and steady. It becomes fascinating and pleasurable to sense the flow of air into and out of the body and to feel the mind becoming still and calm. At this point we pass from *trying* to meditate to meditation itself. We move from the sensuous sphere to the sphere of archetypal form. We become completely engrossed in the breath and we pass through a sequence of four states of absorption which take us to the pinnacle of the mundane chain of conditionality.

The first absorption is the *stage of horizontal integration* when all the energies of the conscious and subconscious are unified. There is, here, some subtle discursive mental activity, usually connected with the object of concentration, but it is relatively peripheral to the mind and attention is almost wholly on the breath. Feelings of ecstasy, as were described in 'link of ecstasy' (p. 160), course through the body and strong feelings of joy and bliss possess one. In the next absorption, the *stage of inspiration*, the process of vertical integration begins and one feels as if one were being nourished with creative energy from some higher source. Ecstasy and bliss are stronger still and the one-pointedness of mind has become so fine that all discursive thinking has ceased. The mind is luminously clear but no thoughts disturb its tranquillity. The third absorption is the *stage of permeation* in which the mind is completely immersed in that higher dimension of awareness which, in the previous stage, appeared only as an outside source of inspiration. All trace of the sensuous world has receded from consciousness and one moves in the sphere of pure form. Ecstasy has ceased because the reservoir of unresolved energies has been exhausted but the bliss and happiness is greater still and the mind is more sharply focused than ever. The breath has now faded from attention – not because the mind has wandered but because it has, as it were, 'passed beyond the breath'. The fourth absorption is the *stage of radiation*. One experiences a state of equipoise and balance which is also dynamic. The powerful positivity of one's mind, passing beyond the bliss of the previous stages, now seems to radiate in great waves of love and well-wishing, a kind of aura of beneficial influence. Although there are other, higher states of absorption which belong to the sphere of formlessness, they are but further refinements of this fully concentrated stage of radiation for there are no more energies to unify – integration is complète. It is only this integrated and refined mind that is capable of seeing reality. If we do not have this basis, whatever insight we may gain will only pertain to the intellectual aspects of our personality. For an insight to transform us, it must be backed by the full weight of our purified and unified mind in which reason and emotion are drawn together and resolved in the faculty of Imagination.

The worlds which correspond to these sublime states of consciousness are themselves sublime. They all belong to those spheres of archetypal form and formlessness which lie beyond the sensuous sphere. Each of the worlds of archetypal form, surpassing the one below it in beauty and delight, does have form, but it is of a subtle kind, communicating itself not by means of sense organs but directly to the mind. Here we may contemplate beauty not clothed in any earthly clay, but in its pure, ideal form. By no means are such forms abstract but they pass beyond sensuous definition. Perhaps the nearest we can get to imagining such an experience is to conceive of a world constructed of beams of light, rainbows, subtle perfumes and chords of music. The formless sphere is even more subtle for not even the pure form of the archetypal world can be perceived. Here we are in contact with the most refined essences of experience: infinite space, infinite consciousness, 'no-thing-ness – in which we go beyond the differentiation of experience into particular objects – and neither perception nor non-perception in which subject and object are so closely merged that we cannot find words to describe the experience. It is to these spheres that we gain access through meditation once we have passed through the more tangible visionary experiences of the gods of the sensuous sphere. The gods on these higher planes are born here as a result of their development of meditative states in previous lives. They are as beautiful and pure as the worlds they inhabit. They are androgynous, perfectly integrating masculine and feminine qualities. No sexual activity is found here because the gods have transcended sexual polarity and joyfully experience within themselves the play of opposites which humans seek in sex.

Immeasurably exalted as may be the highest state of absorption and the beings who inhabit it, human or divine, it is still mundane. It is still possible for evolution to be reversed if the conditions which have brought it about are exhausted and no new merit is accrued. The mundane part of the Spiral is maintained only by constant effort and mindfulness, for the Wheel is still more powerful within one than the Spiral unless it is supported by conscious striving. So strong are the powers of ignorance within us that most people would be incapable of making headway against them on their own. They need the full cooperation and encouragement of the environment and people who surround them. Ugliness, brutality and confusion make it hard to develop positive emotions. Hatred and enmity, or indifference and scorn from the people we live and work with soon wear down all but the strongest. We need a world which is beautiful and peaceful and companions who share our faith and who have more experience on the Path than we do. Without these, we will fall back again and again. No one should underestimate the effort required for the Higher Evolution –

although neither should one underestimate its rewards. If one truly wishes to ascend the Spiral then one must seek spiritual friendship. Without it, even those gods of the highest world of formlessness may slip back into lower states of being. Only with the Transcendental can one no longer fall back and one's progress is assured.

10
The Transcendental Path

After John Milton's death, an acquaintance reported that he had met nobody who could, with any certainty, ascribe motives to Milton's actions. We judge others by what we know and particularly by what moves us. The lesser man cannot, therefore, easily assess the greater because the greater man's psychology is differently based and does not conform to any mechanical pattern. His deeds spring from deeper sources, fed by the Muses and the forces of creative imagination. His personality has not that rigid structure which makes its motions predictable or easy to analyse. Those who have Transcendental attainment are even harder to fathom. They are said to resemble three beings – a ghost, a madman and a child: a ghost, because he appears out of nowhere so that one cannot tell by what agency he arrived; a madman, because his actions will not conform to the logic of convention and seem to make no sense; and a child, because he has all the whole-heartedness, energy and spontaneity of youth. The Buddha himself compared those great beings who have passed the point of no return to strange monsters swimming in the ocean's deep. They live in a quite different medium from us, the medium of Truth, and we cannot properly discern them. All we see is a dark fin breaking the waves, from time to time, or a silver flash beneath the swell. These few glimpses and the wonderful stories which voyagers tell are all we have to picture them by. It is of these great beings, moving in the waters of the Dharma, that we must now attempt to form some impression.

Up to this point, the stages of the Path we have considered have consisted in the progressive refinement of the distinction between subject and object. Experience is still divided into self and world but the self is now very light and open and the world is very subtle and beautiful. Self and world, though distinct, are in harmony and vibrate closely together. Morality has purged away the grosser negative emotions and meditation has unified consciousness, purified it of the remaining taints, and given it strength and sharpness. The mind is now able to see the real nature of things and so, in dependence on absorption, there arises *knowledge and vision of things as they really are*.

Knowledge and Vision of Things as They Really are

For the first time, the veil of delusion is lifted and reality is faced directly. This is not merely intellectual understanding but *vision*, backed by the full force of the intensified emotions and one-pointed mind. Up until this link, we have not seen things as they are at all but distorted and perverted by the greed, hatred and delusion within us. This leads us to see the world as made up of stable entities, forming desirable objects which we think can give us some deep and lasting satisfaction. Moreover, we think of ourselves as isolated units, egos which are fixed and unchanging. Having made the great evolutionary advance of dividing self from other, we attach ultimate significance to the division we have made. Even at the state of absorption, this is our basic attitude, albeit highly sublimated. But now things are seen as they really are: impermanent, insubstantial, imperfect and ugly.

We have, I hope, already sufficiently stressed that everything conditioned is part of a process whose essential nature is change. Nothing, however vast and long lasting, is exempt from this universal law. Probably, no one would deny its truth, at least of the things of this human world, although most of us act as if it were not so. We behave as if we, ourselves, were going to live for ever and we expend much time and energy in the service of things which are even more perishable. Some people maintain that there are higher beings and states that are eternal. This Buddhism denies, asserting that, throughout all the levels of existence, even amongst the highest gods, nothing is permanent and there is no supreme being who stands exempt from the law of change.

Going one step further, one who gains this level of Insight sees that what we usually perceive as things or people are, in reality, compounded of innumerable particles bound together in the complex patterns of objective phenomena. We label these formations as objects or people for the sake of practical convenience but then we attach an absolute metaphysical reality to our own labels. A tree has no reality apart from the sum of the attributes which present themselves to our senses. It is like a pointillist painting, a cloud of dancing atoms, molecules, and perhaps more subtle forces in constant motion. Even these particles are, of course, not realities but are themselves compounded of smaller units which can be subdivided indefinitely. When we analyse any object, we can never come to a substance beyond which our analysis cannot penetrate. We can never find anything conditioned which has an underlying substantial reality. We are, ourselves, constituted of parts, as we have seen in examining the five heaps which make up the psychophysical organism. All things, whether subject or object, are processes linked together in an intricate network of mutual conditions.

That all conditioned things are imperfect follows from the preceding considerations. Conditioned things are fleeting and insubstantial and cannot be sources of ultimate satisfaction or reliance. There is, of course, pleasure to be gained and happiness to be enjoyed but, within the sensuous world, that pleasure is inevitably mixed with pain and suffering. Even in the higher worlds, there is a subtle pain or frustration since consciousness is limited and confined by the constrictions of that conditioned world. Only to be beyond all worlds whatsoever gives lasting satisfaction in the experience of true perfection. One who has Insight has no illusions that conditioned experience can provide him with that perfection.

Finally, conditioned existence is seen as ugly. There is nothing within it that is worthy of man's full approbation. Such experiences as we do have of beauty are more or less pale reflections of an ideal beauty which cannot be found within the mundane. The pursuit and appreciation of beautiful things is, in fact, a search for a beauty that lies beyond the objects in the Transcendental itself.

With knowledge and vision of things as they really are, one sees that conditioned things are quite different from what one normally conceives them to be. The ordinary man is distracted by the bright surface of the world and mistakes this for reality. Of course, the objects and people of this world are real in the sense that we can perceive and interact with them but we do not see them as they really are. Insight now reveals our previous error. But it also reveals that, as it were, behind the conditioned or within its depths, there lies unconditioned reality. That reality is the ultimate nature of both the world and the self. The unconditioned is glimpsed as being permanent for, since it is empty of conditions, it is beyond change. It is seen as ultimately real although it has no fixed characteristics by which it can be defined, even the categories of existence and non-existence cannot apply to it. It is perfect and complete and is the source of the only abiding happiness and fulfilment there can be. And it is Beauty itself, the satisfaction of all desires and the fount of all pleasure. Since it is Transcendental, it cannot be caught by words which inevitably limit in defining it. It can only be perceived by the direct penetrative Insight which this stage represents.

The mundane Path finds its consummation here. The stirrings of intuition that were faith have been confirmed by direct vision. One no longer moves forward with great personal effort based on strong intuition and backed up by reason. One knows for oneself the real nature of things. Although one may still function, and function very effectively, within the world, one is not entirely of it any more. One is now a Transcendental being, not a worldly one. This is the point of no return at which one enters the stream that flows on to full Enlightenment and cannot be turned back. Though this radical change in the orientation of one's being has taken place, there remain still within one the forces of greed, hatred and delusion. Although the Wheel has been overcome, it has not been extirpated and it still exercises a strong, though never decisive, influence. The remainder of the Transcendental Path consists in the gradual eradication of its every trace. The vision has been glimpsed but now the whole being must be transformed so that it becomes its perfect expression. The Stream Entrant begins to move away from the worldly within him and so, in dependence on knowledge and vision of things as they really are, there arises disentanglement.

Disentanglement

Conditioned things have been seen for what they are and no longer are there any illusions about them. Quite naturally, old attachments based upon those false conceptions just fall away. No real effort is required to do this, they simply do not interest or involve one as they used to. Just as a child leaves behind, without really noticing that they have gone, the toys which it once cried and fought for, so one withdraws oneself from the worldly things which previously engaged all one's energies. This is not a mood of grim and moralistic asceticism but a natural movement which arises out of the experience of the supreme happiness and beauty of the Transcendental. It is a joyous and serene detachment, not one which leaves one aloof and isolated from others. One no longer clings to people out of craving, rather one is all the more capable of feeling love and compassion for them. As the Path progresses, metta and compassion become the dominant emotions which underlie one's actions. One becomes, more and more, quite simply, a manifestation of compassion.

Disentanglement marks the changing basis of one's involvement with conditioned things. It gives way to an even deeper and more steady detachment as, in dependence on disentanglement, *dispassion* arises.

Dispassion

So powerful, now, is the effect of one's Insight that one is not stirred by worldly things at all. One feels, not indifference, but an equal love for all things. With one's base in the Transcendental, nothing can disturb the perfect calm and firm tranquillity of one's being.

This great stream, flooding towards Enlightenment, continues at more and more subtle levels and so, in dependence on dispassion, there arises *liberation*.

Liberation

So far, the force of one's Insight has carried one to the limits of the conditioned. One has been liberated from the psychological forces which bind and constrict the mind and which give rise to craving and hatred. But now the most subtle of barriers is attacked. One tears off the bonds of the most finely woven wrong views. One is liberated from the dualism of conditioned and Unconditioned. From our worldly point of view, there is, most certainly, a conditioned and an Unconditioned. When we come to experience the true nature of each, however, we find that that distinction was merely made from our own point of view, although very much to our spiritual advantage. When one sees the conditioned in its depths, one realizes that it has no fixed or definable nature. It is as if one is gazing at smoke, billowing from a chimney: one can never capture its essential shape because it does not have one – it is nothing but a constant flow of ever-changing forms. One's mind can never grasp or fix it and one must simply stand back and enjoy the rich variety of its configurations. The smoke is empty of all definable characteristics. In reality, all conditioned things are like this. We may arbitrarily define them as trees, or neighbours, or whatever, but their real and essential nature we cannot grasp. They are empty of such characteristics and it is that Emptiness which is their inmost nature.

Emptiness, in this most profound sense, is not a black hole of nothingness, but the ultimate unboundedness of things, the fact that nothing can ever finally be tied down. Emptiness is, therefore, infinite potentiality, limitless creativity. If we look deeply into the heart of any object or, more especially, of any person, we will see this Emptiness which is absolute creativity. Everything, seen as it really is, is the perfect expression of transcendent potentiality. This is the true nature of the conditioned. The Unconditioned, too, is devoid of characteristics, indefinable, and it cannot be grasped by the mind. It too is characterized only by Emptiness. The conditioned and the Unconditioned are both empty. If one looks at the conditioned one sees, in its heart, the Unconditioned and if one looks into the Unconditioned there is the conditioned. With liberation, one is freed from that subtle delusion which leads one to separate the one from the other although, it must once more be stressed, it is a delusion from that exalted perspective alone – not from ours for we have far grosser delusions to deal with first. One is liberated then from both the conditioned and the Unconditioned. One's mind is almost identical with that potent Emptiness – that Full Emptiness as it has been called – and there is but an hair's breadth which separates one from it.

The final barrier that stands between one and complete liberation is the very concept of freedom itself, even of Emptiness. One must be freed of freedom, see that Emptiness is empty. All thoughts and views, even the categories of Buddhism itself which have launched one to this point, must be abandoned in the full and direct experience of reality, unmediated by any concept or image. The last trace of any distinction between self and world must be relinquished. In this way, in dependence on liberation, there arises *recognition that the poisonous mental floods have been destroyed.*

Recognition That the Poisonous Mental Floods have been Destroyed

This last link in the evolutionary chain is the point of Enlightenment. Buddhahood is devoid of all negative tendencies whatsoever, for the poisonous mental floods which spring from our defensive egoity and which intoxicate us, filling our lives with their noxious vapours, are completely dried up.

There are three of them, the first of which is the poison of *craving for sense-experience*. This is that familiar longing to fix and confirm the ego by gaining sensuous pleasures, for without their tangible experience we feel weak and insubstantial. The Enlightened person dwells in the utter security of the Transcendental and has, therefore, no need of such hollow sanctuary as the senses afford. He is able to use the senses, even to enjoy them, but he has no neurotic need for their pleasures. Then there is the poison of *craving for existence* on any plane, in any world. The ego craves some definite state, some world in which it can define itself against everything else. Beyond self and other, the Buddha has no need of such embodiment, although he chose to function through a body and in a world in order to help beings to gain freedom. He has also extinguished the most basic poison of all, that of *ignorance*, the refusal to see things clearly out of fear that our ego will be overwhelmed. His mind absorbed in Truth and his heart in bliss, the Buddha has nothing to fear from the non-dual awareness in which he lives. Not the faintest trace of any tendency towards the Wheel is left in him, even in its most rarefied form.

This stage is not only one of destruction of all negative tendencies, it is one of recognition that that is what has happened. The Enlightened individual knows that the poisonous mental floods are dried up, quite clearly, without any self-aggrandisement or inflation. He knows that he is Enlightened. We have passed beyond the power of language to describe his experience.

The whole of the Transcendental Path, indeed the complete evolutionary Spiral, can be traversed in a single human lifetime. Those beings who die at any of the stages on the Path short of full Enlightenment, however, will be reborn according to their level of consciousness and the extent of the influence which the Wheel still has on them. We will now examine the four kinds of Transcendental being and the rebirths which await them.

The *Stream Entrant* is the one in whom vision has first dawned. He has, of course, already traversed the mundane Path and so he combines the qualities of steadfast morality and firm faith in the Three Jewels with that burning vigour, delicacy of feeling and sharpness of mind which the absorptions perfect. He is full of love and goodwill for his fellow creatures and has unfailing positivity. He is said to have broken the first three of ten fetters which tie us to the conditioned: the fetters of personality-view, doubt and dependence on morality and observances as ends in themselves. These are the grosser veils of ignorance which blind us to the full radiance of reality. *Personality-view* is the opinion either that there is an unchanging soul or spirit which survives death or that the personality is identical with the body and, therefore, ceases at death. These two, eternalism and nihilism, render it impossible to see the real nature of things as an ever-changing process. This has been called the fetter of habit, for it is the tendency to see things in a fixed, habitual way without recognizing that everything is constantly coming into being and passing away. We even see ourselves like this, as if we always are and always will be the same.

Doubt as a fetter does not mean the careful refusal to accept something until sound evidence has been adduced but a culpable unwillingness to make up one's mind about things. One prefers to remain in perplexity and continues to throw up objections long after conviction would have been reasonable. Such doubt is emotional in basis. One will not clarify one's mind on any issue because one would then have to act upon whatever conclusion one had reached. So one wavers and dithers and never moves. This has been termed the fetter of vagueness, for the doubter refuses to clarify his mind and likes to keep things woolly and undefined. The Stream Entrant is able to place himself wholeheartedly behind his Insight.

Dependence on morality and observances as ends in themselves is that tendency to superficial practice which constantly threatens those who follow the Path. Instead of observing the precepts in order to develop the underlying ethical sensitivity which they express, we keep them as if they were a list of rules. Instead of meditating in order to develop higher states of consciousness, we merely sit for a few minutes out of habit or to keep up appearances. What start out as important and useful practices and guidelines become quite external activities whose true meaning is lost. This is the fetter of superficiality: we just go through the outer motions without looking for the inner meaning. Precepts, spiritual exercises, ritual and ceremony all have an important place in Buddhism and are very effective means of Higher Evolution but, unless they are performed with an awareness of what is being done and why, then they may actively hinder us. The Stream Entrant has broken through these fetters and, it is said, will gain Enlightenment within seven human rebirths. He may also be reborn into higher realms, from time to time, but he can never again be born in any of the four worlds of suffering.

The *Once-returner* is the next of the Transcendental beings. He has, and surpasses, all the qualities of the Stream Entrant and, in addition, he has weakened the next two fetters: *sensuous craving* and *aversion*. Even at this exalted level these basic negative emotions are still present and, though their power is considerably weakened, they still exert their baneful influence. The Stream Entrant has broken the fetters of confused understanding but the emotions are far harder to transform. The Once-returner has sufficient of the cock, the snake and the pig within him to bring him back to the human world one more time during which he will gain full Enlightenment.

The *Non-returner* finally breaks the fetters of sensuous craving and aversion, which the Once-returner merely weakened. He has broken all the bonds which tie him to the sphere of sensuous experience so that he is no longer reborn into any of its worlds. He has, however, still subtle illusions and tenuous cravings which tie him to the worlds of archetypal form and formlessness. Within these higher heavens, he will traverse the remaining steps of the Path and reach Enlightenment.

The *Enlightened* are the last in this series of four Transcendental Beings. They have broken the remaining five fetters which tie one to the conditioned, even at its most rarefied. Those who have reached this stage have destroyed the two fetters of *craving for experience in the worlds of archetypal form* and *of formlessness*. The desire to achieve and settle down in one of these states is said to correspond to the longing of the theist to dwell in heaven with God. But the Enlightened break through even the most attenuated duality such desires manifest. They break also the fetter of *conceit* which, here, is the last trace of attachment to ego-identity such as the Non-returner still has. The fetter of *restlessness* is the almost imperceptible disturbance produced by that last, faint dividing line between subject and object. This, too, is finally dissolved in the all-pervading bliss of Transcendental non-duality. The last fetter is the chain of *ignorance*. In the mind of the Non-returner there is still a very thin veil covering the full radiance of reality, the most refined delusion of subject and object. This, too, is torn aside and the Truth shines forth, absolutely clear and unobstructed.

One who has attained this state is no longer reborn but this does not mean that he does not exist. It is said that when an Enlightened person dies, he neither exists nor does he not exist – nor both nor neither! He passes beyond our comprehension. There is nothing within our experience by which we can grasp the nature of his being. Our language is built out of our common experience in the sensuous world. It can never adequately describe the Enlightened one for, whatever we say about him, if taken literally, can be misunderstood since Enlightenment utterly transcends the mundane whose language we must use. We can, for instance, describe the state negatively as an absence of all unwholesome emotions, the destruction of those poisonous mental floods and of the Wheel with all its forces. Sometimes, Buddhism resorts to a steady denial of all the categories of thought, saying that Enlightenment is not this, not that, so that we are forced to stop trying to understand with our intellect alone and use some deeper, more intuitive faculty. But this does not tell us what the state actually *is* and may lead us to suppose that it is simply a complete vacuum. We can try using superlatives, describing it as the state wherein all the most positive qualities which we revere are raised to their highest degree. This has the virtue of giving us the image of Buddhahood as something eminently desirable but introduces the danger that we may think of it as being merely the best of the mundane rather than being on another level altogether. Sometimes paradox is used, forcing us to join two contradictory ideas together so that we must intuit something which transcends them both. Perhaps the most effective means of conveying some flavour of the Enlightened state is by appeal to the Imagination through the use of symbols and poetic images. It is this kind of communication of the ultimate goal of human existence which we will be encountering in the next chapter.

11

The Mandala of the Five Buddhas

The potential for Enlightenment lies deep within us. It is no mere abstract possibility but is experienced as an upward pressure within our self-awareness. It could even be said that, from an absolute point of view, we are Transcendental Beings who do not recognize our own true nature. Our ultimate essence is constantly trying to manifest through us, pushing aside the egoistic personality which fights desperately for its own narrow survival. This is, fundamentally, what it is to be human – to have within one the twin currents of the Wheel and the Spiral. We are cut off, therefore, not only from elements of our psychological make-up which must be made fully conscious in the process of horizontal integration but also from our deeper spiritual and Transcendental nature to which we must open ourselves through vertical integration. Whatever we lack in our inner experience, we project on to our environment and its inhabitants. And so we invest sense objects and other people with the qualities of the Transcendental – with permanence, substantiality, perfection and beauty, qualities which they, being conditioned, cannot possess.

Projection, we have found, leads to terrible confusion and pain, for the object of our projection is not seen as it is and our lives are built upon complete illusion. But projection also gives us the opportunity to make contact with the qualities which we have projected and thus to draw them into consciousness. In this way, the one-sidedly masculine person projects femininity on to some other person. But, if he is careful, he may use the act of falling in love to cultivate his own inner femininity. He must take great care not to become tangled with that other person to their mutual disadvantage. But if he can catch his projection in the mirror, say, of poetry, and prevent it from attaching itself to its original object he may make it fully conscious, first of all, as something outside himself and then, within. Similarly, if we can head off our projection of those qualities which are really Transcendental from the world around us we can begin to incorporate them into consciousness or, rather, see that they are, ultimately, the basic nature of our own minds and of the entire universe.

Vertical projection selects either people, physical objects or visionary symbols as the screens upon which it throws its images. When we project on to people the danger arises that they may take advantage of our projection. Thus, if we fall in love, the object of our affections may exploit or manipulate our infatuation – or may fall in love, too. Rather than recapturing our latent qualities, we may end in a confused emotional tangle or, at best, trapped in conventional domesticity. Similarly, if we project idealized spiritual qualities on to someone who does not in fact possess them, he may use our devotion for his own private purposes as many modern gurus so clearly do. If, on the other hand, the object of our projection is worthy of the confidence we place in him – that is, if our projection corresponds to his actual qualities – then he will help us, in our communication with him, to draw out the same latent virtues in ourselves. This aspect of projection is part of the very important principle of spiritual friendship which is one of the keys to human growth.

Physical objects may be the vehicle for our projected potential. A lump of clay or wood fashioned into the likeness of a seated man – a statue of the Buddha – may be a focus for very genuine feelings of devotion. As far as the devotee is concerned, the figure *is* the Buddha – although, at the same time, he knows that it is but a statue. The more devotion he is able to experience and the more readily he is able to feel that, when he bows to the statue, he is bowing to the Buddha himself, the more deeply he will contact his own inner potential for Buddhahood. Some schools of Buddhism have taken advantage of this faculty of vertical projection on to physical objects by developing a very beautiful and effective system of rituals using a rich variety of symbolic implements and forms.

Visionary experiences, in which we see archetypal figures enacting myths which have deep spiritual significance, are also projections of the vertical kind, this time using only the inner eye of Imagination. Some forms of Buddhism have raised this aspect of spiritual practice to a very high level indeed. A system of figures of Buddhas and other beings has evolved which represents, in symbolic form, the Transcendental in its myriad qualities. The contemplation, in imagination, of these figures allows us to project more and more of our own inner nature. They are very beautiful, made of bright and clear colours, richly dressed and adorned with jewels, glowing with brilliant light and so, as we see them more and more vividly, our own sense of beauty is stirred and we are lifted up the mundane links of the Spiral. But the figures are also significant, they carry implements and make gestures which have a Transcendental meaning so that the more cognitive aspect of Imagination is also aroused. The figures embody both Beauty and Truth, and we are led on by our fascination for them until we project not only the spiritual within us but the Transcendental also. At this highest point, the figures are not just beautiful and rich in meaning but they express reality itself. We have seen, as it were, through the form and colour to the Emptiness beyond which is our own true nature.

Of the Buddhist schools which utilize these symbolic forms, each has its own system which varies in detail from the others, although the basic principles are the same for all. There are many hundreds of these figures, each representing Transcendental reality from a somewhat different point of view. Thus the figures each embody a quality such as Wisdom, Compassion, Energy and so forth, all aspects of the Enlightened mind. In a sense, the entire assembly of forms is one figure, viewed from different perspectives in the same way as the many facets of a cut jewel refract the fire at the centre of each in its own surface. Every figure contains all the others and, in its turn, is contained by them.

All the Buddhas and other Transcendental beings arrange themselves in a kind of sacred circle, called a mandala in Sanskrit. A mandala is an harmonious and symmetrical network of archetypal forms placed in a circle about one central figure; it represents the dynamic totality of the Enlightened mind in all its various dimensions.

We are here concerned with the Mandala of the Five Buddhas which consists of one Buddha seated at the centre of the circle with four others at the cardinal points. In a sense, each of the four outer figures is but an aspect of the central one, drawing out his many endowments. At the same time, each of the five encompasses all of the others and each becomes himself the centre of a sub-mandala with his own surrounding figures, elaborating yet further his own particular qualities. In principle, this process of unfoldment could go on indefinitely, each figure emanating more figures which are, at the same time, aspects of the one central figure and themselves the totality of the Enlightened mind. The beings in the Mandala are engaged in a kind of exuberant dance that suggests the infinite creativity of Enlightenment and its perfect completeness and harmony.

The Mandala is set in the midst of space which is perceived as a clear blue sky, stretching to a luminous infinity in every direction. It is surrounded by a threefold wall through which we must pass if we are to glimpse the Buddhas themselves. There is, first of all, a wall of *lotus flowers*. Lotuses are a very common symbol in Buddhist iconography not only because they are magnificent when in full bloom. Though their roots are nourished by the mud at the depths of a lake yet they stand clear of the water, pure and undefiled by the dirt from which they have grown. They suggest, therefore, growth from a grosser to a finer level, and thus purification. In other contexts, as when they form the thrones for the Buddhas in the Mandala, they indicate transcendence, for the lotus stands clear of the earth and water which nourished it and blossoms in the clear radiance of the sun. So, to pass through the wall of lotuses, one must be pure. One must have practised morality and one must be purged of all unskilfulness. A wall of *thunderbolts* meets us next. The thunderbolt is a very rich symbol indeed, often used as the active counterpart of the more soft, receptive qualities which the lotus flower suggests. A thunderbolt is irresistibly powerful and is said to be itself indestructible; yet it can destroy everything in its path as it flashes from the sky. It comes, therefore, to represent, among other things, unshakeable determination, the kind of commitment to realizing the Ideal which allows nothing to stand in its way. One must have this kind of dedication to enter the Mandala. Finally, there is a wall of flames, for flames transmute: they consume gross material substances and change them into the heat and smoke which billows upwards from a fire. Thus flames represent the transformation of every particle of our being. We must die to our old selves, be swallowed up in the fire of spiritual practice, so that we can be reborn within the Mandala.

We enter the Mandala from the East, the direction of the rising sun. Before us there is Akshobya, the Imperturbable, the blue Buddha in his realm of Complete Joy. His skin is the dark blue of the tropic sky at midnight, deep and mysterious, dark yet luminous. He sits, as do all the Buddhas, in lotus posture and he is adorned with silk robes of the same dark blue as his body, covered in golden embroidery. On his head is a golden crown with five crests, delicately worked and covered in jewels. He wears a necklace of gold and other ornaments on his arms and feet and his whole body glows with brilliant light so that he is surrounded by a shining aura. His left hand rests in his lap while his right touches the earth before him. This gesture recalls the legendary incident before the historical Buddha's Enlightenment when he was challenged by the personified forces of evil to state his right to be seated on that spot where all the Buddhas of the past had sat. The Buddha touched the ground before him in this way, calling the Earth Goddess to witness that he had been making his spiritual effort for innumerable lifetimes so that he had a firm basis of ethical and meditative experience. The gesture suggests confidence, deep-rootedness and the same kind of determination which the Buddha manifested at the moment before his attainment of Enlightenment. In the palm of his left hand Akshobya holds a thunderbolt, symbol of irresistible conviction and commitment and of a power which penetrates to the very heart of things. He is seated on a great blue lotus which is supported by two blue elephants which stand with massive strength.

Each Buddha is the head of a 'family' of Transcendental Beings which are further refractions of the aspect of Enlightenment which he embodies and which arrange themselves around him to form a new mandala within the greater one. Akshobya is head of the Thunderbolt family whose qualities are penetrative Wisdom and the destruction of all barriers and obstacles. Many members of the family are shown in 'wrathful' form – powerfully built, surrounded by flames, and with faces glaring with anger – which draws out the associations of strength and positive destructiveness of this clan. All of these subsidiary figures are Bodhisattvas (a term we will explore in detail in the next chapter). Briefly, a Bodhisattva is a being who has dedicated himself to the attainment of Enlightenment for the sake of all beings, out of his deep compassion for the suffering he sees around him. The Bodhisattvas of the Mandala are of such lofty attainment that they come to represent Buddhahood manifesting itself as an active force in all the worlds of the conditioned. The chief Bodhisattvas connected with Akshobya are Vajrapani and Kshitigarbha. Vajrapani, the Thunderbolt-bearer, represents the unconditioned dynamism of Buddhahood. Kshitigarbha is the Bodhisattva who enters the realms of hell in order to help its denizens gain liberation – representing the extent to which active compassion is prepared to go in order to help beings.

Each Buddha is the embodiment of a Wisdom, the five together constituting the full depth and range of Enlightened awareness. The Mirror-like Wisdom shines from the heart of Akshobya as a pure, dazzling white light. Just as a mirror reflects an absolutely faithful image of the object before it, so Akshobya's Wisdom sees things exactly as they are without distortion or interpretation, perfectly objectively.

If we take any feature of conditioned experience and contemplate it deeply enough we will find that it opens out into the Transcendental. The figures in the Mandala thus not only express all Transcendental qualities but also correspond to every aspect of the mundane. Each of the five heaps into which human experience may be divided (form, feeling, recognition, motivation and consciousness) is, in purified form, one of the Buddhas. Some schools have worked out an elaborate network of these alignments which reveal to us the ultimate identity of the mundane and the Transcendental. Akshobya's quality of firmness, solidity and objective awareness corresponds to the more stable and objective elements in our experience – to the heap of form. The passion of hatred, with its destructiveness, corresponds to the thunderbolt aspect of the blue Buddha – his quality of bursting through all barriers and obstacles to the heart of Truth. He is therefore associated with the realm of hell which is the manifestation of hatred.

Following the track of the sun, we come next to the Southern quarter of the Mandala in which we see the Buddha Ratnasambhava, the Jewel Born, in his realm, the Glorious. He is golden yellow, like a field of ripe corn in bright sunlight, and he, too, is richly dressed in royal robes and jewellery and is crowned with a five-pointed crown. His left hand rests in his lap and he reaches forward with his right hand in the gesture of giving. His open palm contains a jewel – the Wish-fulfilling Gem which instantly grants all desires. This is the 'Triple Gem' of Buddha, Dharma and Sangha, the threefold Ideal which alone can ultimately satisfy us. He sits on a golden lotus throne which is supported by two powerful yellow horses. The horse, to a nomadic people, means wealth and in many cultures it has been a sign of aristocracy. It also suggests a journey – a spiritual voyage such as that on which the Buddha-to-be set forth when he left his life at home, riding on his faithful charger. Further, it signifies a messenger bringing news from distant places just as does the Buddhist 'Windhorse' which carries the Three Jewels on its back, to all beings.

In the Jewel family, of which Ratnasambhava is the head, is Ratnapani, He Who Holds the Jewel in his Hand, and Jambhala, a strange figure who squeezes a mongoose with his left hand so that it vomits forth jewels – a kind of Indian cornucopia.

A yellow light shining from Ratnasambhava's heart is the light of the Wisdom of Equality. Everything is perceived as having the same fundamental nature – which is Emptiness. Beneath the external differences of things is one underlying reality – although that reality should not be thought of as a substantial entity but as the principle of absolute creativity which underlies all things. It is this basic nature which Ratnasambhava sees. He sees the creative wealth inherent in all things and the Transcendental beauty which pervades the entire universe – he could even be called the Buddha of Beauty just as Akshobya is often called the Buddha of Wisdom. His Wisdom corresponds to the heap of feeling since the Ideal Beauty which he embodies is the Transcendental counterpart of pleasure. Because he sees all things as having one underlying nature he does not compare himself with others – he therefore transcends the passion of pride. Pride is the failing of the human realm, for self-consciousness can, all too easily, degenerate into self-conceit. Ratnasambhava's realm is therefore aligned with the human world.

In the Western quarter, the Buddha Amitabha, Infinite Light, presides over the realm Sukhavati, the Abode of Bliss. He is deep red, the colour of the setting sun, and is richly adorned. His hands are folded in his lap in the gesture of meditation and in them is cupped a red lotus blossom. He sits on a red lotus throne which is upheld by two peacocks, their shimmering fans uplifted. The peacock was thought to derive the brilliant hues of its plumage from the poison of the snakes on which it was said to feed – a symbol, thus, of purification and transformation.

Amitabha's family is the Lotus family which contains many deeply reverenced Bodhisattvas and Buddhas, the most well known of whom is Avalokiteshvara, the Lord Who Looks Down, the quintessential embodiment of Compassion. The family also contains two historical figures: Gautama Shakyamuni, the founder of the Buddhist tradition, and Padmasambhava, the great teacher who established the Dharma among the Tibetans, by whom he is known as 'the Second Buddha'. Amitabha has a kind of special jurisdiction over our own era and, since he is the Buddha of the West, perhaps over the Western world as well.

Amitabha represents, above all, Love – the active Compassion that shines in the glowing red of his body. A ray of red light, the Discriminating Wisdom, beams from his heart. The Mirror-like Wisdom sees everything as it is and the Wisdom of Equality sees everything as having the same Emptiness as its fundamental nature; the Discriminating Wisdom sees each and everything as unique with its own minute particularities. Amitabha's Love is not mere generalized goodwill, it is a burning compassion, sensitive to the individual needs of every creature. This Wisdom corresponds to the heap of recognition which is the faculty whereby we recognize things and set them off from their surroundings. The intense emotion of Compassion is the Transcendental counterpart of craving which is a strong attachment to particular things. Craving is the poison which drives the hungry ghosts and so their world is aligned with Amitabha's realm, Sukhavati.

The Buddha of the Northern quarter is Amoghasiddhi, Unobstructed Success, who dwells in the Realm of Accumulated Actions. He is green in colour and raises his right hand in the gesture of fearlessness, conveying confidence and serenity. In his left hand, resting in his lap, he holds two thunderbolts crossed – a symbol of immense power in which two forces are united, each of which is irresistible, indicating a Transcendence which harmonizes all fundamental polarities, such as that of subject and object. His throne is supported by two strange creatures, called Shang-Shangs. These are composite animals, birds up to the neck, from which sprouts the upper body of a man who clashes two cymbals as he flies.

Amoghasiddhi's family is the Action family which has, amongst its members, the Bodhisattva Vishvapani, He Who Holds the Universe. Also in this clan is Sarvanivaranavishkambhih, He Who Destroys the Hindrances.

The green radiance from Amoghasiddhi's heart is the All-performing Wisdom. Wisdom is no passive quality, it is not merely the ability to see things clearly. It is also the knowledge of what must be done, what actions will bring about the fulfilment of all beings. It is a very mysterious power, able to see connections and interrelations invisible to ordinary cunning, so much in tune with the fundamental rhythm of the universe that it can act with complete confidence of success. This Wisdom is very subtle and Amoghasiddhi's movements are barely perceptible as he fulfils his aims. The end to which his efforts are always directed is the highest happiness of all creatures. Amoghasiddhi, since he is the Buddha of Action, corresponds to the heap of motivation, for his compassionate activity is the Transcendental counterpart of volition. The poison of envy leads to very aggressive and competitive behaviour, all undertaken to surpass or confound rivals. Amoghasiddhi's activity is even more vigorous but it is directed to the welfare of others. The world of the titans, who are motivated by envy, aligns with his realm.

In the centre of the Mandala is Vairochana, the Illuminator, and his realm is the All-Pervading Circle. He is, in a sense, the sum of all the Buddhas and combines all their qualities. He is therefore pure white, since white light is a blend of all colours. Each of the Buddhas is the idealization of an aspect of Enlightenment, particularly as exemplified in the career of the historical Buddha. Thus Amoghasiddhi sums up that determination and steadiness which Gautama displayed when he touched the earth to call the Earth Goddess to witness. So Vairochana is the idealization of what might be termed the central function of a Buddha, the teaching of the way to the Transcendental. The occasion which has come most closely to represent this in Gautama Buddha's life is the teaching of his five former ascetic disciples immediately after his Enlightenment. This is known as the First Turning of the Wheel of the Dharma. Probably this eight-spoked golden wheel which has come to symbolize the Dharma was originally a solar disc in Indian tradition; and it later came to be considered an attribute of kingship. The king was the one who occupied the position of the sun in society and so he held the sun-wheel as a symbol of his authority. The Buddha occupies that same position in the universe from a spiritual point of view. He is the source of the nourishing light of Truth and, when he turns the Wheel of the Dharma, it sends forth golden beams which illumine the hearts of men, darkened by ignorance. So Vairochana, the Illuminator, is the ideal form of this teaching function of the Buddha and, like a great sun disc, he holds the wheel of the Dharma to his heart and turns it so that it burns ever more brightly. Vairochana is a kind of Transcendental Sun-King, blazing at the centre of the Mandala. His white lotus throne is supported by two great white lions for the lion is the king of beasts and, it is said, when he roars all other beasts fall silent. The Buddha's teaching is a lion's roar because all lesser teachings are silenced by its depth and grandeur. The family of Vairochana is the Buddha family and its principal member is Manjushri, the Bodhisattva of Wisdom.

The blue light which shines from Vairochana's heart is the Wisdom of the Sphere of the Dharma. The whole of existence, from the lowest hell realm to the most refined heaven, is seen as Truth. Wherever one looks, whatever one contemplates, one is faced by the Dharma. The Transcendental is perceived as non-different from the mundane, the mundane as non-different from the Transcendental. At one and the same time, with the Wisdom of the Sphere of the Dharma, conditioned things are seen as objects and people and also as Empty, as manifestations of Absolute Reality.

The heap of consciousness which illumines the objects of perception is the mundane equivalent of the Transcendental Wisdom of Vairochana, the sun of Truth. The absolute brilliance of his awareness corresponds to the darkness of ignorance. The gods, who are at the summit of mundane existence as Vairochana is of all reality, are separated from the Transcendental only by their ignorance of the real nature of things and so their world aligns with Vairochana's realm. That realm is the All-Pervading Circle, a kind of circle without centre or circumference. For though Vairochana represents centrality and kingship, it is of a Transcendental kind. The centre is everywhere, at every point in the unverse, for Transcendental awareness is not identified with any particular place in space or time. Though he is at the heart of the Mandala, he is also at every other point within it . . . and outside it.

The Five Buddhas in their Mandala with their attendant Bodhisattvas present in symbolic form all the qualities of Enlightenment. The contemplation of their shapes and colours, their various emblems and figures, will help us to project more and more of the Transcendental qualities which are within us. The more vividly the Mandala is seen and the more beautiful and brilliant the whole vision appears, the nearer to reality will we approach. In the end, the Five Buddhas are not really to be found in their symbolic forms. One must go beyond their shapes and colours to their very essence. To see the Five Buddhas in their true form, one must see the Transcendental face to face – one must gain Enlightenment.

12
The Bodhisattva and the World

In the infinite blue sky of absolute space, the Buddha Amitabha sits, poised in the perfect peace of Transcendental Meditation. His body glows the fiery red of the setting sun, an aura of universal love that penetrates the entire universe. On his calm features is the faint smile of ineffable bliss, mingled with highest Wisdom and Compassion. From his heart, a ray of ruby light shines forth, out into the furthest reaches of the cosmos. At the end of this piercing beam, the glorious figure of a young prince manifests itself. His skin is pure white, the colour of virgin snow when the sun first gleams on its surface. He is dressed in richly coloured silken robes, embroidered with golden flowers. On his head, he wears a crown with its five Wisdom crests and the jewels of the six Perfections adorn his body. His finely proportioned figure is strong but lithe and graceful. His features have all the fineness of Wisdom and the fullness of Compassion. His eyes are clear and penetrating and they are filled with tears. He is Avalokiteshvara, the Lord Who Looks Down in Compassion, the Bodhisattva of Compassion and he weeps as he beholds the manifold sufferings of all the beings in the six realms and three spheres of existence.

As he gazes down at the universe, he feels utterly helpless. Transcendental being though he is, he cannot help everyone. So intensely does he enter into the individual agony of every creature that his body cannot absorb or express the power of his emotion and it bursts into fragments. His head splits into eleven pieces, each of which forms another head, searching yet more intently for beings in need: one faces in the direction of each of the four cardinal and four intermediate points, one to the zenith, one to the nadir and one in the centre. No being, however minute, goes unnoticed. His shattered body sprouts a thousand arms which fan out in a great circle around him. In the palm of each hand is an eye, the eye of Transcendental Awareness which sees

each creature with complete clarity. In each of the hands is an implement: a weapon, book, jewel, food, fire, whatever is needed by any
being to help him to grow beyond his suffering. The hands reach out to
every corner of every world, however remote, bringing the aid appropriate to each individual. Tirelessly, joyfully, Avalokiteshvara works,
his eleven heads seeking out suffering and his thousand arms bringing
relief. Although he feels the pains of every other being as if they were
his own, yet is he inseparably immersed in the supreme bliss of Transcendental Realization and, though he works without ceasing out of
his bottomless Compassion, he feels his work to be a joyous play. He
vows that he will not cease that playful activity until the last being has
been helped to pass beyond suffering.

Even now, he considers that more must be done and, from his heart,
he radiates six beams of light: white, green, red, dark blue, light blue
and yellow. Each of the rays enters one of the six realms of existence
and there manifests a Buddha who comes in a guise appropriate to the
beings to whom he appears. In the realm of hell, a dark-blue Buddha
brings ambrosial ointment which he pours on the hell beings, soothing
their sufferings. In the world of the hungry ghosts, a red Buddha bears
food and drink which will at last give them true nourishment.
Amongst the animals, a light-blue Buddha appears carrying a book
which gives them the culture and vision to lift them beyond their
instincts. In the world of the titans, a green Buddha, wearing full
armour, wields a flaming sword. It is the sword of Wisdom and he
shows them how to fight against ignorance and darkness. In the
human world, a yellow Buddha comes wearing the orange robe of a
monk and holding a begging bowl and staff, teaching them how to
lead the spiritual life. Finally, a white Buddha plays a lute to the gods.
His tune is the melody of impermanence which wakes the gods to the
transience of their present pleasures.

Avalokiteshvara manifests himself at every level of existence and
brings to every single living being the means for his liberation – if he
will only take it. His Compassion is, at once, completely universal and
impartial and, at the same time, responsive to the particular needs of
every single individual. His field of activity is infinite space and his era is
eternity. He never ceases to help all living beings to gain Enlightenment. He is the true Bodhisattva.

The image of the six Buddhas, manifestations of the Bodhisattva
Avalokiteshvara who appear in the six realms of the Wheel of Life, is of

very profound significance and provides us with a suitable symbol around which to synthesize all we have discussed so far and to bring it to its culmination. In the first place, the image tells us something about the spiritual needs of beings in the various worlds. In each, the needs are different and the Bodhisattva responds in an appropriate form. Even within our human world, people are of varying temperaments and types and thus have different spiritual requirements. There is, in principle, but one evolutionary Path, for the same Ideals, the same ethical values, the same truths hold good for everyone. But the outward form which that one principal Path will take will vary from one individual to the next. Buddhism has always applied this truth and has developed new ways of expressing the one eternal Dharma in each new culture and age. Moreover, Buddhism presents, even within one school, fashioned for a particular time and place, many different approaches so that each person moves forward from his own particular point of contact with the Dharma. Some people respond more to meditation, others to study, and for others it is work for the Dharma which draws them. While all aspects of spiritual life must eventually be brought into harmony, initially it is likely to be one or another which attracts. The Dharma, though universal in its appeal, is individual in its application. It is not an abstract set of quasi-mathematical theorems but a living communication between the Enlightened mind and the individual unenlightened being. The Bodhisattva does not impose his preconceived notions of growth upon the beings he encounters or try to fit them to the procrustean bed of his dogmas. He sees beings as they are and he gives them what they need in order to unfold for themselves their own inner potential.

To the hell beings he brings soothing balm for their sufferings. Someone in that state of extreme hatefulness needs very careful handling. One must guard against their tendency to see a threat where none was intended and, if possible, some objectivity must be introduced into their experience. In this way, they will be able to recognize their own hatred as the source of their pain and frustration. But, first of all, the Bodhisattva relieves their agony. Wherever there is suffering, whatever its source, he tries to remove it because excess of pain so dominates the mind and numbs awareness that it is almost impossible to rise to any higher level. Only when the agony has abated will it be possible to absorb the Dharma. So the Bodhisattva soothes the fury of the demon, removes the torments that torture him, and then teaches him the Dharma.

The hungry ghost is filled with neurotic longings but the objects that he craves cannot nourish him and, indeed, only increase his pain. He suffers from a sense of inner emptiness which he tries to fill with external gratifications. The Bodhisattva brings substantial food which will nourish him. He makes him face up to his own emptiness and recognize what it is that he really wants. If his desires are simply repressed instinctual needs then he can satisfy them in a healthy way and if they are of a deeper nature he can find fulfilment for them in the Dharma.

The animal is totally immersed in the body and has no wider perspective on life than food, sex and sleep. Avalokiteshvara's emanation brings him a book, representing culture. He awakens him to the life of the mind and heart, to beauty and to the Imagination. For the first time, the animal raises his head from the grass on which he is grazing to see the limitless expanse of the sky. He begins to see that his life has some meaning and that he has a destiny.

The titans, in their intense envy, battle and intrigue to dominate and to possess the wish-fulfilling tree. They must be met with a power they will respect and so the Bodhisattva appears as a warrior, clad in armour and brandishing a sword. Yet he does not harm anyone with his weapons. He teaches the titans to channel their inordinate energies into the battle for the Higher Evolution and to use their might, not to destroy but to cut through confusion and ignorance and to reveal the Truth.

In the human world, there is communication and cooperation so that culture can come about. But that culture can easily be perverted so that the human world degenerates into one of the worlds of suffering. There must be a higher aspiration if the human state is to endure. The human being must commit himself to following the spiritual Path. So the Bodhisattva appears in the guise of a full-time follower of the Dharma and he encourages others to Go for Refuge to the Three Jewels and to lead a life based upon them.

The Bodhisattva approaches the gods on their own terms. Lapped already in pleasure, they respond to the beauty of the melody he plays upon his lute. It has, perhaps, a haunting quality. It is lovely, but it can never be caught and savoured to eternity: the music always flows on, but eventually it comes to an end. Just by listening to it the gods are reminded of mortality, for in their extreme happiness and delight they hardly notice the passing of time. They are shaken from their complacency and spurred to reach yet higher on the Spiral of Evolution and to change the brittle pleasures of heaven for the permanent bliss of the Transcendental.

The Bodhisattvas in each realm represent the Transcendental within the mundane. Whatever our state of mind, whatever the world we occupy, Enlightenment is still there. If we only could see clearly enough or enter the full depth of things we would see them as they really are. And if we see the conditioned as it is then we also see the unconditioned. Each world, looked at with the eye of Truth, is fundamentally Empty, the field of limitless potentiality. Within each and every world, there is the Bodhisattva.

Not only do the Bodhisattvas signify the unconditioned principle immanent within the conditioned world – the transcendence of the object – but also the Enlightened consciousness within self-consciousness – the transcendence of the subject. The Bodhisattva represents the evolutionary force inherent within all consciousness. It is part of the basic nature of consciousness that it seeks to expand to higher levels. Because we fear for the loss of our present level of self-consciousness, we fight against that tendency to grow with all the vigour of greed, hatred and delusion. Our efforts are directed to preventing our own growth, it seems! Among all the forces, however, that have shaped the world in which we find ourselves, forces generated by our own past volitions, there is, at least, some trace of the evolutionary urge. This is the force which drives consciousness at every level to go beyond itself. Self-consciousness is driven to burst the boundaries of subject and object at its lowest levels, and then to swell beyond each new, more refined duality. Evolution essentially consists in this process of self-transcendence at higher and higher levels until self is finally fully transcended in Enlightenment. This force is the Bodhisattva within each being.

The Bodhisattva is the link between the mundane and the Transcendental. He represents the drive within the mundane to fulfil itself in the Transcendental. But also, as the emanation of Amitabha, one of the Ideal Buddhas of the Mandala, the Bodhisattva is the movement of the Transcendental towards the mundane. The Bodhisattva within us is aided in his upward struggle by the Bodhisattva from without who, as it were, descends to pull us up by his outstretched hand. In this sense, the Bodhisattva is a being who, motivated by Compassion, strives to lead others on the Path of the Higher Evolution. He is the leader who embodies the evolutionary principle.

193

'Bodhisattva' is a Sanskrit word which means 'the Being of Awakening'. This is variously interpreted as the being who is set upon gaining Enlightenment or the being whose basis is Enlightenment. The Bodhisattva, properly speaking, is one who has vowed to gain Enlightenment for the sake of all beings. He does not see Enlightenment as a personal goal at all but as a basis from which he will be able to help others. He is motivated not only by his experience of the imperfections of the world and his faith in the Three Jewels, but by his feelings of sympathy and compassion for others. This is no mere mundane altruism. It is not just his ability to empathize with others based upon healthy self-love. Admirable as that certainly is, his Compassion goes far beyond it. The true Bodhisattva no longer makes any distinction between himself and others. He has seen through the dichotomy of subject and object to the extent that he feels the sufferings of others as keenly as his own. He is concerned only with the removal of suffering and he does not trouble to distinguish whose it is. He unites both the qualities of Wisdom and Compassion. By his Wisdom he breaks the barriers of subject and object and by his Compassion he acts for the welfare of all.

So lofty is his state of mind, so far has he gone beyond the mundane ego that, in a certain sense, he scarcely seems like a person any more. It is more as if the evolutionary urge has become fully conscious and functions through him, driving him to ever higher levels of self-transcendence, pushing aside all egoistic desires. He is the highest manifestation of that creative force which lifts every living thing beyond itself.

We have, so far, viewed the spiritual Path mainly in terms of psychological states and of worlds. It can also be looked at from other points of view: for instance, in a sociological perspective or as a system of practices and exercises. The Bodhisattva represents another, very important, way of seeing the whole Path, this time in terms of our relations with other people. The Bodhisattvas are those same Transcendental beings whom we have already encountered, considered in the light of their altruistic approach to their fellow men. The Path of the Bodhisattva is the same Higher Evolutionary Path as the Stream Entrants tread. What the Bodhisattva teaches us is that our spiritual development must take other people into account. In the first place, our lives are so bound up with other people that we can scarcely develop unless we consider and work upon our relations with them.

Ultimately, one cannot be fully at peace oneself while others suffer. No man, truly, is an island and spiritual development consists in realizing our interconnectedness with others on ever deeper levels until we are identified not with the ego at all but with the whole field of consciousness.

The evolution of our relations with others begins in the group, the human equivalent of the animal herd. The group provides its members with the important benefits of security and support but it demands of them absolute conformity with its conventions. Such a group may be positive or negative. In the former case, it encourages healthiness and happiness in its members and is upheld by a higher vision. The negative group holds together only out of the overlapping self-interest of its members and unwholesome mental states predominate within it. Within either kind of group, relationships are based upon need. Each person sees the others primarily as sources of definite advantages to himself, providing biological fulfilment, practical aid or psychological support. In the positive group, since its members are, at their own level, happy and contented, these relationships are on the whole friendly and beneficial. The atmosphere of the negative group, on the other hand, is poisoned by suspicion, resentment and exploitation. The group member belongs more to the group than he does to himself. His consciousness, by and large, is an expression of the group's consciousness. From immersion in the network of needs that is the group, mature individuality slowly emerges.

The individual has identified himself as a separate awareness from others. He is, therefore, for the first time, able to feel a genuine disinterested friendliness, for he can rise above his own immediate self-interest and appreciate the separate being of others. More especially, since he is aware of himself not only in the present but in the past and the future as well, he is aware of himself as having a continuity of identity and therefore he can enter into enduring relationships with others based upon mutual goodwill. Friendliness becomes friendship.

True friendship is based upon self-awareness, but self-awareness itself contains, in its full form, awareness of the evolutionary forces within consciousness. In other words, real friends are aware of themselves and each other as developing individuals whose lives are based upon an Ideal. Without that vertical dimension, what passes for friendship can only be based upon mutual self-interest and soon falls to the level of the group. Friendship, properly speaking, is spiritual friendship, based upon common commitment to the Higher Evolution. The culti-vation of such friendships is one of the principal aspects of the Path and one of its principal delights. The Buddha is reported as saying, on one occasion, that spiritual friendship is the whole of the Higher Evolution.

The first aspect of spiritual friendship is metta. Usually, we pick friends because of shared interests or some sort of temperamental affinity between them and us. Metta teaches us to go beyond that and to see other people apart from our conditioned predispositions. We should be able to feel goodwill for any conscious entity and we should be capable of friendship with anyone who is sufficiently an individual to form friendships himself. Spiritual friendship is a matter of responding to the evolutionary potential in the other person, of being attracted by his positive qualities. Friendship, it has been said, is the mutual recog-nition of the virtuous and cannot be known by the vicious.

Friendship does not blossom overnight, for it takes some time for two people to get to know each other. It is by communication that friends are made – communication in the sense of that mutual aware-ness and openness that we have already noted. As friendship develops, the parties to it are able to reveal more and more of themselves to each other and to be themselves more fully. Since true friendship is based upon Ideals, then it will be possible to relate freely to one's friends at one's best and highest while ordinary acquaintances might have no appreciation of those ideals and might even ridicule them. One's spir-itual friends will place the Three Jewels at the heart of their lives and spiritual commitment will underlie all one's communication with them. In this way, vision is intensified and reinforced. Where one person is less developed than the other, he is raised up by his contact with his spiritual friend. His own latent qualities are activated by the actualized virtues of his friend. In this vertical sense, spiritual friendship forms a chain running from the highest to the lowest levels of the Higher Evoluton. The more developed give their friendship to the less, drawing out their evolutionary potential, and the less developed respect them and value the friendship they receive. From the Buddhas and Bodhisattvas down to those who feel the first stirrings of a desire to develop, the whole Path is linked by friendship.

This great network of friends, stretching from one end of the Evolutionary Spiral to the other, is the Sangha, the Spiritual Commu-nity, in its widest sense. All those who share a spiritual vision share, in a sense, the same world and they have more in common with their fellows on the Path than with those who inhabit the same physical world as they do. They are all trying to go beyond themselves, to give up their limited ego-sense – not by regressing into the unconscious harmony of the group but by joining together in a fellowship which is on a level where self and other merge. In order to realize this ideal of spiritual community as a concrete reality, an Order is formed which is a living embodiment of the Ideal of Sangha. Those who have joined it try, in their relations one with another, to transcend themselves and to experience a level of consciousness in which their egoistic interests are merged in mutual love and respect. It has even been said that they aspire to a kind of 'collective consciousness'. This term could be misleading: collective consciousness does not mean the submersion of individuality in the undifferentiated sea of unconscious group identification. Rather, the members of the Sangha try to share individually in a common state of consciousness which transcends the individual. By their care and concern for one another, by their communication, by their work and practice together, they each try to go beyond themselves to realize a true Spiritual Community. For Sangha, in its highest sense, is the brotherhood of those who have transcended the distinction between subject and object. It is the community of the Stream Entrants, the Once-returners, the Non-returners, the Liberated ones, the Bodhisattvas and the Buddhas. They dwell in a state of consciousness in which self and other are merged in a non-dual awareness to which our normal categories of understanding do not apply. They are, each of them, completely unique individuals but they are also all manifestations of one unconditioned reality. It is this Transcendental community which the members of the Order seek to bring about on earth by their love and cooperation with each other.

Other people are our principle pathway to self-transcendence. They are part of the objective aspect of experience yet they are themselves subjects who will not easily bend to the dictates of our egos. If we enter into friendship with them and join with them in a spiritual community then we must consider their needs and desires as much as our own. This means we must go a little beyond ourselves. The more intensely we can harmonize with them, the more we will transcend ourselves until eventually we will go beyond subject and object altogether. This is the Bodhisattva Path.

The Path of the Bodhisattva is divided into two major phases: the stage of the novice Bodhisattva and that of the Bodhisattva of the Path. The novice feels the urge to self-transcendence and he has faith in the Three Jewels and in the Bodhisattva Ideal itself. He wants to go beyond himself so that he can, like Avalokiteshvara, become the manifestation of Compassion let loose in the world. As yet, however, these are aspirations, though noble, and not realities. He must work hard upon himself in order to bring them about. He strives to cultivate six virtues which are, in the true Bodhisattva, natural qualities, spontaneously expressed. There is, first of all, the virtue of *generosity*. He strives to overcome his tendency to meanness and egoistical self-seeking by giving in many different ways. He gives material things to those who need them, his assistance in time and energy and, wherever he can, he gives the Dharma or, at least, helps to provide the conditions under which others may find the Dharma. Whatever situation he finds himself in, he tries to act creatively, giving freely of himself. In this way, he begins to go beyond himself.

The next virtue he tries to cultivate is *morality*. He cultivates that sensitivity to others, which is completely natural to the full Bodhisattva, by applying the precepts to his life as closely as he can. His behaviour is not only moral in the broadest sense but it is civilized. His interaction with others is decorous and considered, and he is polite and dignified in his every movement.

The novice Bodhisattva tries to practise *patience* as the next virtue. He attempts to overcome his own reactive hatreds and cravings. He does not blame others for his own misfortunes and feels no enmity for those who do cause him harm. He forbears from seeking vengeance and he does not try to assert his own ego against that of others. He is receptive to other people, able to listen to them and, if possible, learn from them. He is always ready to absorb spiritual truth, however much it may undermine his own present understanding. He is cooperative and amenable, able to work with others and to drop contention on trifling matters. He has what have been called the feminine virtues – he is able to respond with warmth and to care for and help others.

Energy is the virtue which, as it were, balances patience. It is the masculine quality of initiative and vigour, of actively seeking the good. Since the Higher Evolution can only occur on the basis of effort, energy is indispensable to growth. It is the drive to self-transcendence, the positive urge which takes us beyond ourselves. It also expresses itself in work, particularly for the sake of the Dharma.

The novice Bodhisattva cultivates *meditation* as a virtue. He systematically trains his mind so that he experiences more and more positive states. He tries to raises his consciousness so that he dwells for some time each day in the state of absorption.

Wisdom is the last and most crucial virtue which he tries to develop aided by all the other virtues. It is specifically courted by the study of the doctrinal formulations of the Dharma and by meditations which are directed to Insight. It is the dawning of Wisdom which turns a novice Bodhisattva into a Bodhisattva of the Path. With the eye of Wisdom he sees that all things are ultimately indefinable, unconditioned, Empty. He himself is Empty, all other beings are Empty. He sees that the basic nature of all reality is that ungraspable openness which is called Emptiness. Once more, it is not a blank nothingness but such a plenitude that all our ordinary categories of thought diminish and belittle it. Based in his Wisdom, he now strives to convert all the virtues into Transcendental Perfections, the spontaneous expressions of his Insight into non-duality. He gives perfectly out of his immediate and heartfelt response to need, without any preconceived idea of himself as a donor or of the recipients as beings to whom he is giving – he does not even have an idea of an act of giving. He is both the giver, the receiver and the gift. He has the perfection of morality because he acts spontaneously out of his Wisdom without any idea of trying to cultivate precepts or etiquette. His behaviour is naturally moral. He is perfect in patience. He feels no anger towards those who harm him because he is as much concerned for them as he is for himself. He has to make no effort to curb or control his reactions – he simply has none. He has the Perfection of energy because, by now, evolution works through him, he has to make no effort in order for it to manifest. His energy arises freely and without limit to help living beings. Perfect meditation is his because his mind is always calm and balanced, always one-pointed and refined. He no longer struggles to become absorbed – absorption is his natural medium. And he has Perfect Wisdom, the realization that all things are empty; which raises virtues to Perfections.

The historical Buddha, Gautama Shakyamuni, is said to have pursued this Path of the Bodhisattva over innumerable lifetimes during which he cultivated and perfected each of the virtues. Countless aeons before the life in which he gained Enlightenment, the story goes, he made his great vow before the Buddha of that era. This vow arises in all

Bodhisattvas when they become Bodhisattvas of the Path and it represents their spontaneous response to the sufferings of all beings. They feel, very deeply, their interconnectedness with all life and they vow that they will gain full Enlightenment for the sake of all. They see that spiritual life is not a matter of personal evolution alone but of bringing the entire universe to perfection. The perspective of the Higher Evolution is the infinitude of space and the endless sequence of time and it involves all living creatures. The story of the Bodhisattva career of the historical Buddha is told in a series of tales, many of which are not considered canonical. Some of them are, quite clearly, folk stories, like Aesop's fables, but the general emphasis of all the stories, whether they are taken as literal records of the Buddha's previous lives or not, is clear. In each incident, the Bodhisattva goes beyond himself and in going beyond himself he leads other beings with him. The Bodhisattva, in each story, takes the initiative, leading others on the road of evolution.

Buddhist history is filled with great teachers and sages who showed those same Bodhisattva qualities in full measure – men who, sometimes under very difficult circumstances, led their fellows on the Path to Enlightenment. Indeed, it is that Bodhisattva spirit which has kept Buddhism alive to this day, not as a set of scholarly philosophies or exotic customs, but as a living network of spiritual friendships in which individuals are evolving. The Ideal of the Bodhisattva has inspired and still inspires countless men and women to see their own development and the welfare of others as two aspects of one Path. While they work vigorously to raise their own consciousness, they also devote themselves to helping others. The Bodhisattva Ideal has thus found expression in the lives of many human beings. Many have, as novice Bodhisattvas, tried to bring about those six virtues in their own conduct. They have assiduously cultivated feelings of metta and have deepened their spiritual friendships. They have participated in that Sangha-consciousness which transcends but does not negate the individual. They have worked directly for the welfare of others. Some have, in this way, broken through to a new level of Wisdom, the level of the Bodhisattva of the Path. Their virtues have become Perfections and their active Compassion has sprung from their Transcendental Insight.

The Bodhisattva principle also finds expression in archetypal form. By that process of vertical projection, figures have been envisioned which are the personification of the essential qualities of the

Bodhisattva. Existing on the loftiest plane of Enlightenment, they embody the active nature of Enlightenment, as the force of good in the world. There are four principle Ideal Bodhisattvas who are reverenced in most Buddhist countries as the archetypes of the Bodhisattva's virtues.

Avalokiteshvara, the Bodhisattva of Compassion, we have already encountered at the beginning of this chapter with his eleven heads and thousand arms. Like all Bodhisattvas, he is represented not only in visual form but as a Mantra. A Mantra is a sound-symbol which carries the qualities of Enlightenment just as does the shape, colour and gesture of the visual image. The Mantra *is* the Bodhisattva in terms of sound. It does not really mean anything, or rather what literal meaning it has is scarcely relevant. It has its effect by virtue of the associations it has gathered to itself in the course of centuries. (The Mantra of Avalokiteshvara is the famous Om Mani Padme Hum which is sometimes translated as 'Om, the jewel in the lotus, Hum' – Om referring to absolute reality, the jewel being the jewel of Enlightenment in the lotus of the mind, and Hum being absolute reality as manifested in the conditioned world.)

Manjusri, the Gently Auspicious One, is the Bodhisattva of Wisdom. He, too, is a young prince of great beauty, decked in silks. On his head is the crown of the Five Wisdoms and on his body are the jewelled ornaments of the six Perfections. His body is a fiery orange colour, 'like a lion's eye', and from him there glows a resplendent aura of reddish gold. He is seated in the cross-legged posture and his right hand is raised aloft, wielding the flaming sword of Wisdom whose razor-sharpness cuts effortlessly through all confusion and ignorance. It is the sword of non-duality which slices away suffering and imperfection. With his left hand, he presses a book to his heart, the book of Perfect Wisdom, the highest knowledge that there is. Manjusri is a kind of Buddhist Apollo although on a far loftier, transcendental plane, for he is the patron of all arts and sciences, the bringer of culture and learning. His mantra is Om Ah Ra Pa Cha Na Dhih.

The Bodhisattva of energy is Vajrapani, the Bearer of the Thunderbolt. He is often depicted in wrathful form to emphasize the force and positive destructiveness of the Transcendental, bursting through all barriers, annihilating ignorance and burning up all limitations. He is an enormous, dark-blue figure with a barrel chest and massive arms and legs, rippling with heavy muscles. He stands, stamping his right foot

upon a prostrate corpse and raising in his right hand a golden thunderbolt as if to hurl it. His left hand is held to his heart in a gesture of
teaching. His face is scowling and his three bloodshot eyes glare in
rage. His teeth are pointed and drip blood. Around his body is an
aureole of flames. Although the Tanscendental being has nothing but
love for every member of the universe, to those who are completely
identified with their own ignorance and who do not wish to grow, his
uncompromising honesty and unfailing energy appear terrifying and
threatening. Even this horrific figure of Vajrapani is, in reality, the
calm and serene Buddha, sitting in perfect peace. His Mantra is Om
Vajrapani Hum.

Tara, the Saviouress, is the female Bodhisattva of Compassion. She
is said to have been born out of a lake formed by the tears of
Avalokiteshvara as he wept for the sufferings of the world. She is a
beautiful young princess, a delicate jade-green in colour. She sits with
her left leg drawn up in meditation and her right leg stepping down
into the world to save living beings. Her left hand holds to her heart
the stalks of three lotuses whose dark-blue flowers are at her left
shoulder; one in bud, one half open, and one in full bloom, symbol-
izing the different stages of maturation of beings. Her right hand is
extended before her left knee in the gesture of generosity. She symbol-
izes the very quintessence of that sympathy for all creatures which is the
Bodhisattva's nature. Her Mantra is Om Tara Tutare Ture Svaha.

The career of the Bodhisattva, in his path from the earliest efforts of
the novice to the complete Enlightenment of a Buddha, may take
many, many lifetimes. During his career, the Bodhisattva will try to
help as many other beings as he can. The more advanced he is, the more
beneficial and widespread his aid will be. He will gradually form
around him a field of influence which will raise up all those who are
open to it. In the final stages of his career, the Bodhisattva creates a
kind of Ideal world by the power of his own Compassionate volitions.
Everyone who makes spiritual contact with him and who is receptive
to him will be reborn in that world which is called a Pure Land. In it
everything is favourable to development and nothing hinders or
obstructs. It is the perfect environment for the leading of the spiritual
life for one is always in the presence of the Bodhisattva whose pure land
it is and who now becomes a Buddha. Everywhere, in the Pure Land,
one hears the Dharma and the only beings there are members of the
Sangha. All bodily and psychological wants are immediately satisfied

merely by wishing for them and the whole world is of exceptional beauty and purity. It is like the highest of the heaven worlds suffused with the influence of the Transcendental.

The Bodhisattva on the threshold of Buddhahood creates a Pure Land at a very high level of refinement. The human Bodhisattva, whether novice or of the Path, tries to create a Pure Land on Earth. More especially, he works with others, with the Sangha, to create the best possible conditions for growth, here and now. He tries to bring into being a movement of people who are inspired by the vision of the Three Jewels. He tries to establish the institutions in which people can live and work together on the basis of those Ideals. He tries to bring about a culture which carries the full perspective of the Higher Evolution to as many people as possible. All his efforts are directed to forming a new society which has spiritual evolution as its central value.

He does not work alone for he seeks out and cooperates with others who share his vision. Some may see it more brightly and clearly than he does and he willingly follows their guidance. Others are less spiritually mature than he is and he leads and encourages them as best he can. With all, with this total Sangha, he is united in bonds of brotherhood and mutual self-Transcendence.

This is the Buddhist life, the life of the Higher Evolution. It is an unending, yet joyous struggle to unfold the best and noblest qualities from within oneself. It is an ever-deepening harmony with one's spiritual friends and fellows in the Sangha so that one moves with them as if all were different manifestations of a single higher consciousness. And it is the heroic effort to draw as many people as possible on to the Path so that they may fulfil their own innermost nature. The Buddhist life, in the end, is the truly human life, a life dedicated to the transformation of self and world.

Further Reading

Coleridge, S.T., *Biographia Literaria*, Dent.

Conze, Edward, *Buddhism: Its Essence and Development*, Cassirer, 1951.

Conze, Edward, and others, *Buddhist Texts Through the Ages*, Cassirer, 1954.

Evans-Wentz, W.Y., *The Tibetan Book of the Dead*, Oxford University Press, 1960.

Guenther, Herbert V., *Philosophy and Psychology in the Abhidharma*, Shambhala, 1976.

Head, Joseph and Cranston, S.L., *Reincarnation: The Phoenix Fire Mystery*, Julian Press/Crown, New York, 1978.

Nanamoli, Bhikkhu, *The Life of the Buddha*, Buddhist Publication Society, Kandy, 1978.

Peele, Stanton with Brodsky, Archie, *Love and Addiction*, Sphere, 1977.

Sangharakshita, Ven., *The Bodhisattva: Evolution and Self-transcendence*, Windhorse Publications, 1983.

Sangharakshita, Ven., *Going for Refuge*, Windhorse Publications, 1983.

Sangharakshita, Ven., *Human Enlightenment*, Windhorse Publications, 1980.

Sangharakshita, Ven., *Mind Creative and Reactive*, Windhorse Publications, 1985.

Sangharakshita, Ven., *A Survey of Buddhism*, Shambhala, 1980.

Sangharakshita, Ven., *The Three Jewels*, Windhorse Publications, 1977.

Sthiramati, Dharmachari, *Imagination: The Faculty Divine*, Windhorse Publications, 1982.

Story, Francis, *Rebirth as Doctrine and Experience*, Buddhist Publication Society, Kandy, 1975.

Subhuti, Dharmachari, (Alex Kennedy), *Buddhism for Today*, Element

Books, 1983.

Woodward, F.L. (trans.), *Some Sayings of the Buddha*, The Buddhist Society, 1974.

Index

Index

Kshitigarbha: 183

lama: 73
lotus: 17, 43, 182, 184, 185, 187, 201, 202
love mode: 58, 59, 77, 79

man('s): viii, ix, 18, 20, 26, 27, 29, 35, 36, 41, 44, 80–81, 84, 86, 94, 104, 139, 141, 171
mandala: 43, 181
Mandala of the Five Buddhas: viii, 18, 39, 181ff, 188
Manjushri: 187, 201
Mantra: 201–202
masculine: 132ff, 167, 179, 198
  – masculinity: 134, 135, 138, 148
materialism: 70, 71, 75, 86, 87, 102
  – materialist: 70, 71
meditation: viii, 16, 21ff, 30, 43, 55–56, 68, 74–75, 93, 97, 100, 107, 116, 160ff, 170, 185, 189ff
merit (s): 77, 86, 149, 150, 154, 159, 167
metta: 54, 55, 56, 57, 59, 65, 77, 79, 140, 146, 156, 163, 173, 196, 200
Mettabhavana: 55, 56, 122
mindfulness: 67, 78, 79, 94, 122, 150, 156, 160, 167
  – of breathing: 22, 165
moral: 140, 142, 144, 146, 149–150, 159, 198–199
morality: 21–22, 24, 68, 77, 79, 86, 146, 150, 156ff, 182ff
motivation – see also five heaps: 63, 65, 95, 100, 121, 160, 184, 186
myth: 11, 37, 38, 71, 131, 180

nihilism: 85, 87, 88, 89, 95, 106, 176
Non-returner: 177, 197
nuclear family: 137

Once-returner: 177, 197

Padmasambhava: 185
pagan: 142, 143
parturition: 93, 116
Path: 20ff, 29, 33, 43, 57, 73, 76, 89, 94, 108, 155ff, 163, 164, 167, 169ff, 191ff
  – Bodhisattva: 194, 197, 199
  – Mundane: 151, 163, 172, 176, 181
  – Spiral: 18, 24, 29, 31, 35, 53ff, 68, 79, 105, 112, 141ff
  – Spiritual 33, 48, 54, 59, 119, 155
  – Transcendental: 151, 172, 174
Path of the Higher Evolution – see Spiral Path: 49, 76, 154, 193, 194
patience: 17, 198, 199
peace: 151, 158, 162, 163, 195
perception: (s) 27, 30, 33, 37, 38, 62, 85, 89, 98–99, 101–102, 113
Perfections: 189, 199–201
personality view: 176
pig: 39, 44, 47, 48, 49, 53, 177
pleasure: 51, 66, 67, 86, 87, 103, 104, 105, 106, 107, 109, 131, 139, 143, 147, 148ff, 171ff, 185ff
power mode: 58, 59, 79
precepts: 22, 78, 79, 108, 176, 198, 199
pride: 143, 144, 185
projection: 34, 57, 117ff, 135, 137, 140, 179, 180
  – vertical: 118ff, 180, 200
proto-man: 58, 141–142
Pure Land: 202, 203

rapture: 150, 161, 162
Ratnapani: 184
Ratnasambhava: 43, 184, 185
reactive: 19ff, 34, 101, 105, 154, 198
  – reactions: 85, 152, 156, 199
reality: 70, 80, 82, 87ff, 100, 102, 112, 114, 115, 118, 135, 146, 151, 155, 156, 166, 170, 171, 174, 176, 178, 181, 185, 188, 197, 199, 201
reason: 11, 14, 35ff, 71, 85, 134, 157, 166, 172
rebirth: 68–77, 91–97, 109, 112, 116, 120, 130, 134, 136, 138, 139, 149, 151, 175, 177
recognition - see also Five Heaps: 73, 97, 99, 100, 151, 174, 175, 184, 186, 196
religion: 71, 88, 108, 130, 139

209

Index